About Island Press

Island Press is the only nonprofit organization in the United States whose principal purpose is the publication of books on environmental issues and natural resource management. We provide solutions-oriented information to professionals, public officials, business and community leaders, and concerned citizens who are shaping responses to environmental problems.

Since 1984, Island Press has been the leading provider of timely and practical books that take a multidisciplinary approach to critical environmental concerns. Our growing list of titles reflects our commitment to bringing the best of an expanding body of literature to the environmental community throughout North America and the world.

Support for Island Press is provided by the Agua Fund, The Geraldine R. Dodge Foundation, Doris Duke Charitable Foundation, The Ford Foundation, The William and Flora Hewlett Foundation, The Joyce Foundation, Kendeda Sustainability Fund of the Tides Foundation, The Forrest & Frances Lattner Foundation, The Henry Luce Foundation, The John D. and Catherine T. MacArthur Foundation, The Marisla Foundation, The Andrew W. Mellon Foundation, Gordon and Betty Moore Foundation, The Curtis and Edith Munson Foundation, Oak Foundation, The Overbrook Foundation, The David and Lucile Packard Foundation, Wallace Global Fund, The Winslow Foundation, and other generous donors.

Water War in the Klamath Basin

Water War in the Klamath Basin

MACHO LAW, COMBAT BIOLOGY,
AND DIRTY POLITICS

Holly Doremus
A. Dan Tarlock

ISLANDPRESS
Washington · Covelo · London

Doremus, Holly D.
Anatomy of a water war in the Klamath basin : macho law, combat biology, and dirty politics / Holly Doremus, A. Dan Tarlock.
p. cm.
ISBN-13: 978-1-59726-393-1 (cloth : alk. paper)
ISBN-10: 1-59726-393-1 (cloth : alk. paper)
ISBN-13: 978-1-59726-394-8 (pbk. : alk. paper)
ISBN-10: 1-59726-394-X (pbk. : alk. paper)
1. Water resources development—Law and legislation—Klamath Basin (Or.) 2. Klamath Basin (Or.)—Water rights. 3. Water-supply, Agricultural—Klamath Basin (Or.) 4. Freshwater ecology—Klamath Basin (Or.) I. Tarlock, A. Dan, 1940- II. Title.
KF5590.K53D67 2008
346.795'9104'691—dc22 2007040656

Printed on recycled, acid-free paper 

Manufactured in the United States of America

10 9 8 7 6 5 4 3 2 1

Keywords: Klamath Basin, Klamath Project, water scarcity, endangered species, Western water issues, water conflicts, federal irrigation project

In memory of my father, Stanley D. Doremus, who began his career as a civil engineer on a Bureau of Reclamation irrigation project, and from whom I learned both the importance and the challenges of public service.

—HD

To the memory of my mother, Fay Ollerton Tarlock, who introduced me to the craft of writing, the beauty of the West, and first explained how water got from mountain streams into ditches.

—ADT

Contents

Illustrations

Abbreviations

BiOp	biological opinion
cfs	cubic feet per second
COPCO	California Oregon Power Company
ESA	Endangered Species Act
ESU	evolutionarily significant unit
FERC	Federal Energy Regulatory Commission
FPA	Federal Power Act
FPC	Federal Power Commission
FWS	U.S. Fish and Wildlife Service
NEPA	National Environmental Policy Act
NMFS	National Marine Fisheries Service
NRC	National Research Council
NWR	National Wildlife Refuge
TCID	Truckee-Carson Irrigation District

Preface

Our careers have been largely devoted to studying the clash of the laws adopted in the environmental decade (1969–80) with earlier legal regimes that sought to encourage exploitation of the West's resources. The Endangered Species Act (ESA) has been of special interest to us. It is often at the heart of fights for control of the beautiful and fragile western landscapes we love. These fights are bitter ones because the statute has a greater capacity to disrupt settled expectations, especially with respect to the use of water, than any other law. Environmental advocates have become passionately devoted to the ESA because it appears to be the best hope for species and ecosystem conservation. Conversely, it is the worst nightmare of the entitlement holders who suddenly find themselves in harm's way. Ultimately, though, as we and many other students of the ESA have recognized, it is an inadequate tool for ecosystem conservation. And it can exacerbate conflict by purporting to frame as purely scientific, issues that in fact are a wickedly complex brew of science, ethics, and public policy.

Science has been a special focus of our work. Scientists have long argued that environmental law should seek to define, protect, and manage large ecosystems to maintain some semblance of their historic functions. Since the 1990s, the goal of ecosystem management has been widely accepted both within the federal and state resource management agencies and by the larger stakeholder community. Still, little progress has been made in translating these broad, science-based principles into effective laws or, more important, results on the ground.

In the 1990s, all of these themes came into sharp focus in a remote, water-short area in Oregon and northeastern California, the Upper Klamath Basin. The Upper Klamath is home to one of the earliest federal irrigation projects, a tight socioeconomic community founded on family farming, and an Indian tribe trying to come back from federal termination. It is connected by the Klamath River to the Lower Klamath Basin, an area of deep canyons largely unsuitable for farming but home to a white community economically dependent on fishing and several Indian tribes whose cultural identity is intimately bound up with salmon.

The ESA listing of two freshwater suckers in the Upper Klamath Basin and a salmon run in the Klamath River provided new hope to the tribes and environmental advocates, but it stretched the region's water supply to the breaking point. After modest cutbacks to irrigation deliveries during droughts in the 1990s, in 2001 the two federal agencies charged with administering the ESA decided that more needed to be done for the dwindling fish. They ordered the Bureau of Reclamation to leave more water in Upper Klamath Lake for the suckers and also to send more down the Klamath River for salmon. That left essentially nothing for irrigators dependent on the Klamath Project. For the first time, the headgates of a federal irrigation project were closed, denying irrigators use of their state water rights, in favor of conservation.

The reaction was immediate and furious. The Klamath conflict became the poster child of the hour for what is wrong with the ESA, and by extension with environmental law in general. The political fury was enhanced by the report of a blue-ribbon scientific panel appointed by the National Research Council (NRC). To the consternation of environmental interests and the glee of irrigators, the panel concluded that the shutoff was not supported by science. It also concluded that the ecosystem was in serious need of repair and that there was no support for the high levels of water the Bureau of Reclamation wanted to withdraw for irrigation, but those messages were drowned out by the fury over the wildlife agencies' "junk science." Eventually, the protests fizzled, and even with the NRC report and Bush administration support for the irrigators, Congress did not gut or repeal the ESA. The government agencies, the irrigators, the Indians, and downstream fishing communities were left with the unenviable task of picking up the pieces.

We were drawn to a case study of the Klamath Basin water conflicts in part because of the drama of the ESA's impact but even more because the story of the Klamath raises all the key problems of managing ecosystems on living landscapes occupied by real people with settled expectations. There are many stories that one could tell about the Klamath. One could focus on the plight of the irrigators, the Indians, or the line government officials faced with the impossible task of applying the ESA in the face of internal and external pressures. However, as lawyers, with some science background,* we have chosen to focus on the legal institutions, the accretion of unintegrated resource management and environmental laws that make ecosystem conservation so difficult in small areas with deeply entrenched property rights. Most of the lessons we draw are negative; the Klamath experience demonstrates the poor fit between our current laws and institutions and the goal of creating more environmentally sustainable landscapes. We believe that the Klamath holds lessons for other basins in the West and for other water-stressed areas around the world. Our hope is that the lessons of the Klamath can improve the ability to anticipate and respond to future water crises.

The title tries to capture what we see as the most salient features of events in the Klamath Basin from the late 1990s through 2007. Describing the water conflicts as a "war" may seem dramatic, but not all wars are military. The term reflects the deep divisions and antagonisms among those who seek to control the water future of the basin. "Macho law" refers to two inflexible, winner-take-all legal regimes—prior appropriation and the Endangered Species Act—that the protagonists tried to use to impose their vision for the basin on their opponents. We have borrowed the term "combat biology" from a biologist who used it to describe the plight of scientists in the basin, squeezed between the demands of conducting science as they learned it in graduate school, the macho legal regimes, and political pressures from various constituencies. Politics has always played a role in resource management, but that role was amplified after the 2001 installation of George W. Bush as president. Evidence continues to leak out that members of the Bush administration, from the vice president down, went to the legitimate limits of their office and perhaps beyond, into the realm of improper, "dirty" interference with the implementation of congressional mandates.

Many people generously shared their experience and expertise with us during the course of this project, including Gail Achterman, director, Institute for Natural Resources, Oregon State University (2006 and 2007 College World Series champion); Reed Benson, formerly of Water Watch Oregon and now a professor of law at the University of Wyoming; Kristen Boyles,

*Professor Tarlock barely made it through "Rocks for Jocks" in his first year of college but received a wonderful postgraduate science education working with National Research Council committees for over thirty years and is a National Associate of the National Academies. Professor Doremus earned a PhD in Plant Physiology from the same university, Cornell, where Professor Tarlock struggled with geology, and also has extensive experience with National Research Council studies.

EarthJustice; John Engbring, U.S. Fish and Wildlife Service; Charles Howe, professor emeritus of economics at the University of Colorado; Matt Jenkins of High Country News; Ron Larson, U.S. Fish and Wildlife Service; Cecil Lesley, Bureau of Reclamation; Matt McKinney of the University of Montana; Jeff Mount, professor of geology, University of California Davis; Larry MacDonnell, former director of the Natural Resources Center, University of Colorado School of Law; Peter Moyle, professor of wildlife, fisheries, and conservation biology, UC Davis; J.B. Ruhl, professor of law, Florida State University; and Paul Somach of Somach, Simmons and Dunn. Of course, none of them bears any responsibility for our interpretations or errors. Mona Badie, Justin Bosch, Megan Jennings, Julie Ogilvie, and Andrew Zabel provided invaluable research assistance. We thank the staff of Island Press for their unwavering support for this project and for their design and editorial assistance. In particular, Barbara Dean, Erin Johnson, and Kat McDonald made the publication process as painless as possible. Finally, we are grateful to our spouses, Gordon Anthon and Vivien Gross, who showed more patience with this project than we had any right to expect. Professor Tarlock is also grateful to his black labrador, Benjamin, for early morning walks along the shore of Lake Michigan that helped bring the pieces of the Klamath kaleidoscope into some kind of focus.

Long Canyon, on the East Fork of the Stuart's Fork of the Trinity River
Lower Klamath Basin
July 2007

CHAPTER 1

A Water Crisis Exposes Political Fault Lines

The old West rubs elbows with the new in Klamath Falls.

Works Progress Administration, *Oregon: End of the Trail*

In 2005, the Klamath irrigation project observed its hundredth birthday, but the celebration was muted by persistent fears about the project's future. Since the early 1990s, Klamath irrigators have struggled to maintain an irrigation economy in the face of demands that more water be dedicated to the preservation of endangered species and downstream fisheries, as well as the stresses of the national and global agricultural economy. After simmering for a decade, the tension between irrigation and species conservation came to a head during the exceptionally severe drought summer of 2001.[1] For the first time in its history, the United States Bureau of Reclamation was forced to make an absolute choice between irrigation deliveries and species conservation. Believing that the law left it no choice, the bureau closed the headgates of the Klamath Project to comply with its conservation duties under the federal Endangered Species Act (ESA) (see fig. 1).[2] This drastic action was taken after the two federal agencies responsible for the administration of the ESA, the U.S. Fish and Wildlife Service (FWS) and the National Marine Fisheries Service (NMFS), issued biological opinions (BiOps) concluding that summer irrigation releases from the project's main storage source, Upper Klamath Lake, would threaten the survival of protected Lost River and shortnose suckers and coho salmon.[3] On April 6, 2001, the Department of the Interior announced that it would deliver no water from Upper Klamath Lake that summer.

FIGURE 1
The headgates of the Klamath irrigation project stand closed in 2001. For the first time, irrigation deliveries from a federal water project were halted to protect endangered and threatened fish. (Photo by Seth Zuckerman.)

That decision would have shocked the utopian reformers and engineers who together created an irrigation-based society in the arid West in the early twentieth century. It startled and enraged the irrigators presently enjoying the benefits of a century of federal largesse. To comply with the ESA, the Bureau of Reclamation had begun to cut back water deliveries as early as 1988, but those cuts had been mild. In 2001, irrigation deliveries were reduced by 90 percent in order to protect fish. The approximately fourteen hundred farmers who rely on the Klamath Project were either unable to plant or faced severe losses on the roughly 210,000 acres they farm.[4] The cutbacks triggered violence, street protests, some comic political drama, and a wide variety of other responses that continue to reverberate throughout the West.

The decision to close the headgates was made in April of 2001, before the start of the irrigation season. On May 7, thousands of area residents formed a bucket brigade to bring water from Lake Ewauna, where the Upper Klamath Lake reservoir spills into the Klamath River, to an irrigation canal near the local high school. This initial protest was peaceful and symbolic, modeled on the civil rights protests of the 1960s. But the situation soon became increasingly volatile as local frustration mounted and anti–federal government activists from across the West poured into Klamath Falls. Some protestors saw the conflict in biblical terms and called on a just God to consecrate the area as a place of liberty.[5] However, impatient farmers quickly turned to an old remedy: self help. The headgates were illegally forced open several times in early July, and later a pipe was run from Upper Klamath Lake around the headgates to an irrigation canal. The local sheriff observed the trespasses and other illegal acts but refused to intervene. As a result, federal

FIGURE 2

Protest signs in the Upper Klamath Basin. When the water was shut off in 2001, protest signs sprouted throughout the Upper basin. These were two of the mildest. (Photo by Seth Zuckerman.)

marshals and FBI agents were brought in to defend the headgates, recalling images of the forced integration of southern schools and universities after the U.S. Supreme Court declared segregation unconstitutional.

Tensions briefly eased that summer when Secretary of the Interior Gale Norton "found" an accounting error in the estimates of the amount of water stored in Upper Klamath Lake, allowing the Bureau of Reclamation to release about 70,000 acre-feet of water for irrigation without defying the FWS and NMFS BiOps. When those small deliveries ended, however, the protests resumed. They culminated in late August with a "Convoy of Tears" bringing sympathizers from around the West to a rally in downtown Klamath Falls that was characterized by some as "the vanguard of a citizen revolt against federal water and land management policy."[6] In an extreme example of hyperbole, former Idaho congresswoman Helen Chenoweth-Hage compared the struggle to the American Revolution. A variety of signs deploring the shutoff and attacking federal control sprouted throughout the basin that summer, as shown in figure 2.

The terrorist attacks of September 11, 2001, indirectly ended the Klamath Falls protests. The protesters withdrew to allow redeployment of federal law enforcement officers to more important national security assignments.[7] A year later the headgates were demolished, replaced by multimillion-dollar new works. The events of the summer of 2001 are now officially history, as a three-hundred-pound chunk of the old headgates, like a remnant of the Berlin wall, has been put on display at the Klamath County Museum. The broader story, though, remains unfinished.

Understanding the Klamath Conflict

Since the summer of 2001, the Klamath Basin water conflict has been a symbolic rallying cry for people on both extremes of a fierce national debate about environmental protection in general and the Endangered Species Act in particular. On the one hand, this conflict is used as an illustration of the ways that property rights are "disrespected" and farmers callously pushed off lands they have sacrificed for generations to improve. One farmer characterized the headgate closure as a "land grab,"[8] and the Internet is filled with sites inveighing hysterically against the ESA as a totalitarian weapon used by urban environmentalists to cleanse the rural landscape of all human imprint. Behind the invective lie powerful images with a deep grip on our national psyche, images of the Jeffersonian yeoman farmer and the romantic western cowboy. Appeals to those images allow irrigators to present themselves as victims of modern environmentalism and their battle to restore the status quo as a selfless defense of true constitutional and moral government.[9]

Environmentalists, too, have used the Klamath water conflict as a symbol, albeit in somewhat more measured terms. For them, it illustrates the extent to which the current federal government is willing to ignore both law and science to protect the historic resource extraction economy, supported by legal regimes put in place during the heyday of the disposition of the public domain that have brought the West's environments to the brink of ruin. Defenders of Wildlife, for example, emphasizes the role played by White House political advisor Karl Rove in making sure that Department of the Interior officials understood that the White House favored the farmers over the fish in water allocation decisions following the 2001 crisis. The organization describes the Klamath conflict as one of several in which the George W. Bush administration "ignored science altogether in order to promote the interests of its corporate supporters—to the immediate and direct detriment of endangered species."[10]

In this book, we dig below these superficial views for lessons from the Klamath experience. Those lessons are larger than the basin itself. They extend at least to the many other water conflicts throughout the irrigated West, from California to the Missouri River. Because a variety of environmental conflicts feature many of the same key elements, we believe the lessons extend well beyond the water resources of the West. They apply, in some measure, not only to all river basins but to all conflicts over limited natural resources.

In some respects, of course, the Klamath conflict is unique, shaped by the particular characteristics of this basin and its people. The basin's geography both exacerbates and relieves water stresses. Topographically, the basin reverses the usual pattern; it is dry and flat near the headwaters and steep and wet near the mouth. That makes water conflicts tougher because it means there is no way to store water to carry the project through a dry year. By the same token, the Klamath Basin's isolation has long helped to shield it from conflicts that have engaged the region and the nation. It remains far removed from the major urban and agricultural centers in California and Oregon. Its remote location made it one of the last areas of the Pacific Northwest investigated by trappers and one of the last opened to white settlement.[11] Klamath Falls, the major community in the Upper Klamath Basin, was not served by railroad until 1909, and the railroad did not effectively tie the region to the urban centers of the West until 1926, when Klamath Falls became a stop on the main Southern Pacific Line from the Bay Area to Portland.[12] Today, Klamath Falls remains the largest community in the basin, with a population just less than twenty thousand. Unlike many areas in the West, the Klamath Basin has no growing cities to compete for its scarce water. That is both a blessing and a curse with respect to water conflicts: Although it means one less source of pressure on the resource, it also means an important source of political leverage, one that has been used in other basins to pry water away from agricultural use, is missing.

The human communities of the Klamath Basin are unique in their particulars, but they are also, in general, representative of others across the West. The waters of the West are stretched nearly to the breaking point throughout the region.[13] The Klamath Basin was simply the first place the breaking point was actually reached. The Klamath conflict brings into sharp focus the elements that make water conflicts so difficult to resolve. Upstream there are farmers and the communities that have grown up around them. Some farmers rely on federal irrigation water, while others use private irrigation works. Some grow high-value crops, while others produce only forage or pasture. Downstream there are some agricultural communities, as well as communities that are heavily dependent, economically and socially, on commercial and recreational fishing. Both upstream and downstream there are Indian tribes, struggling to maintain cultural traditions and join the economic mainstream. There are also important transient communities, visitors drawn to various parts of the basin to experience the environment.

Recurring Themes in Environmental Conflict

Looking at this conflict through the eyes of outsiders to the basin but longtime observers of environmental conflicts, we find the similarities to other contested landscapes striking. Throughout the arid West, disparate human and nonhuman communities share landscapes with limited, and highly variable, water supplies. Everyone seems to agree, on the most general level, that all the various human communities, as well as the natural community, should be respected, and that ideally all would thrive. But priorities differ radically. To us, the fundamental questions are the same across the West, across the country, and indeed around the world: Can sustainable human communities coexist with a functioning natural environment? How should conflicting demands upon limited natural resources be balanced? How can current unsustainable patterns of resource use transition into something more closely approaching harmony with the natural world?

The Klamath conflict illustrates four general themes fundamental to understanding conflicts over natural resources anywhere: the historic entrenchment of resource entitlements granted without recognition of competing interests; the clash of fundamental values closely intertwined with natural resource use; pervasive uncertainty, not just over the environmental impacts of activities but also over the priority to be assigned to competing entitlements; and a "problem-shed" extending across political and other boundaries. Each of these features helps to explain how these conflicts develop and why they are so difficult to resolve. We explore each in detail.

The Past Is Prelude

The first theme is the power of the historical context to create strong expectations that the status quo should be maintained. Environmental crises do not develop overnight. They are typically created by patterns of behavior with firm historical roots. People are often slow to realize the effect they are having on the world around them, and even on their ability to achieve their own goals. It can take a long time for the harmful effects of decisions made in good faith to become apparent. At the same time, societal goals evolve. Past decisions aimed at achieving one goal can produce consequences out of step with modern sensibilities. Yet patterns, both of private behavior and of governance, once set in place are highly resistant to change. They may become so ingrained that the idea of change is simply inconceivable to some people. Changing the law is often a necessary aspect of correcting anachronistic behavior patterns, but it is rarely sufficient for that purpose. Implementing the law in new ways is often a struggle, one that requires committed leadership to achieve success.

The fallibility of human decision making and the continuing power of past decisions are on full display in the Klamath Basin. Irrigated agriculture is the root of an environmental and social crisis that was long in the making. One of the first people to notice that crisis was Rachel Carson. In her landmark 1962 book, *Silent Spring*, she linked a large bird kill in the Tule Lake and Lower Klamath Lake National Wildlife Refuges to the presence of agricultural chemical residues. She prophetically observed, "All of the waters of the wildlife refuges established on . . . [Upper Klamath and Tule lakes] represent the drainage of agricultural lands. It is important to remember this in connection with recent happenings."[14] Forty years later, the crisis was apparent to any informed observer. The Upper Klamath Basin included sites with "some of the worst water quality in the state."[15] Naturally nutrient rich, Upper Klamath Lake had become hyper-eutrophic, leading to constant massive algal blooms, largely as a result of agricultural runoff.[16] Oxygen levels in the upper Klamath River fell low enough to kill thousands of fish in 1986,[17] prompting the Klamath Tribe to close its c'waam fishery.[18] The first-order consequences of a severe drought in an already stressed basin, like those of hurricanes and other foreseeable natural disasters, were widely understood long before the crisis came to a head. In 1999, the Oregon Water Resources Department issued a report, *Resolving the Klamath*, which warned the farmers that relying on the luck of rainfall that happened to be above average for a few years "will not solve the underlying problem."[19] Even the project irrigators now recognize the foreseeability of the crisis, although they accept none of the responsibility for it. In litigation seeking damages from the United States for failing to deliver their contracted water in 2001, they claimed that if the United States had taken conservation steps well before 2001, cutting off irrigation that dry summer would not have been necessary.[20] Not surprisingly, though, reducing irrigation deliveries is still not on their list of acceptable conservation steps.

Even in light of societal goals at the time they were made, the water allocation decisions in the Klamath Basin were questionable. Conversion of native wetlands to farming, expansion of irrigation, and even homesteading continued until after World War II, publicly justified largely by the founding vision of the Bureau of Reclamation. That vision, in which communities of small farms provided an ideal social, political, and economic organization, was never well suited to the high desert environment. The harsh climate and remoteness from markets have always made the Upper Klamath Basin a challenge for profitable agriculture. Furthermore, the vision of rural society as the ideal was an anachronism in the United States long before the end of settlement in the Upper Klamath Basin. For better or worse, the United States was urbanizing throughout the twentieth century. By the time of the final homestead allocations in the basin, it was apparent that cities were, and would remain, the nation's social, political, and economic centers of gravity.

The water allocation decisions made in the first half of the twentieth century in the Klamath Basin, like those in other parts of the West, have proven highly resistant to change. Only recently has growing recognition of the environmental crisis, coupled with rising political fortunes for environmental and tribal interests and the waning economic and political importance of agriculture, finally forced a confrontation. The environmental movement set the stage for change in the 1970s by winning new federal laws that, taken together, made the newly minted concept of environmental protection a legal responsibility of the federal agencies in charge of managing natural resources. The new laws endorsed what then seemed to many a heretical idea: that human beings might have to limit their demands on natural resources in order to ensure the continued functioning of the environment. The Endangered Species Act of 1973, in particular, imposed conservation duties on all federal agencies, including those, like the Bureau of Reclamation, that had previously had single-minded development missions.

Passing environmental laws did not immediately change water use in the basin. For one thing, the new conservation mandates were simply overlain on the existing missions of resource agencies. The task of reconciling new environmental goals with the promotion of irrigation, the facilitation of grazing, and the production of timber was left to the future. Some of the new laws explicitly exempted agricultural practices from their reach. The Clean Water Act (CWA), for example, required permits for most channelized discharges but exempted irrigation return flows.[21] The permit requirement forced industries and cities to install improved pollution control equipment to reduce their waste discharges. Farmers, however, were allowed to continue their historic practices, shielded by the view, endorsed by the National Research Council, that irrigated agriculture was not just another industry but "more a culture—the way people live and part of the national identity."[22]

Other new laws, like the ESA, lay dormant until stakeholders learned how to push for listings and use the leverage listings could provide. Environmental protection came to the Klamath as a means to another end: the preservation of Indian tribal cultures in the face of a history of annihilation, dismemberment, and misguided efforts to impose whiteness. The Klamath tribes, once almost destroyed in the name of assimilation, partnered with the state and environmental groups to gather information about declining sucker species and to bring that information to the attention of federal authorities, ultimately resulting in listing the two species under the ESA.[23] Together with the Yurok, Karuk, and Hoopa tribes in the Lower Basin, the Klamath tribes also have advocated for protection and restoration of Klamath River salmon runs. The tribes' efforts to push their rights under treaties, as well as under the ESA, have been an essential catalyst for moves toward ecosystem management in the region. But those moves remain halting at best.

Culture Wars

The second big theme in natural resource conflicts is the role of human values and cultures in shaping attitudes toward, and societal responses to, rapid, dislocating change. Frequently, opponents of natural resource protection caricature conflicts as "fish versus farmers" or, more generally, "environment versus people." In every case, however, natural resource conflicts are fundamentally conflicts between people with differing values. The differences in values arise in part from dependence on different economies. The economic fortunes of farmers in the Upper Klamath Basin are dependent to some degree (although not entirely) on the amount of irrigation water made available from the project. Similarly, the income of ocean salmon fishers is tied to abundance of that resource, and the wealth of the tribes is connected to their ability to harvest fish. The water conflicts in the basin are in part an illustration of the inevitable tension between an extractive economy and an ecosystem service economy.

Focusing solely on the economic impact of water allocation decisions on farmers, fishers, and tribal members, however, elides the emotional overtones of those conflicts, which are often the strongest driving forces. Farmers, fishers, and tribal members are not simply the calculating economic actors that Chicago-school economics posits.[24] They are people striving to realize their differing but deeply held views about what makes a human life satisfying and worthwhile. Their self-images, aspirations for their children, and sense of obligation to their predecessors are closely bound up with their interactions with the natural world. We refer to such noneconomic attachments to lifestyle generally as "cultural" claims. The centrality of decisions about natural resources to the culture of various groups makes those conflicts more intense and harder to resolve. It is difficult for the contending groups to empathize with, or even to understand, the claims of their opponents because their own point of view is so ingrained. From an economic perspective, they may react "irrationally" to proposals to resolve the dispute. If fishing produces more net income than farming, for example, an economist might suggest either that the fishers should buy out the farmers or that the government should buy out the farmers and recover some or all of the cost of that buyout from the fishers. But if the decision to farm is based more on emotional connections to the land and community than on economic calculation, the farmers will not be satisfied with that outcome. Indeed, to the extent they see a policy choice as denigrating their cultural identity or placing another culture above theirs, they are likely to fiercely resist it even if it provides for economic compensation. The law formally recognizes such culture-based claims on the part of Indian tribes, but not on the part of farming or fishing communities, which do not fit the model of racial, ethnic, or religious groups at high risk of majority oppression. Nonetheless, culturally based appeals from such groups may carry substantial political power.

In the Klamath Basin, as along the Colorado, Columbia, Missouri, Platte, Rio Grande, and Sacramento–San Joaquin rivers, the ESA is driving efforts to find a new balance between intensive consumptive uses of water resources and the restoration and maintenance of functioning ecosystems. These efforts are intensely controversial because change is seldom good for those trapped in the path of rapid displacement, especially when it comes to water use. The opposition to transition can be summed up in one word: fear. People understandably fear the loss of existing entitlements, of the political and economic power associated with those entitlements, and of the culture that has grown out of the small western communities sustained by irrigation.

As the National Research Council has observed, "To participate in the transformation of deserts and wetlands and to bring out their potential productivity have been viewed as inherently moral and civilizing activities."[25] Environmental protection threatens to topple that old moral order. Given the context, fears that change will bring loss of power, livelihood, and even cultural identity must be acknowledged as both real and legitimate.

But cultural identity cuts both ways in this conflict. The ESA, by finally forcing at least some reduction in irrigation deliveries, helped the Klamath tribes obtain a small measure of reparations for a long history of efforts to eliminate their tribal identity. Tribes in the Lower Klamath Basin were also delighted that the government finally took some steps to restore traditional sacred salmon fisheries that had long been in decline due to upstream dams and diversions. Environmentalists have been pleased that the ESA has protected threatened and endangered species and, incidentally, focused attention on watershed restoration. The Klamath Basin seems to many the perfect focus for such attention, because the irrigation culture there appears so clearly unsustainable and inefficient.

Unfortunately, the cultural dimensions of the conflict encourage both sides to treat it as a high-stakes, winner-take-all dispute. A 2004 *Washington Post* editorial dramatically captured what has seemed to be the prevailing view on all sides: "In the Klamath Basin, there is no middle road: Either the farmers move away, or the fish die."[26] When the contesting parties see a problem in this light, solutions are not likely to come easily.

Another kind of culture conflict often simmers under the surface. That is a conflict between levels of government and even between agencies within a single government. Because of their different histories, missions, and employees, the Bureau of Reclamation takes a different view of the priorities for water allocation in the basin than the Fish and Wildlife Service or the National Marine Fisheries Service. The law can strengthen the hand of one side or the other in interagency disputes, but leadership, personalities, funding, and standing within the administration are likely to be just as important.

Science Wars

The third fundamental theme is of uncertainty and its consequences for conflict resolution. Efforts to use science to mediate conflict lie at the root of this theme. High levels of uncertainty about the causal connections between actions and environmental impacts, about the extent of those impacts, and about the relative importance of various causes of environmental degradation typically pervade environmental conflicts. The Klamath conflict shows such uncertainty in abundance. Little was known of the endangered species before they were listed; not much more is known today. The Klamath Basin ecosystem as a whole is just as poorly understood.

There is a close relationship between the values that underlie the cultural elements of these disputes and dealing with scientific uncertainty. Culture- or values-based claims can be uncomfortable to argue about and typically offer little in the way of direct legal purchase. As a result, disputes fundamentally grounded in the differing values of the disputants often end up being characterized (and even genuinely perceived) by all sides as scientific disagreements.

Framing disputes in scientific terms cannot remove values from the equation, but it can make their role less apparent. Because uncertainties and information gaps are rampant, even in well-studied systems, management decisions frequently depend on the extent of information demanded before the status quo is changed, on which data are accepted as reliable, and on whose interpretations of that data prevail. Those decisions, in turn, are inevitably determined by values. People who believe in, and benefit from, the status quo will demand strong proof of harm as a predicate to change and a high level of certainty that the proposed change will address that harm. They will also be inclined to interpret uncertain or incomplete data as supporting their position. The opposite is true of those who place a high value on environmental protection: They will demand change on the basis of much less certain data. The Klamath is a microcosm of these debates, which take on a Miltonic dimension nationwide, with proponents of the status quo demanding that "sound" (as opposed to what they call "junk") science support any policy move that threatens to destabilize existing entitlements.

One side or the other often seeks review by outside scientists and blue-ribbon panels to resolve scientific uncertainties or disputes. Because even scientists cannot be totally objective when the evidence is incomplete or uncertain, background assumptions and values play a role even in the outcome of high-level outside reviews. Most obviously, research scientists have often deeply internalized the highly conservative norms about burden of proof that are typically applied to research science. Those norms may be so deeply ingrained that reviewing scientists will apply them automatically to management decisions, calling for very high levels of certainty before the status quo is changed without reflecting on whether the management context calls for different assumptions.

Factual uncertainty plays a key role in natural resource conflicts, but other kinds of uncertainty are also important. Often, the law itself is uncertain, as well as how it applies to the specific situation. The law of water allocation is a prime example, for a number of reasons. Appropriative water rights depend on diversion and actual use, but use is only infrequently directly monitored.

Water rights with very early priority dates have been implicitly reserved across the West to support federal interests, but those rights have rarely been quantified, or even defined in any but the vaguest of terms. The Klamath crisis unfolded in the middle of a lengthy process in Oregon of comprehensive state determination of all the water rights in the Upper Klamath Basin. Until that process is completed, all entitlements, public and private, are only presumptive, and it remains unclear who holds what rights to the basin's waters.

Overlain on that layer of uncertainty are two more layers added by the environmental regulatory system. The first is uncertainty over what steps the environmental laws require. Research science can pursue interesting questions regardless of their immediate societal relevance, advancing gradually toward robust causal explanations by incremental narrowing of the band of uncertainty. Environmental regulation, in stark contrast, requires that regulatory science answer extraordinarily difficult causal questions immediately. It is often difficult to precisely sketch the obligations imposed by the ESA because the exact survival needs of protected species are poorly understood. Nor is it easy to gain that information over time. Tightly controlled, laboratory-style experiments are impossible to conduct in large-scale natural systems, even if they were politically acceptable. That means there is almost always lots of room for wrangling and political maneuvering over precisely what conservation measures are required or authorized.

Added to that is uncertainty over the interrelationship between the law of water allocation and that of environmental protection. The federal legislature, which until very recently has been the primary driver of environmental protection law in the United States, has long recognized water allocation as primarily the domain of the states. Although it is clear that the United States has the legal authority to override state water allocation law in the pursuit of valid federal goals, Congress has been reluctant to do so strongly or openly. Environmental laws, therefore, often contain provisions that encourage federal authorities to consider state water law, or reserve authority over allocation to the states. Those provisions, while they have proven to be weak reeds in litigation, can lead water rights holders to overestimate the strength of their entitlements and federal regulators to underexploit the scope of their authority.[27]

In total, this litany of uncertainties places significant barriers in the way of resolution of water conflicts. Classic market solutions, in which the government or environmental groups would purchase water rights from farmers and dedicate those rights to fish, do not work if there is high uncertainty about what the farmers actually own. It is difficult for negotiations of any sort to be productive if each side, its view colored, of course, by its cultural lenses, is able to believe that it holds strong entitlements and its opponents do not.

Square Pegs in Round Holes

The fourth and final recurring theme is that the available problem-solving tools are ill suited to addressing environmental conflicts. Natural resources simply do not respect the many levels of artificial political and institutional boundaries created for human convenience. For these disputes, therefore, boundaries are often a hindrance to finding solutions.

Political boundaries are the most obvious problem. The Klamath Basin crosses two states and is divided geologically and socially into two distinct parts. The Upper Basin is a transition zone between the Sierra-Cascade range and the basin and range province of the intermountain West; the Lower Basin runs through a wet and mountainous region to the Pacific Ocean. The Upper Basin lies mostly in Oregon; its economic and social hub is Klamath Falls. The Lower Basin is entirely in California and lacks a cohesive center. But they share a single river system; water and land use in the Upper Basin dramatically affects the Lower Basin, and, conversely, Lower Basin water demands can limit Upper Basin options.

More subtly, resource conflicts in the United States almost always straddle the invisible boundary between state and federal government jurisdiction. That is especially true of water conflicts, because the states are primarily responsible for water allocation decisions, while the federal government is principally responsible for operating the large irrigation systems that make water rights valuable and for regulating the environmental effects of allocation decisions.

Even within the scope of federal efforts or those of a single state, conceptual, institutional, and legal boundaries can limit perceptions of an environmental problem and, therefore, of potential solutions. In the Klamath Basin, the federal regulatory response has focused almost entirely on operation of the Klamath Project, because that appears to be the variable most vulnerable to regulatory control. A host of other federal, state, and private actions with effects on the basin's water resources have been nearly ignored. Those include actions within and beyond the geographic boundaries of the basin. Through California's intricate plumbing system, the Klamath River watershed is connected to the entire California agricultural and urban water delivery system, from Lake Shasta, just south of the basin, to the Mexican border. The Trinity River, the largest tributary of the Klamath system, is dammed as part of the Central Valley Project. Up to 90 percent of the Trinity's average flow can be diverted into the Sacramento River to augment Central Valley Project supplies. The future of the Klamath watershed is intimately bound up with ongoing efforts to restore some part of the Trinity River's natural flow, but until recently the two have been addressed in isolation.

Finally, many of the problems in the Upper Basin are related to water quality, but neither federal reclamation law nor state water law effectively integrates water quality considerations into allocation decisions. As a result, water quality problems are largely unaddressed. The regular blooms of algae toxic to humans and pets in two reservoirs along the upper main-stem Klamath are just the latest and most extreme manifestation of those problems.

Learning from a Train Wreck

Since the summer of 2001, irrigators, federal and state governments, environmental organizations, and Indian tribes have struggled to find ways to balance the needs of endangered species with irrigation in the Klamath Basin. Some progress has been made. A combination of wet years, last-minute rains, a water bank, increased groundwater pumping, and the issuance of a ten-year operating plan allowed the Bureau of Reclamation to maintain normal irrigation deliveries from 2002 through 2007. Collaborative efforts to restore the land, water, and spirit of the basin have been launched. New commitment to ecosystem-wide management has been voiced on all sides.

While they are submerged for the moment, however, the underlying problems and the bitterness that came to the surface in 2001 remain. The arid West remains vulnerable to periodic drought and may become even more so as global warming exacerbates the natural wet and dry cycles. The water needs of fish and irrigators have not changed. Some watershed restoration efforts have received renewed attention, but the ecosystem is still distressed. Low salmon returns to the Klamath in 2006 led to drastic curtailment of ocean fisheries, despite a seemingly healthy run on the nearby Sacramento River. Efforts have been made to improve scientific understanding of the basin, but much remains unknown. Threats to the ESA have abated for the moment with the return of Democrats to power in the Congress, but underlying uncertainty about the extent to which that law can or should be aggressively implemented to promote comprehensive ecosystem management remains. Operations of the Klamath Project have not been substantially modified, although some small changes have been made. The economic pressures facing agriculture, especially trade policies that promote cheap imports, have only worsened. Those pressures have increased recently in the Klamath Basin as PacifiCorp, the utility that operates the hydropower dams along the Klamath River, has gained regulatory approval to raise the highly subsidized rates irrigators have been paying for power. Meanwhile, the license issued by the Federal Energy Regulatory Commission (FERC) for operation of PacifiCorp's dams is up for renewal. Those proceedings have become the latest battleground in the Klamath conflict.

In short, the crisis of 2001 led to a variety of ad hoc efforts to find an accommodation among the competing interests. Those efforts have produced a great deal of important new information, but in the end they have only expanded the problem-shed and the range of interested parties. They reveal the lack of effective legal or social strategies to manage the transition from the old to the new West, from rivers harnessed solely to serve human economic needs to rivers that do ecological as well as economic work. Another crisis is inevitable unless the root cause of the 2001 shortfall, too many demands competing for too little water, is addressed. It is entirely human, but unrealistic and ineffective, to rely instead on the hope of a quick fix and annual prayers for sufficient rain.

Finding a Way Forward

Combining the four key themes mentioned earlier, the basic lesson of the Klamath story is that natural resource conflicts are far more complex than the simplistic "fish versus farmers" picture painted by most of the media and many of the participants. Just as the conflicts are not simple, neither will the solutions be. The challenge in the Klamath Basin, and across the West, is enormous. Creating landscapes that are both economically and ecologically sustainable will require vanquishing history, recognizing divergent and deeply held human values, addressing pervasive uncertainty, and nourishing institutions capable of acting across traditional boundaries.

The question, of course, is how to get there in an age of minimal government, with the influence of environmentalism seemingly in decline. To date, the combatants in the Klamath Basin have called on four interrelated but in some ways inconsistent strategies to solve this conflict: absolute faith in science, strict application of the law, infusions of emergency federal money, and stakeholder negotiation. Taken alone, none of those strategies is sufficient, but each is necessary to a lasting solution.

Resort to science is understandable, and indeed inevitable in the current legal structure. The ESA, the law that brings these conflicts to light, is strongly science based. The question of how much water must be left in a lake or sent down a river to sustain an endangered species certainly has strong scientific elements. The ESA reinforces the importance of science by directing the regulatory agencies to apply the best available science to their decisions. Moreover, science is widely viewed as an objective basis for making difficult decisions, one that all parties should accept. Ultimately, though, even the best science cannot eliminate the need for policy judgments and hard decisions about the appropriate level of precaution against future environmental risks. The hard truth is that science alone cannot determine how water should be allocated among competing demands. It is a mistake to insist, as the law currently does, that scientists identify the magic point at which agricultural water withdrawals can be precisely balanced with environmental protection. That point may not exist. Even if it does, it will be impossible to identify. The futile search for the magic point will only continue to escalate controversy, satisfying no one.

Neither can law alone resolve these conflicts, for two related reasons. First, law cannot create new social landscapes; at best, it can serve as a catalyst to trigger the political negotiations needed to do that. Second, law is often not rigorously enforced in the face of stiff opposition. It can easily end up as a symbolic statement of societal priorities with little impact on the ground. The strong, substantive mandates of the ESA have at times been a catalyst for positive changes, in the law and in water institutions.[28] But while the ESA can focus attention on a problem, and can prod those advantaged by the status quo to the table, its political vulnerability limits its transformative power. A priori, one might speculate that an ESA-driven water crisis in the Klamath Basin would generate strong federal and state leadership in an effort to identify solutions consistent with the act's requirements but also fundamentally fair to all stakeholders in the basin. We believe that one of the most important lessons of the Klamath conflict is that reliance on the hammer of the law to trigger transitions to sustainable landscapes has serious limitations.

Modern environmental law has encouraged emphasis on litigation as an agent of social change. In the 1960s, environmental law was created out of whole cloth, first by courts and then by Congress. This new invention was, of necessity, built on two related premises: (1) the environment can be saved only by suing the bastards who are mucking it up;[29] and (2) the enforcement of all environmental laws must be strict, which requires that responsibility be shared between the government and citizens or nongovernmental organizations. After courts liberalized standing rules to allow citizen suits to protect environmental values, Congress routinely put citizen suit provisions in the major environmental law programs.

Over the years, environmentalists have deliberately provoked political crisis through litigation. Students of modern environmental policy have argued that a perceived crisis can trigger political and legal action and produce lasting solutions. Some evidence does support that view. Severe air pollution episodes triggered local and state laws in the first half of the twentieth century and played an important role in the enactment of the Clean Air Act.[30] In the 1970s, some litigation achieved similar results. To cite one of the best-known examples, a federal appellate court held that the nineteenth-century statute governing management of the national forests required that each tree be individually assessed and marked before it could be cut. That decision brought clear-cutting to a halt and led directly to enactment of the National Forest Management Act.[31] The use of litigation to spark increased environmental protection remains the key premise of many environmental groups; indeed, the preference for litigation enjoys renewed vigor today in light of the George W. Bush administration's moves to roll back much of the environmental safety net constructed between 1969 and 1980.

In today's political climate, though, litigation can be a positive or a negative catalyst. A successful suit may harden opposition to change, sowing the seeds of long-term political loss, especially for a law like the ESA, which appears far more politically vulnerable than pollution laws that protect human health. As the United States and the Soviet Union discovered during the Cold War, weapons can be so powerful that the costs of using them become "unacceptably high."[32] Overaggressive use of the ESA might prove to be a self-defeating "nuclear option." Furthermore, in the years since the environmental revolution of the 1970s, extractive interests have learned that the courts can also work to their advantage, as judges sometimes seize on any excuse to avoid vigorous application of laws that seem to pay too little attention to human economic concerns.[33]

Nonetheless, in 2001 the Bureau of Reclamation was willing to risk a crisis by acquiescing in strict enforcement of the ESA. In that particular drama, it thus played the provocateur role commonly taken by environmental groups. Many environmentalists vigorously supported the decision to close the Klamath headgates because they assumed that consensus-building efforts would follow the falling of that hammer.

Using public interest litigation to provoke a crisis, however, is now a game that anyone can play. In the Klamath Basin, the irrigators enthusiastically embraced the theory that crisis can move policy. In one of the legal run-ups to the summer of 2001, the irrigators successfully used the citizen suit provision of the ESA to challenge limitations on irrigation deliveries from the Klamath Project. The case reached the U.S. Supreme Court, where the majority held that those seeking to block enforcement of the ESA had just as much right to be heard in court as those seeking to promote it. Justice Scalia felt compelled to bolster this plausible reading of the ESA with the wholly implausible claim that besides conserving species, "another objective (if not indeed the primary one) [of the ESA] is to avoid needless economic dislocation produced by agency officials zealously but unintelligently pursuing their environmental objectives."[34] Perhaps buoyed by this earlier success, agricultural interests hoped that the 2001 crisis would at least bring them an individualized exemption from the ESA and perhaps even spark broader amendment of the act. Farmers did not win an exemption and lost a suit in the federal court of claims for $1 billion in damages. However, in the immediate aftermath of the crisis of 2001, the farmers have managed to maintain the status quo, in which their water needs enjoy practical priority over those of fish and tribes.

In addition, the farmers succeeded in opening the federal and state treasuries to keep a fragile, marginal agricultural area of the Upper Basin alive. As we detail in chapter 7, farmers received substantial emergency payments for lost crops, the Bureau of Reclamation funded a water bank, and the states pumped money into the basin for new wells and other remedies. Money is the key to any ecosystem restoration, but most of the public expenditures so far do not contribute to sustainable solutions; they simply move some water from Klamath Basin farmers to wetlands and refuges. They are designed only to preserve the status quo and paper over the ongoing crisis by allowing farmers to survive until the next wet cycle.

Unlike many people who enthusiastically embrace the decline of the New Deal state and the shift to bottom-up, stakeholder-driven processes to govern the use of natural resources, we are skeptical of collaborative planning as a panacea for these sorts of conflicts. Across the country, governments and well-organized stakeholder groups have jumped head first into large-scale ecosystem restoration experiments without a clear understanding of the goals and incentives needed to make them work. These ad hoc efforts are substituting for large-scale federal landscape planning, which has been off the political agendas of federal, state, and local governments since New Deal efforts were ended in 1943. In the place of plans with fixed objectives, process has been substituted for substance through collaborative governance. The best example perhaps is the California Bay Delta Program, which began, with great hope, during the Clinton administration. Millions of dollars were spent on meetings, workshops, research, and environmental assessments in an effort to find ways to protect a sustainable San Francisco Bay–Delta ecosystem without taking water away from farmers. However, that bold experiment did not produce consensus on the difficult water reallocation questions, and the state-federal collaboration collapsed. After years of talk, study, and important but ineffective decisions, a Klamath-like crisis looms; in March of 2007 a California superior court judge ordered the massive pumps shut down to conserve the declining delta smelt. Although that shutdown was averted, the fate of the entire delta remains in the courts, in December 2007 the court ordered changes that could reduce water deliveries by as much as 30 percent. The place that consensus process was specifically intended to avoid.

The moment for these experiments may be passing. They ultimately depended on each stakeholder assuming that there was a worst-case scenario to be avoided. For the extraction and irrigation communities, the worst case was strict enforcement of the ESA. If that is removed as a credible threat, winners under the status quo will have little incentive to negotiate new approaches.

To resolve the Klamath and similar conflicts, we suggest the following basic principles:

1. The keystone principle is the articulation of some workable vision of a sustainable landscape. At the outset, we reject the polar extremes, the ideal of pristine nature and the ideal of the nineteenth-century irrigation society. Both have been overtaken by history, and neither allows the vision needed to achieve a workable balance for the future.
2. That vision must be based on the much contested concept of carrying capacity. As Garrett Hardin has written: "We can, of course, increase carrying capacity somewhat. But only hubris leads us to think that our ability to do so is without limit. Despite all our technological accomplishments—and they are many—there is a potent germ of truth in the saying of Horace (65–8 BC): Naturam expelles furca, tamen usque recurret. 'Drive nature off with a pitchfork, nevertheless she will return with a rush.' This is the message of Rachel Carson, which has been corroborated by many others."[35]

   Carrying capacity is not a magic number or set of numbers but an ethical construct informed by science and stakeholder values. It requires articulation of a vision of what people should be and what a desirable world would look like, not just of what is necessary to fulfill basic biological needs. Thus, developing a vision of a sustainable landscape requires that the community struggle through difficult, forthright political debates. Ultimately, policy makers should understand that they are dealing with a clash of cultures and must make value choices. But they cannot avoid putting the competing cultures at risk; all choices carry some risk to some deeply held human values.
3. The vision of a sustainable landscape should be independent of the existence of endangered species or current crop patterns. We advocate this heretical view because the focus on either conserving listed species or maintaining the status quo leads to tunnel vision and a preference for quick fixes rather than sustainable solutions. The ultimate objective is a balance between biodiversity conservation and human use.
4. The process must be science based to the maximum extent possible. We are acutely conscious of the limits of science but equally

recognize the necessity for continued reliance on it. We reject all simplistic approaches to the use of science, such as the dichotomy between "good" and "bad" science, the notion that scientific evidence that is not determinative is valueless, and the idea that value judgments such as the precautionary principle can be used to substitute for the teachings of science. The application of science is an essential element of fairness, legitimacy, and long-term effectiveness. Nonetheless, a more realistic vision of what it means to make effective use of science in resource allocation decisions is needed. That vision would separate scientific from policy judgments to the extent possible, provide greater transparency about those judgments, and include a firm commitment to improving our understanding of the problem over time.

5. The process must start in the Klamath Basin, but it cannot end there. Both the vision and the plan for sharing the pain should come from the basin. Many consensus processes try to minimize the second factor, but we are guided by the words of a leading antifascist Italian diplomat, who described his objective in negotiating a post–World War I treaty with the newly created Yugoslavia as ensuring "that the causes of discontent should be equally divided between the two nations."[36] Of course, for that purpose the basin must include all its inhabitants, both Upper and Lower. The Upper Basin irrigators cannot be permitted to define the Lower Basin out of the problemshed. The basin is too poor to implement the solution on its own, so the necessary funds must come from a variety of sources; but they should not flow until whatever process survives to grapple with the problem develops realistic, substantive goals.

Once the vision and specific targets are established in the Klamath Basin, the institutions used or created to implement the vision must be given the capacity to deliver truly basin-wide solutions. One of the problems of consensus processes is the guest list. Hikers and recreational fishers in the Lower Basin, environmental groups without strong in-basin representation, and beleaguered California farmers 300 miles to the south all have a legitimate interest in any outcome. In the end, distinctions between primary and secondary stakeholders will have to be made, and some interests will have to be represented by proxies.

Earlier, we dismissed characterizing the problem as a choice between farms and fish as too simplistic, but ultimately, society must either choose between farming and fish in the Klamath Basin or find a way to accommodate both. Avoiding or putting off the debates will not make them any easier.

Delay simply courts another train wreck, a future that offers no promise to any of the competing groups. For farmers, the best chance of maintaining their culture may be to make peace with the ecosystem. They will have to accept the fact that the West's ecosystems are a resource of increasing value and scarcity and that the future of western irrigation is one of gradual downsizing. Environmentalists will have to accept the fact that humans are also part of any sustainable landscape. We return to these themes in the last chapter.

A repeat of the summer of 2001 could be tragic for fish and wildlife, farmers, and the West more generally, yet it is inevitable without deeper structural change than has yet been attempted. We join the call of Ed Marston, the distinguished founder of the *High Country News*, for a new spirit of reclamation, one that seeks to reclaim both the land and those left behind by the engine of "growth, progress and technological mastery" that the original reclamation vision produced.[37]

CHAPTER 2

A Remote, Upside-Down Watershed

> If Klamath peaks stand on their heads, the major rivers . . . seem to run backward—looking-glass rivers. While driving upstream beside the Klamath where it begins to rise from its deep, forested gorge into the bare buttes of the volcanic plateau, I began to see cormorants and sea gulls as though I were approaching the river's mouth instead of its upper reaches.
>
> David Rains Wallace, *The Klamath Knot*

In the relatively remote Klamath Basin, nature's unkind geological tricks lie at the root of the water allocation puzzle. An irrigation economy developed in the driest, least watered portion of the basin and a commercial and recreational fishing economy in the wettest. That unusual combination has proven difficult to sustain.

The Klamath River drains a vast, lightly populated region in south central Oregon and northern California. The river originates in Upper Klamath Lake, a broad, shallow lake fed by snowmelt from high in the Cascade Mountains of Oregon. After reaching California, the river is augmented by the flows of the Scott, Shasta, Salmon, and Trinity rivers. Ultimately, it empties into the Pacific Ocean within the boundaries of Redwood National Park. Overall, the watershed of the Klamath River covers some 12,000 square miles,[1] an area roughly the size of Maryland and bigger than eight other U.S. states.

As can be seen in figure 3, a map of the Klamath watershed resembles an hourglass tilted on its side. Its two nearly equal regions are geographically, biologically, and socially distinct. The Upper Basin lies primarily in Oregon,

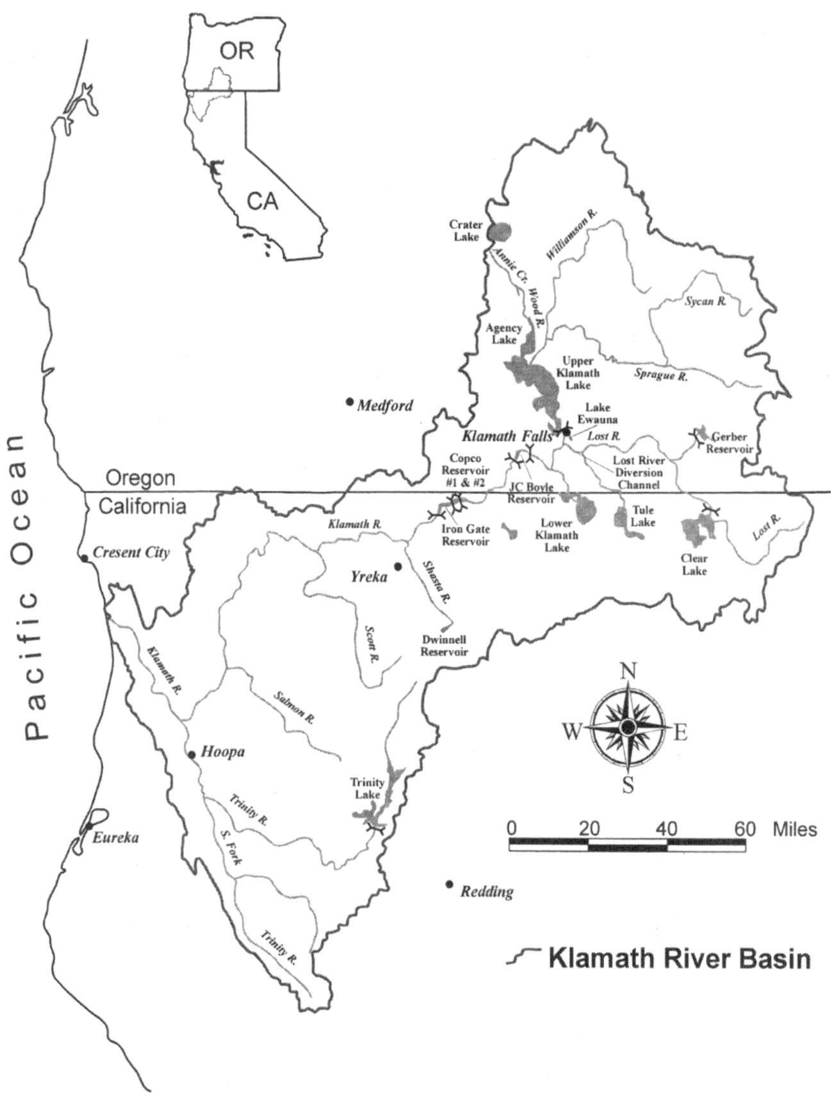

FIGURE 3

The hourglass-shaped Klamath River Basin. The Upper Klamath Basin straddles the Oregon-California border, while the Lower Klamath Basin forms the far northwest corner of California. The major dams on the Klamath and Trinity systems are noted. (Independent Multidisciplinary Science Team, *IMST Review of the USFWS and NMFS 2001 Biological Opinions on Management of the Klamath Reclamation Project and Related Reports*, Technical Report 2003-1 [Salem, OR: Oregon Watershed Enhancement Board, 2003], 9.)

spilling over into far northern California. It includes all the lands that drain into the Klamath River above Iron Gate Dam, located just across the state line in California. Lying entirely in northern California, the Lower Basin encompasses the watershed of the Klamath River and its major tributaries from Iron Gate Dam to the Pacific Ocean.

The two pieces of the basin are put together upside down or backward, depending on how you look at it.[2] The typical watershed is steepest and wettest in its upper reaches, near the source of the river, and flattest and driest near its mouth. The Klamath reverses that pattern. The rivers there are older than the mountains, which arose recently near the coast as the tectonic plate that carries North America collided with the plates of the Pacific.[3] The Klamath River originates in the Cascades, flows through high sagebrush plateaus, then cuts back through mountains to the sea. The Lower Basin is a rugged, inaccessible jumble of steep peaks and small valleys. Most of the runoff in the Klamath watershed occurs in this lower region, far downstream from the primary agricultural lands.[4]

The watershed's unusual topography plays an important role in its water problems. As the National Research Council has observed, "Unlike most watersheds, the Klamath watershed has its greatest relief and topographic complexity in the lower half rather than in its headwaters."[5] The steep canyons and deep valleys of many watersheds allow substantial storage in reservoirs upstream from agricultural demand. The upper Klamath watershed does not offer those sites. Instead, the storage of project water is primarily restricted to broad but shallow Upper Klamath Lake. In addition to enjoying most of the precipitation, the Lower Basin has the best water storage topography in the watershed, the deep canyons favored by Bureau of Reclamation engineers in the first half of the last century. The late Marc Reisner described the bureau's view of the Lower Klamath as "a perfect example of how God left the perfection and completion of California to the Bureau of Reclamation."[6] The Bureau once planned a dam near the river's mouth, but that plan died in 1981, when the Lower Klamath River was added to the federal Wild and Scenic Rivers system.

Despite their proximity and the river whose troubled waters they share, the two halves of the Klamath watershed are in many respects isolated from each other. The Upper Basin lies predominantly in Oregon, while the lower is exclusively in California. Roads in the region are few and slow, complicating travel between the Upper and Lower basins. Their economies, although similarly lethargic, depend on different engines. Their people tend to share an independent streak and a suspicion of outsiders, to limit their sense of community to others within their own sub-basin and even within that area to those who share their economic and cultural interests.

A Closer Look at the Upper Klamath Basin

Located in south central Oregon and extreme northern California,[7] the Upper Klamath Basin is an ancient volcanic area that straddles the basin-and-range and High Cascades geologic provinces. Unlike most waters of the basin and range, the Klamath River finds an outlet, to the Pacific Ocean. Thus, the use and allocation of its waters affect coastal as well as interior environments and economies. The Upper Basin sits on a 4,000- to 6,000-foot-high plateau that lies in the rain shadow of the Cascadia margin, the line of volcanoes, some still active, that extends from Washington state into northern California. The basin includes a small portion of the High Cascade mountains. Its most striking element, and the one most familiar to outsiders, is Crater Lake, the deep blue lake that fills the caldera left by the catastrophic eruption of Mount Mazama some seven thousand years ago. But the dominant physical feature is a flat, high agricultural plateau lying just west of the ridge that marks the beginning of the forbiddingly arid Great Basin. Klamath County, the site of most of the lands irrigated by the federal Klamath Project, covers the northernmost part of the Upper Basin.

The region has the wet winters and dry summers typical of the Pacific Coast states. Because much of it lies in the rain shadow of the Cascades, the Upper Klamath Basin is predominantly an arid, high desert area. Although some of its high peaks receive more than 40 inches of precipitation annually,[8] the basin averages only about 27 inches per year, about half of which falls as snow. Klamath Falls averages only 11 to 14 inches per year. As in much of the western United States, precipitation is highly variable from year to year. Periodic droughts are the norm. Agricultural water demand exceeds supply in about seven out of every ten years.[9]

The Upper Basin is not an easy place to farm. It enjoys good volcanic soils, but because of the severe climatic conditions, none of the lands in the region fall in the U.S. Department of Agriculture's highest productivity class.[10] The growing season is short, only 100 to 125 days per year. Killing frosts can happen in any month of the year. Despite these difficulties, with the help of a federal water project, a relatively diverse agricultural industry has developed in the area.

An enormous volcanic lake covering more than 1,000 square miles once occupied much of the Upper Basin. A climatic warming period split the lake into three smaller pieces, known today as Upper Klamath, Lower Klamath, and Tule lakes. At the time of white settlement, a vast wetlands complex encompassing roughly 185,000 acres of shallow lakes and freshwater marshes dominated the Upper Basin, earning it recognition as the Everglades of the West. Early settlers were not enamored of the wetlands, however.

Masses of water snakes entwined on lake and river banks frightened early residents with their hissing, and frogs were thick enough to make walking in Klamath Falls difficult.[11]

While unpopular with settlers, the Upper Basin's marshes and lakes attracted millions of ducks, geese, swans, and other migratory waterfowl.[12] Today, with less than 25 percent of the historic wetlands remaining, migratory bird populations are much reduced. Nonetheless, they remain impressive. The cluster of national wildlife refuges in the Upper Basin supports the greatest concentration of waterfowl in North America, providing "a migratory stopover for about three-quarters of the Pacific Flyway waterfowl, with peak fall concentrations of over 1 million birds."[13] It also harbors the largest wintering bald eagle population in the continental United States from December to February.[14] The birds draw hundreds of thousands of visitors to the refuges each year.[15]

Upper Klamath Lake, the dominant hydrologic feature of the modern Upper Basin, is fed primarily by the Williamson and Wood rivers, which arise in the forests to its east and north. Upper Klamath Lake has the largest surface area of any lake in Oregon,[16] and it is reportedly the largest freshwater lake in the West.[17] But it is extremely shallow, as much marsh as lake, averaging only 8 feet deep when full and falling to as low as 3 feet on average in a dry year.[18] Other large shallow lakes and marshes remain in the Upper Basin, including Lower Klamath, Tule, and Clear lakes, although the area of each has been substantially diminished by conversion to agriculture. The Klamath Project, described in the next chapter, severed the connection between Lower Klamath and Tule lakes and the Klamath River.

The marshlands of the Upper Basin historically supported robust populations of two large, long-lived fish, called *qapdo* and *c'waam* by the Klamath Indians, for whom they provided a major food source. They were dried, as shown in figure 4, to provide a long-term food supply. The Lost River and shortnose suckers, as they are now known, are large—the Lost River sucker can reach more than 3 feet, and the shortnose sucker nearly 2 feet[19]—and exceptionally long lived, with some individuals known to have survived more than forty years.[20] They spend most of their lives in the shallow lakes, ascending tributary rivers annually to spawn. They once inhabited all the major lakes of the Upper Basin and their tributaries, supporting multiple canneries. One naturalist described Upper Klamath Lake in 1884 as "more prolific in animal life" than any other water body he had seen.[21] Another wrote of the "incredible numbers of Lost River suckers, the most highly prized food fish in the basin, running up the rivers in spring."[22] Recreational and tribal fishing for suckers in the Upper Basin persisted into the 1980s, when the catch declined sharply.[23]

FIGURE 4

Drying suckers, 1898. C'waam and qapdo, as the Lost River and shortnose suckers were known, were a primary food source for the Klamath Indians until the 1980s. (Photo courtesy of the Klamath County Museum.)

In recent decades, the Upper Basin has struggled economically. Like the northern Great Plains, it did not share in the boom times experienced by much of the "new" West.[24] After rapid population growth in the 1970s, Klamath County lost population in the 1980s. It rebounded with modest growth in the 1990s, but out-migration still exceeded in-migration, the population was aging, unemployment rates were high, and per capita income was below the national average.[25] Weyerhaeuser closed its Klamath Falls sawmill in the 1990s. The mill was designed for old-growth ponderosa pine, which is essentially gone from the basin. Second-growth timber will not mature until well into the twenty-first century, and timber harvesting on federal lands has been constrained by the Northwest Forest Plan, developed to protect the northern spotted owl.

The precarious economic position of the region is perhaps best illustrated by the fact that the largest share of household income is imported from outside the basin, in the form of government transfer payments, dividends, and wages from jobs outside the area, rather than locally produced.[26] Within the Upper Klamath Basin, agriculture, forest products, education, and public administration (government employment and federal and state payments to local governments) are the largest generators of jobs and income.[27] Total nonfarm payroll employment was about thirty thousand in 2006, with most of the jobs in the service sector. The Kla-Mo-Ya Casino, a joint venture among three tribes, opened in 1997, but how much new revenue it will bring to the area is not known. Given its remote location, it is likely to simply shift leisure spending within the area, rather than attracting substantial funds from outside. Agriculture, like the other extractive industries that sustained the West up to a generation ago, generates an ever-smaller proportion of the local, state, and regional economy. Income from agriculture has fallen with the prices of agricultural commodities.[28]

Yet farming remains an important part of the Upper Basin's identity. There are some 2,239 farms in the Upper Basin, 1,744 of which are irrigated.[29] Farm and ranch families have more than money at stake in the Klamath water conflicts. Like many small irrigators, they view farming not as a business but as a way of life. In many cases, they have chosen to farm knowing that they could make more money if they moved elsewhere and pursued other livelihoods. Their attachment to farming is tied to a sense of heritage and obligation to preceding and succeeding generations of basin farmers.[30] Not surprisingly, they resist the notion that economic value alone should determine the distribution of the basin's waters. Like other economically marginal farmers, they have come to see themselves as an embattled cultural minority, adopting the rhetoric of minority protection more typically associated with Native American or small Hispanic communities in the West to buffer themselves against threatening political and economic currents.[31] They have also accepted the basic moral critique of the use of economics to make public resource choices. The Klamath farmers make essentially the same argument as environmentalists, but with a different goal in mind. Mark Sagoff, a leading environmental philosopher, writes that "policies that protect the ecological and historical character of the shared environment do not necessarily maximize its economic product, but construct a common heritage."[32] Change "ecological" to "cultural," and the statement could aptly summarize the Klamath farmers' defense of the status quo. This said, the Klamath irrigators place their faith in the liberal theory that people are better protected by individual civil rights than by group rights.[33] As subsequent chapters explain, the farmers have vigorously asserted their individual rights to protection of their investments through the takings clause of the federal Constitution.

Downstream to the Lower Klamath Basin

The Klamath River runs from Iron Gate Dam to the Pacific Ocean through a sparsely populated, well-watered area. The Lower Klamath Basin, lying entirely in California, is dominated by timber-covered slopes and mountainous wilderness areas. Geologically, the Lower Basin is an area of rapid tectonic uplift, which accounts for the steep, forested terrain through which the Klamath and its major tributaries—the Trinity, Salmon, Scott, and Shasta rivers—run. In the words of David Rains Wallace, the mountains of the

Klamath region are "intricately and tortuously folded, faulted, and upthrust, forming a knot of jagged peaks and steep gorges."[34] This fractured topography proved extraordinarily confusing to early white explorers such as Jedediah Smith, who found it nearly impossible to follow the basin's rivers. It limited exploration and development of the area even after gold was found along the lower Klamath, Trinity, and Scott rivers in the late 1840s. Roads were difficult to construct, and the swift rivers were barely navigable.[35]

Today, the region's topography ensures its continued isolation. The four California counties that lie wholly or partially within the Lower Basin together have a population of only about 215,000 people, fewer than half of those actually within the boundaries of the Lower Basin. The largest communities in the Lower Basin are Yreka, along Interstate 5, with just over 7,000 residents, and Weaverville, a town of roughly 3,500.[36] The population numbers can perhaps be best understood by comparison to those for California as a whole. The state has some 35 million residents, an average (across the entire state) of 217 per square mile. The Lower Basin counties, by contrast, have a population density of just over 15 people per square mile, even including the relatively urban communities of Eureka and Crescent City, which lie outside the geographic basin.

The Lower Klamath Basin lies within the Klamath-Siskiyou bioregion, recognized by the International Union for the Conservation of Nature and the World Wildlife Fund as an area of global biotic significance.[37] This is Bigfoot country, sufficiently remote, densely forested, and mysterious to make tales of 8-foot-tall hairy hominids difficult to refute. The forests of the region support a remarkable range of plant species; "winters are mild enough and summers moist enough for species to grow together that elsewhere are segregated by altitude or latitude."[38] Most of the lower-elevation forests have been logged over, and many of the streams of the Lower Basin show the lingering effects of the nineteenth-century gold rush.[39] A high proportion of the land in the Lower Basin is owned by the federal government. The highest peaks, with their associated alpine lakes, provide recreation for backpackers and llama trekkers in places like the Marble Mountains, Trinity Alps, Red Buttes, and other wilderness areas.

Because its aquatic environments are radically different from those of the Upper Basin, the Lower Basin harbors distinctly different fishes. Its cold, swift-running waters once offered ideal habitat for salmonids. The Klamath River and its tributaries in the Lower Basin once teemed with coho and chinook salmon,[40] providing million-pound annual harvests for the region's Indians.[41] Anadromous salmon are remarkable fish, beginning their lives in freshwater, adapting to saltier conditions as they move downriver to the ocean, and returning after several years to their natal rivers to spawn. Some of the anadromous fish of the Klamath system, including chinook, steelhead, and possibly coho, historically traversed the boundary between the two halves of the basin, ranging as far inland as warm, murky Upper Klamath Lake. Iron Gate Dam now blocks all fish passage just below the California border.

The Lower Basin's salmonids, in addition to being more charismatic than the Upper Basin's suckers, still support valuable commercial and recreational fisheries. Concerns about species decline are intensifying in the Lower Basin, however. Many of the native fish are drastically reduced from their historic runs,[42] although so far only the coho salmon has been listed under the ESA.

Coho, also known as silver salmon, are fairly large, typically weighing as much as 13 pounds at spawning age. The spawning males are imposing, with hooked jaws, humped backs, and dark red sides. Coho occupy coastal streams from central California to Alaska. Populations are isolated from one another in those streams but not entirely so. They mix in the ocean, and every year a small proportion stray into streams other than those of their origin to spawn.[43] That is typical of salmon, which have complicated and variable life cycles. Within a single species, runs can become isolated enough to diverge genetically from one another simply by spawning in different streams at different times. That poses a challenge for the identification of entities for protection under the ESA, whose drafters assumed that species were easy to differentiate.

Coho in the Lower Klamath Basin spend just over a year in freshwaters before migrating to the ocean. At the age of three years they return to freshwater to spawn, mostly in the forested tributaries rather than the main-stem Klamath, over coarse gravel substrates. That upriver migration occurs in the fall, the earliest spawners arriving in September and stragglers sometimes coming as late as mid-December.[44] Young coho emerge from the eggs in spring. They do best in cool waters but can survive higher temperatures if food is abundant, predation is low, and the high temperatures are not constant.[45]

By 1997, when they were listed under the ESA, coho salmon in southern Oregon and northern California had declined from historic runs of 150,000 to 400,000 spawning fish annually to only about 10,000.[46] They have been extirpated from nearly half of the coastal streams they used to inhabit.[47] Only a small population of wild coho remain in the Klamath system, spawning primarily in the small tributaries, which are less degraded than the large ones.[48] Two hatcheries, one at Iron Gate Dam and the other on the Trinity River just below Trinity Reservoir, are believed to dominate current coho production in the system. Both hatchery runs descend primarily from stock imported from outside the Klamath Basin.[49]

The most abundant anadromous fish in the Lower Basin are chinook, also known as king salmon. Chinook are the largest Pacific salmon; the record chinook recorded in California weighed in at 85 pounds.[50] They lack the strongly hooked jaws and bright coloration of spawning coho. Historically, robust fall and spring chinook runs spawned in the main-stem Klamath and its tributaries as far as the Wood, Williamson, and Sprague rivers that feed Upper Klamath Lake.[51] Today, the spring run is almost gone, and the fall run is greatly reduced.

The historic size of the fall chinook run is not known with precision, but river harvests as late as the 1920s were in the range of 500,000 to 1,000,000 pounds, or as many as seventy thousand fish.[52] They supported robust recreational as well as commercial fisheries. Fall-run fish used to enter the river in July and August; today their migration peaks in September and continues through October.[53] Within a month, as river temperatures decrease, they reach their spawning grounds, spawn, and die. The young emerge in the stream; travel at varying speeds through spring and summer to the river's estuary; and by fall enter the ocean, where they remain until they are three years old and ready to spawn.[54] Like the coho, young chinook in the river system do best at cool temperatures. In the laboratory, optimal rearing temperatures are in the range of 55°F to 60°F. Juveniles can tolerate exposure to temperatures over 80°F, however, for short periods.

The National Marine Fisheries Service recognizes fifteen distinct populations of Pacific chinook. Klamath Basin chinook fall in two of those populations. Chinook from the lower Klamath River, below the confluence with the Trinity River, are lumped with others from coastal streams in southern Oregon as far south as San Francisco Bay. From the Trinity confluence upstream, Klamath and Trinity river chinook are placed in their own distinct population.[55] Neither group is currently protected by the ESA, but wild spawning fish in both groups are greatly reduced from historic levels.

During their ocean phase, Klamath chinook are believed to mingle with salmon from the Sacramento River and other basins off the coast of northern California and southern Oregon. Although Klamath Basin chinook account for a relatively small proportion of the region's ocean salmon catch, they have been the driver for management measures for the past several years. Salmon from the various basins cannot be readily distinguished in the ocean. As a result, reduction of one run can force the regulatory curtailment of ocean fishing even if other runs are abundant. That happened in 2005, when low Klamath chinook returns led to severe restrictions on the salmon fishery despite abundant (hatchery-supported) returns in the Sacramento system. Even more severe restrictions were imposed in 2006, reducing salmon fishing revenue in the region by more than $15 million from recent averages and prompting the Department of Commerce to declare a "fishery resource disaster."[56]

Steelhead, which are anadromous rainbow trout, remain fairly abundant in the Lower Klamath Basin. They are more tolerant of high temperatures than other salmonids, can return to spawn more than once, and show greater variation in the number of years they spend as juveniles in freshwater and as adults in the ocean.[57] These traits make them less sensitive to adverse stream conditions. Although considerably reduced from historic numbers, steelhead spawning runs remained about 100,000 in the late 1980s.[58]

Other important anadromous fish of the Lower Basin include the green sturgeon and the Pacific lamprey. Green sturgeon are enormous prehistoric fish. They migrate up the Klamath River to spawn between February and July.[59] Individual sturgeon weighing as much as 1,000 pounds were taken from the Klamath River in the nineteenth century.[60] The largest sturgeon taken from the Klamath in recent years was almost 9 feet long and weighed nearly 400 pounds.[61] Hoopa and Yurok tribal fisheries take a small number of sturgeon each year. The NMFS regards green sturgeon in the Rogue, Umpqua, and Klamath rivers as a single population, distinct from the population farther south, in the Sacramento River system. In 2006, the agency listed the Sacramento population as threatened but concluded that the northern population was not in danger of extirpation.[62] The Klamath population is currently monitored as a species of concern. Little is known of the biology of the eel-like Pacific lamprey, which has never been an important food or sport fish for European Americans. It did once provide a major food source for the Klamath Basin Indians,[63] and it remains culturally important to several Pacific Northwest tribes.[64] Lampreys tend to move upstream at night, and they may spend several months in freshwater before they spawn.[65]

The economy of the Lower Klamath Basin, together with much of the California coast around it, is more sensitive than that of the Upper Basin to the loss of ecosystem services. Commercial fishing in the ocean and sport fishing in the basin's rivers are important elements of the resource-dependent economy. The first commercial fishery on the Klamath River was established in 1876; by the 1890s, there were several canneries and a Fisherman's Union in the Lower Basin.[66] Commercial river fisheries were abandoned in the 1920s,[67] but ocean fishing continues. Today, the economic value of the ocean salmon fishery that includes the Klamath runs far exceeds that of agriculture in the Upper Basin. Even with recent ocean fishing restrictions imposed to protect Klamath fish, chinook salmon landings in northern California in 2006 were valued at roughly $5.25 million.[68] According to a fishing advocacy group, regulatory limitations on ocean salmon fishing have cost the coastal economy some four thousand jobs and $78 million annually for the last decade.[69]

Sport fishing is also important to the Lower Basin, although recreational fishing interests have sometimes been at odds with commercial fishermen over allocation of the allowable catch. In 1986, anglers spent a total of about 200,000 fishing days in the Lower Basin. At that time, according to an environmental group, each salmon caught brought $86 to the local economy, each steelhead $172. In 2004, the California Department of Fish and Game estimated that ocean recreational fishing caught about 220,000 chinook salmon statewide.[70]

In addition, logging remains important to the economy of the Lower Basin, although timber harvests throughout California have declined by about 60 percent from their peak in the late 1980s. The decline in the federal land timber harvest has been especially dramatic.[71] Many lumber mills in the Upper and Lower basins closed in the 1990s, victims of both reduced timber harvests and their own inflexibility; mills designed for old-growth wood are not readily adaptable to smaller trees and other species. A number of lumber mills remain in the region, however, and over the past several years timber harvest levels have stabilized or even increased in several of the basin's counties.

Economists have urged western communities to make the transition from the old cowboy economy to a modern economy based on the value of their ecosystem services, including ecotourism. Since the 1970s, it has been generally accepted that resource valuation should include such "soft" values as ecosystem services and aesthetic value, and even "non-use" values such as the desire to pass on ecosystems undisturbed to future generations or the pleasure derived by people who will never see them from knowing that unspoiled areas persist.

A blue ribbon panel of economists concluded in 1993 that those values are as legitimate as more traditional economic use values.[72] Nonetheless, they remain difficult to measure. Reported nonmarket values sometimes swamp the market values of resource extraction. For example, a recent U.S. Geological Survey study concluded that the nonmarket benefits of restoring Klamath River fish runs would greatly exceed the costs of restoration.[73] Even if one overcomes doubts about the validity of methods for measuring such nonmarket values, however, the problem, from the point of view of those whose livelihood depends on resource extraction, is that these paper benefits do not generate paychecks.

The Lower Klamath Basin, for example, has tried to develop a nature-based tourist economy, but so far without much success. The mainstem Klamath River, designated in 1981 as a national Wild and Scenic River, is one of the longest remaining undammed rivers in California. It draws some whitewater rafters, but its remoteness from population centers limits interest. The Lower Basin also includes portions of Redwood National Park and its associated California state parks near the Klamath River's mouth. About 400,000 people visit the Redwood National Park complex every year,[74] and the wilderness areas in the Lower Basin are popular with backpackers. But visitors to those areas, like the visitors who raft the river, tend not to leave a lot of money in the region.

Like the farmers of the Upper Basin, the fishing communities of the Lower Basin believe that more than money is at stake in resolving the Klamath Basin water conflicts. In the United States, fishing is not a livelihood people choose to become rich. Rather, it offers benefits sufficient, for some, to offset the danger and low economic returns. Fishers often say they are "called to the sea."[75] Fishing provides them with a way of life, a social identity, and a culture, not just an income. It allows them to be independent, to follow family traditions, and to live in coastal areas that may offer few other employment opportunities. Also like farmers, commercial fishermen and the communities that have grown up around their harbors face modern economic pressures. Because they see themselves on the ragged edge of economic viability, fishermen tend to see water conflicts, and regulatory conflicts,[76] as culture wars, threatening their ability to pursue a distinctively desirable lifestyle.

Common Threads: People, Economies, Environments

Although the two halves of the Klamath watershed are isolated and depend upon different economic bases, they are similar in many ways to each other, and to much of the rural, resource-dependent West. Their economies share a traditional dependence on boom-and-bust commodity production industries, including logging and agriculture in the Upper Basin and logging, mining, and fishing in the Lower Basin. Culturally, their people share an independent streak and suspicion of outsiders. They have long resented both federal and state governments, which they view as remote. In the 1850s, community leaders in the southern Oregon Territory and northern California sought recognition as a separate state, arguing that their region was distinct and was ignored by state and territorial governments.[77] They also criticized the federal government for failing to provide sufficient resources to protect them from the local Indian tribes, which frequently clashed with miners and other settlers. Calls for northern California and southern Oregon counties to break off as a separate state persisted well into the twentieth century and are not entirely forgotten. In 1941, a brief "secession" movement claimed to have established the new state of Jefferson. Cars traveling the highway through Yreka, California, the center of the "rebellion," were stopped, and their drivers were handed fliers proclaiming that the locals intended "to secede each Thursday until further notice."[78] The timing could hardly have been worse. Theaters across the country were scheduled to show a newsreel short about the Jefferson secession the week of December 8, 1941, but the attack on Pearl Harbor intervened. The stillborn state of Jefferson is not forgotten locally. References to it turn up in odd places. The public radio station broadcasting from Ashland, Oregon, for example, which can be heard throughout much of the Upper and Lower Klamath basins, calls itself "Jefferson Public Radio."

Finally, the aquatic environments of both halves of the Klamath watershed, like their counterparts across the West, show the strain of a century and a half of careless development. Fish are the most endangered animal group in North America. Particularly in the arid West, where water projects, timber harvesting, agriculture, and grazing have modified many streams nearly beyond recognition, large numbers of aquatic and riparian species are declining. The Klamath fish illustrate two common types of problems. In the Upper Basin, the endangered sucker species typify the problems of many Great Basin watersheds. The inhospitable, isolated streams of the Great Basin have produced many distinctive endemic species. Diversion of water from surface waters and springs for agriculture and livestock use has left many of those species barely clinging to existence. In the Lower Basin, there is nothing unique about the precarious status of the coho and other anadromous species. Pacific salmonids are in trouble throughout their range. Twenty-seven runs of salmon and steelhead have been listed under the ESA since 1989. Salmon are the canary in the coal mine of western cold-water river systems, clear indicators that conditions in those systems are seriously amiss. Although the specific social and environmental conditions of the Klamath Basin led it to the crisis point first, many other western watersheds could reach their own boiling points before long.

CHAPTER 3

Reclamation Comes to the Klamath

> Without question, water is the single most valuable resource of the Klamath Basin.
>
> Oregon Department of Water Resources, *Resolving the Klamath*

The Upper Klamath Basin, high, cold, and dry in the summer, had little value for agriculture in the absence of irrigation. This chapter explains how two developments made irrigation possible—fueling white settlement of the Upper Basin—and remain at the root of conflicts in the Klamath Basin. The first was a legal innovation, the American development of appropriative water rights, which exalted the value of water extracted from streams at the expense of instream flows. Although appropriative water rights were intended to provide clear property rights, a great deal of confusion remains about who holds what rights in the waters of the Klamath Basin. The second was the federal reclamation program, which firmed up appropriative rights and provided generous national subsidies for large-scale irrigation works, with little concern for the needs of nonagricultural communities or the environment. Although the reclamation era has ended, the Klamath Project remains, and project irrigators continue to hold a strong hand in the basin's water conflicts.

Western Water Law: An Engine for Extraction

The Klamath irrigators are among the beneficiaries of the doctrine of prior appropriation, which was perfected in the late nineteenth century. All over the West, the doctrine of prior appropriation allowed early irrigation settlements to claim almost all the available water in small arid basins and to maintain those rights, and thus their control of the landscape, over time. State law created "hard" irrigation water rights before 1902, and the federal government accepted those rights in the 1902 Reclamation Act.

The emergence of state-created water rights largely immune from federal control was a historical accident. Technically, all water rights in the West should have been riparian rights derived from federal land grants, known as *patents*, since the federal government once owned virtually all the land along western rivers. However, settlement of the West preceded effective federal control of the region. By the time Congress began to think of asserting a long-term federal interest in the public lands, the western states were politically powerful enough to persuade the nation to confirm the status quo. It was not until the progressive conservation era that the federal government began to assert its rights, and by that time it was too late.

As the West turned from livestock and mining to irrigation to sustain itself, it adopted a law of water allocation designed to facilitate diversion and damming of rivers. The Anglo-American common law of water rights, the law of riparian rights, was designed to share water among nonconsumptive users, primarily mills. Originally, all owners of riparian land had equal rights. None could diminish the natural flow of the river or divert the water for use beyond the lands bordering the river. The riparian system ultimately accommodated the demand for consumptive rights by weakening the rights of riparian owners, so that they had a right only to make reasonable use of water, rather than to enjoy the natural flow unimpeded in quality and quantity. Nonetheless, uncertainty over the extent of riparian rights and over the rights of riparian owners to divert or dam streams led to rejection of the riparian rights system throughout the West, with the notable exception of California. As the Colorado Supreme Court explained in 1882, "Imperative necessity, unknown to countries which gave [the riparian system] birth, compels the recognition of another doctrine. . . .[1]

Following the discovery of gold in California, miners fanned out across the landscape, extracting what they could get from the largely unsupervised federal lands. In the absence of effective government institutions, the miners kept a semblance of order among themselves by developing and enforcing customs for the allocation of resources. History tells us that one custom they adopted was to award water rights to the first person to dam and divert a stream. Later comers could divert for their own use whatever remained but assumed the risk that their use would be curtailed in favor of their predecessors in times of scarcity. This custom became the basis for the doctrine of prior appropriation, which was eventually adopted by nineteen western states. Its rugged individualism was tempered by a requirement, borrowed from the collectivism of the early Mormon settlements in Utah,[2] that the water claimed be continuously put to a "beneficial use"—that is, that it serve current human needs, rather than being "wasted" or held for speculation.

In theory, federal land patents should have been the source of water rights. There were almost no private land claims in the West, and the federal government did not begin to dispose of the public domain until the Homestead Act of 1862. There was no indication at the time that the federal government intended to sever water from land when it privatized the public domain. Thus, all western landowners should have taken their land with common law riparian rights, and state judicial decisions and legislation adopting prior appropriation should have raised important Fifth Amendment property rights issues. Politics and a series of Supreme Court decisions, however, solved that problem.

During most of the nineteenth century the federal government, along with the states, saw the public domain as the foundation of western settlement and assumed that the government would quickly divest itself of its lands. Even the goal of maximizing revenues from the liquidation of public lands was subordinated to those of encouraging settlement and facilitating private use of those lands remaining in public ownership. The decisive moment came in 1866. From 1847 to 1865, a weak federal government distracted by the question of slavery and the discontent of the South with the Union had allowed miners to enter where they would on public land and take whatever they found. To replenish the federal treasury, which had financed the Civil War by issuing paper money, some members of Congress proposed to reassert federal ownership of the mines and to charge the miners a royalty. By the time the legislation emerged as the General Mining Law of 1866, however, the western states had used their political power to flip its purpose.

The Mining Law confirmed all existing uses of the public domain and explicitly opened the public domain to private mining claims. That policy was reaffirmed by Congress twice, culminating in the Desert Land Act of 1877, which provided that all water not actually appropriated "shall remain and be held free for the appropriation and use of the public for irrigation, mining and manufacturing. . . . The western states relied on this language to propound a theory that Congress had severed all water from the public domain and acquiesced in the adoption of prior appropriation. Put differently, the states argued that Congress had promised never to assert federal water rights. Eventually, the Supreme Court adopted this theory, but it also held that each state was free to choose its own system of water rights.

This history is important for the Klamath Basin, because Oregon and California arrived at prior appropriation by different routes than other western states did. For example, Colorado law posited that the common law of water rights was never the law of the state. In contrast, California and Oregon always recognized the superior title of the federal government. The courts in both states reasoned that the states acquired sovereignty when they entered the Union but that the federal government retained proprietary rights in the public domain.[3]

Initially, California limited prior appropriation to water users on federal lands. Once the land was patented into private ownership, the doctrine of riparian rights prevailed. California did not adopt a permit system for prior appropriation until 1909 and continues to recognize preexisting riparian rights.

Oregon also recognized the federal government's paramount title, but it departed from the California theory of dual riparian and appropriative rights. Like California, Oregon adopted a prior appropriation system in 1909. Unlike California, Oregon terminated unused riparian rights. In effect, it turned many riparian rights into appropriative rights. To claim a pre-1909 riparian right, the user had to show either that the water was put to a beneficial use before 1909 or that the necessary diversion works were completed within a reasonable time after 1909.[4]

In upholding the state's power, the Oregon Supreme Court used the federal Desert Land Act of 1877 to justify its decision.[5] In 1935, in *California Oregon Power Co. v. Beaver Portland Cement Co.*, the U.S. Supreme Court validated Oregon's logic but recognized pre-1909 riparian rights.[6] The *California Oregon Power* decision has been treated by the western states as an eternal compact calling for federal deference to state water law. Despite the conservation era, revivals of Indian sovereignty, and the modern environmental movement, deference to state water allocation decisions remains a bedrock principle of western water law.[7] This constitutionally erroneous history has the power of a cultural bedrock myth. It explains why today the idea that the ESA, or any other environmental law, can displace appropriative rights strikes many western water users as both heretical and shocking.

Prior appropriation created relatively firm property rights and eliminated the watershed-based restrictions of riparianism. Nonetheless, the appropriative rights system generated considerable uncertainty and litigation. Claims were exaggerated and overuse occurred.[8] Still, priority provided sufficient legal security to induce irrigators to build dams, canals, and ditches, although it has taken additional government support, administrative systems, and millions of dollars to firm up appropriative rights to the satisfaction of their holders.

Originally, an appropriation was perfected simply by posting a notice at the point of diversion, but pressure from irrigators for a more orderly system gradually mounted. In 1878, a young engineer in Colorado named Elwood

Mead proposed that the state adopt an administrative permit system to ensure that only the amount of water normally available in each stream would be allocated. That idea was too radical for Colorado, but it soon won the support of irrigators and a progressive territorial governor in Wyoming, where it was adopted by the first state legislature. Mead, who became Wyoming's first state engineer,[9] later recalled that when he began to survey the state's water claims, "the first thing that was manifest was that the virtue of self-denial had not been conspicuous on the part of the claimants."[10] Eventually, all western states except Colorado adopted a permit system.

Mead's legacy permeates the modern West and influences the ultimate rights of both Indians and non-Indian irrigators in the Upper Klamath. Mead was a perfect representative of the progressive age. He combined technical training with a vision of a scientifically developed western irrigation society centered around the family farm.[11] However, during the formative stage of his career, he believed his vision could be achieved only through state control of water. Between 1899 and 1907, Mead served as the irrigation expert in the Office of Experiment Stations in the Department of Agriculture, where he was able to influence President Theodore Roosevelt's thinking about reclamation. Mead convinced Roosevelt that a federal reclamation program should recognize state water rights.[12]

It is one thing to create a system for allocating water rights; it is another thing to effectively administer it. Permit systems have brought a measure of order to water use, but they have not eliminated the fundamental problem that brought them into existence: There are more water claims than can be satisfied in dry years. To "firm up" water rights, an additional, costly, step is necessary.

Because of their dependence on continued beneficial use, appropriative water rights are inherently uncertain. In the 1970s and 1980s, many western states sought to increase certainty by quantifying all water rights through basin-wide proceedings known as *general* or *basin adjudications*. Certainty, however, has proved to be illusory, or at least extraordinarily costly to obtain. States have sought ways to streamline the process of adjudication and facilitate settlement. Adjudication is basically complete in some western basins, but in others, like the Klamath, it grinds on. Adjudications are relatively rare in California, where water allocation has traditionally consisted of the distribution of large blocks of water through water supply contracts from federal and state water projects.

The problem with firming up water rights is that they are inherently correlative. Prior appropriation limits users to their actual beneficial use over a period of time to make sure that later comers have a chance of using available water. Thus, adjudication is nowhere near as simple as just adding up all the state-issued permits. Actual use over time must be determined, and any water user can challenge another's use as excessive or nonbeneficial. To make matters worse, despite the Supreme Court's disclaimer of federal riparian rights in *California Oregon Power*, some federal water rights still exist. Those rights are not quantified by permits, but they can be claimed in state adjudications.

State Water Rights in the Klamath Basin

The Klamath illustrates all the problems of modern water administration. First, inchoate pre-1909 state riparian rights exist. Like states on either side of the intermountain West, Oregon briefly recognized the common law of riparian rights, only to have the legislature abolish it in 1909.[13] Pre-1909 riparian rights were virtually eliminated in Oregon by a 1987 state law requiring all riparian claimants to register their claims by the end of 1994 on pain of forfeiture.[14] Because the Klamath Basin was in the middle of the adjudication process at the time (a process that remains unfinished), it was exempted from the registration law; it is the last basin in the state to operate under the pre-1987 law.[15] Second, as explained in the next chapter, the basin's tribes enjoy inchoate federal water rights that need not be registered and have never been quantified.

The uncertain status of the Upper Basin's water rights under Oregon law carries over into the interstate allocation regime. Interstate allocation of the waters of the Klamath, as in many other western basins, is governed by an interstate compact, negotiated by the affected states, and approved by Congress. Disputes between competing irrigation interests in upstream and downstream states are common in compact negotiation. In the Klamath Basin, however, the fact that the Klamath Project irrigates lands in both states, together with the topographic unsuitability of the Lower Basin for agriculture, allowed irrigators in California and Oregon to make common cause. Since both are beneficiaries of the same project, they pulled together to make sure that water stays in the Upper Basin.

Negotiation of the Klamath River Basin Compact was triggered by a proposal for a new hydropower facility. In the 1950s, the California Oregon Power Company (COPCO), which already operated power plants at Link River and just across the California border, proposed a new plant in the Klamath River Canyon below Keno, midway between Klamath Falls and the California border. COPCO claimed that unappropriated water was available, and that the use of water to generate power should take priority over future irrigation in the Upper Basin. Upper Basin irrigators, supported by the United States, took the traditional position, a legacy of the progressive conservation era, that any power development should be both public and subordinate to irrigation. More generally, the 1950s were the height of the big dam era, when engineers could dream big and politicians would listen. Farmers in the remote Upper Basin, acutely conscious of their political isolation, feared that Klamath River water would some day be diverted from the basin to irrigate farms in California's Central Valley.

The Klamath River Basin Compact, negotiated by California and Oregon and approved in 1957 by the U.S. Congress, gave the Upper Basin irrigators everything they wanted. It confirmed all vested rights to waters originating in the Upper Klamath Basin, defined as above the state boundary. It guaranteed that future irrigation of up to 100,000 acres in California and 200,000 acres in Oregon would have priority over hydroelectric power generation and in general placed domestic and irrigation use above all other beneficial uses.[16] It also prohibited out-of-basin diversions, with the exception of a small preexisting diversion serving farmlands in Oregon's Rogue River Valley, just west of the Cascades.[17]

Oregon has been slow to use its authority to quantify water rights in the Klamath Basin. Its system for basin adjudication, formulated in 1909, includes both an administrative and a judicial component. It begins with the state engineer, who performs a hydrologic survey and prods water users to file their claims. The engineer then develops a proposed order, specifying water rights and their priority, which is filed with the appropriate district court.[18] At that point, each individual claimant must prove his or her claim, subject to challenge by third parties and the state on a wide range of grounds. Challenges are costly, and resolving them is a lengthy process.

A general adjudication of the Upper Klamath Basin instituted in 1975 remains unfinished.[19] The reasons for the delay are many. The sheer numbers of claims and challenges are daunting. Over 700 claims have been filed, subject to more than 5,600 challenges. The Forest Service filed 216 claims for 416 water rights. The Bureau of Land Management, the National Park Service, and the U.S. Fish and Wildlife Service filed a total of 94 claims, and the U.S. Bureau of Indian Affairs filed 393 claims on behalf of the Klamath Tribe alone. The Bureau of Reclamation filed claims to irrigate 218,654 acres and to store 463,830 acre-feet in Upper Klamath Lake.[20] In addition, the United States put the process on hold for several years with a lawsuit, ultimately unsuccessful, arguing that the United States and the Klamath Tribe could not be compelled to raise their federal claims in Oregon's adjudication.[21] The existence of unquantified early riparian and federal reserved rights in the basin further complicates the adjudication process. In short, the slowness of the adjudication, which is not unusual across the western states, reflects the high costs of due process.

The West Embraces Reclamation

The roots of the current Klamath water conflict can be traced to the late-nineteenth- and early-twentieth-century efforts of the federal government to populate the West by promoting sustainable irrigation settlements. The Klamath Project was one of the first reclamation projects built under the 1902 federal reclamation program. Its construction allowed permanent dedication of the vast majority of the Upper Basin's waters to agriculture and the support of a diverse agricultural community. One hundred years later, changes in the economy and societal values suggest that, at a minimum, room should be made for other interests. But the legacy of the reclamation era stands in the way of change.

At the end of the nineteenth century, the West's future was very much in doubt. Only 10 percent of the nation's people lived in the region. The boom-and-bust cycles of mining- and livestock-dependent economies seemed to doom the West to remain, in effect, a permanent colony of eastern and European capital. Arid lands reclamation was one of the many progressive, even utopian, social engineering experiments that emerged before World War I to improve conditions in the West. Reclamation responded directly to the crippling droughts of the 1880s and the economic depression that followed the Panic of 1893, but also on a larger scale to the collapse of the cattle and mining economies that had drawn people to the West. A number of interests, from the Northern Pacific Railroad to utopian social reformers, came together to support the creation of a federal reclamation program. To settle the West permanently, the proponents of reclamation harked back to the book of Genesis, advocating a powerful but untested vision of the future of this remote region. Promoters imagined that modern engineering techniques could transform the harsh landscape into a modern Garden of Eden.

During the reclamation era, the desirability of exploiting nature for human betterment was taken as a given, on the grounds that it was biblically ordained or represented sociocultural progress or both. For example, William E. Smythe, one of the great irrigation promoters, emphasized the conflict "between the civilization of irrigated America and the barbarism of cattle ranching."[22] Proponents of irrigation saw a federal reclamation program as a way to complete the settlement of the continent, to feed the nation, to absorb some of the burgeoning immigrant population that crowded cities under unsanitary conditions, and to apply science and technology to realize the Jeffersonian dream of a critical mass of self-sufficient farmers.[23] The leading historian of the reclamation era, Donald Pisani, has described federal water policy between 1902 and 1935 as "an almost primal impulse to 'complete' the evolutionary process dictated by God and culture."[24]

Irrigation was not new to North America in 1900, but it flourished only in a few places in the West. Various Native American groups had long irrigated fields in places like northern New Mexico and the Salt River Valley of what is now Arizona. The Spanish Conquest of North America brought the Moorish legacy of irrigation to additional parts of Texas, New Mexico, southern Arizona, and California. The national irrigation movement that emerged at the end of the nineteenth century, however, was inspired primarily by the success of irrigation practices in Mormon settlements in Utah. Brigham Young's early settlement policies were collectivist and utopian. The Mormons set out to redeem the promise of Isaiah to "give waters in the wilderness, and rivers in the desert" to sustain a chosen people. Irrigation soon spread to Idaho and Wyoming, parts of which were colonized by Mormons sent out from the Salt Lake Valley, and to Montana. By the 1870s, irrigation was emerging as a discrete western settlement strategy and ideology. Wine and citrus colonies had been formed in Southern California and other areas were taking up the idea.[25]

An irrigation society is hard to build. The Mormons succeeded because the church could mobilize dedicated labor at very low cost. Other communities found the task more difficult. In 1880, there were only 300,000 acres under irrigation. Irrigated acreage increased rapidly, though, to over 4.1 million ten years later.[26] These early efforts were entirely private, many of them fueled by speculation; irrigation companies built their distribution works in the hope of profitable sale. As a leading historian has observed, these private companies "had a reputation in the West for being grasping and unscrupulous. Often they contracted to deliver water they could not deliver in the dry part of the summer."[27] Private irrigation efforts succeeded in some areas, but during the depression years of the early 1890s many irrigation concerns went under. In 1894, Congress amended the Desert Land Act to support the growing reclamation movement. The Carey Act, which allowed each public-land state to select 1 million acres of desert land from the public domain if the lands were irrigated by private companies and sold in 160-acre tracts,[28] is generally regarded as a failure.[29] Its slow progress helped make the case for more aggressive federal support for irrigation settlements.

The federal reclamation program was intended to rationalize the early private efforts and to correct the central defect in the Carey Act. Experience showed that in most areas private initiative simply would not produce irrigation projects. The federal government had to assume the initial responsibility for project construction. Keeping planning and construction in federal hands would replace what proponents of federal reclamation saw as the generally small, unsound, and speculative private irrigation enterprises with well-planned and engineered federal projects.[30] Frederick Newell, the first director of the Reclamation Service, enthused that "the dead and profitless deserts need only the magic touch of water to make arable lands that will afford homes for our overcrowded Eastern cities. . . .[31] The federal government jumped enthusiastically into the irrigation business in 1902 with passage of the Reclamation Act.[32]

Today, most historians agree that the reclamation program neither lived up its ideals, which were soon washed from the program, nor promoted the regional irrigation development originally envisioned by its sponsors. Instead, it became a welfare program. Large farmers benefited from subsidized water prices as the Bureau of Reclamation failed to enforce the limits that were supposed to be imposed on farm size. Cities benefited from cheap power. That said, the Klamath Project fits the original reclamation vision of an irrigation community better than most, which helps explain the intensity of support for the project in the Upper Basin.

From Private Irrigation to Reclamation

The story of the conversion of the Upper Klamath Basin to an irrigation economy is typical of white settlement of many parts of the West. Fur trappers entered the Upper Basin in the 1820s. John C. Frémont visited Klamath Lake in December of 1843, during his second major western reconnaissance. Earlier fur trappers had described its riches, and Frémont believed that the lake formed a tableland between the Sacramento and Deschutes rivers. During his survey, he commented on the abundance of grasses for livestock. Frémont returned in 1846, but permanent non-Indian settlement did not begin until 1867, when the civilian supplier of Fort Klamath, constructed in 1863, built a store near the Link River. He established the small village of Linkville, which was renamed Klamath Falls in 1891.

The early white settlers of the Upper Basin were livestock ranchers, who were able to cut wild hay from the lakeshores to feed their stock in the lean seasons.[33] As was typical in the West, irrigation began in the Klamath to support the cattle ranches in the area. Overgrazing in the West quickly led to the destruction of open range and to the collapse of the cattle market. Ranchers were instructed by the federal government to drain wetlands and plant them in hay.[34] In the Klamath Basin, land along the meandering Lost River was reclaimed for pasture starting in 1868. Settlement was held back, however, by the settlers' inability to obtain arable land. Much of the Upper Basin had been transferred to the state of Oregon in 1860 under the Swamp Land Act of 1850, a much abused effort by Congress to encourage the reclamation of "unwanted" swamp and overflow lands.[35] "Swamp grabbers" tried to exact monopoly rents for land adjacent to the lakes, so early settlers had to settle for more arid uplands. When the livestock population outgrew the natural supply of forage available on ranching lands, the settlers began building irrigation works so that they could grow more hay and produce row crops on those uplands.

The earliest irrigation projects in the basin were constructed privately by landowners for their own use. The Linkville Ditch and Water Company was incorporated in 1878.[36] By the 1880s, private irrigation works irrigated several thousand acres. William Steele's canal irrigated about 4,000 acres. In 1882, two canals were started along the Oregon-California border. In 1884, the Steele canal absorbed the Linkville Ditch Company, diverted water from the outlet of Upper Klamath Lake, and effectively blocked further irrigation development.[37]

After passage of the Reclamation Act of 1902, the federal government began to look for irrigation projects to finance. Typically, federal attention turned to existing, often marginal, private efforts. The Klamath Basin was one of the first beneficiaries of the federal reclamation program and has been one of the last to experience the problems of reclamation's decline. Local residents petitioned for inclusion in the program when it was first established, and the Klamath Project was among the first wave of reclamation projects authorized in 1905.[38]

Even at the time, the Upper Klamath Basin, with its harsh climate and flat headwaters topography, could be seen as an odd choice for a major federal project. The basin seems to have been the beneficiary of two external forces. The first was President Theodore Roosevelt's desire to spread reclamation projects throughout the West rather than concentrate on a few well-planned ones.[39] Then as now, politicians wanted to curry favor by delivering pork to their constituents. Second, the area impressed Frederick Newell because of the amount of land and water available for irrigation. Newell, an engineer, saw reclamation as a scientific exercise rather than a grand social experiment. The Klamath Basin fit that vision. It was full of pragmatic farmers, not utopian dreamers. The social cohesion that allowed some communities to develop successful irrigation on their own arrived in the Klamath Basin only in the wake of federal reclamation dollars. In 1905, the Klamath became the twelfth project, and the largest to that point, authorized under the Reclamation Act of 1902.

As was typical of early reclamation projects, this one incorporated existing private irrigation works. Most of the small canal companies were happy to sell and were readily folded into the project.[40] Only one large land and canal company, the Klamath Canal Company, actively competed with the federal project until the government succeeded in buying a crucial canal.[41]

The Klamath Canal Company had filed under Oregon law for rights to appropriate all the water on the Link River. This filing exposed one of the central problems of the reclamation program, which persists to this day. While the federal government determined the location and scope of reclamation projects, it lacked control over the waters to be delivered by those projects. This problem is explored in detail in chapter 4, but suffice it to say here that the federal government aggressively asserted various theories of federal water rights until it was rebuffed by the Supreme Court.[42] In the Klamath Basin, the federal government first opposed the Klamath Canal Company's filing as an interference with navigation. Eventually, it fell back on another time-honored federal strategy, buying out the company's water rights, for $150,000 in 1905.[43] With the dog in the manger eliminated, the Klamath Project was able to federalize almost all the existing irrigation activities in the Upper Basin.

The government imposed three conditions on the Klamath Project. The first, that all vested water rights be adjudicated, remains unfulfilled to this day. The second, the surrender of all riparian rights to the waters of Lower Klamath and Tule lakes, and the third, transfer to the federal government of Oregon and California's title to the beds of Lower Klamath and Tule lakes, were quickly met.[44] Finally, Congress authorized the draining of the lakes for reclamation.

Construction of the Klamath Project began in 1906 with the East Canal. Figure 5 shows the newly completed headgates of the project in 1907, just before the first irrigation deliveries began.[45] The Lost River Dam was added in 1912. The roaring twenties saw the expansion of the project, which was only about half completed in 1920 due to technical problems and labor shortages. Gerber Dam, the Miller Diversion Dam, and several diversion dams on the Lost River were added to substitute for the loss of the natural lakes that had been converted to farmland.

The original plan of the Reclamation Act was simple. Federally owned land to be irrigated by the project would be sold to farmers, the proceeds deposited in a trust fund dedicated to financing the initial irrigation works and later the reclamation of additional lands. Land sale proceeds were never sufficient to keep up with construction costs, however, which instead were subsidized by general government funds and dedicated bonds. Construction of the Lost River Dam, for example, had to wait until Congress amended the Reclamation Act to allow the issuance of bonds, which were to be repaid from the trust fund. Consistent with the strong antimonopoly philosophy of the original reclamation program, federal lands within the boundaries of the Klamath Project were initially sold in 80-acre tracts. Farmers agreed to pay yearly maintenance and operation costs and to repay their assigned share of the

FIGURE 5
The headgates of the newly constructed Klamath Project, 1907. The picture was taken just before the breaching of a temporary dam that held back the waters of the lake during construction. (Bureau of Reclamation photograph.)

construction costs within ten years.[46] Klamath farmers originally thought that maintenance and operation costs would be about $20 per month per tract, but in 1908 the Reclamation Service announced that the charges would be $30 a month. Farmers balked at that increase until Secretary of the Interior Richard Ballinger suspended federal construction. Despite this publicly tough stance, from the start the government was lax about collecting payments and about penalizing farmers who farmed more lands than were entitled to water.

Like much of America, the Upper Klamath Basin benefited from European emigration. The Klamath Project drew some of the last waves of Czech immigrants fleeing the decaying and increasingly authoritarian Austro-Hungarian Empire. Many residents of the rural areas south of Klamath Falls are descendants of fifty early Bohemian settlers who came in 1909 after a colonization club in Omaha selected the area because it had a number of desirable features: a large supply of water, the recently arrived railroad, cheap lumber for building, a mild climate, and flocks of ducks and geese.[47] Malin, Oregon, is named for a small town in what is now the Czech Republic.

The California farmers around Tule and Clear lakes are the survivors of harsh early experiences that drove many away. The area is not for most people. Because of its inhospitable location, Tule Lake was one of the sites selected for internment of Japanese Americans during World War II. It housed those Japanese Americans who refused to formally declare their loyalty to the United States; those who were suspected of "disloyalty" for other reasons, such as their failure to adopt a sufficiently "Americanized" way of life; and family members who refused to be separated from the "disloyal."[48] The remote harsh location also meant that homesteading in the Klamath Basin continued later than in many other areas. Homesteads, concentrated in the California portion of the Upper Klamath Basin, around Tule and Lower Klamath lakes, were distributed both to encourage agricultural settlement in the region and to reward the nation's veterans. After World Wars I and II, homestead applicants were selected by lot, with preferences for veterans. The final allocation of homesteads occurred between 1946 and 1948, when 216 applicants were selected from over 2,000 veterans. Many of the farmers in the Upper Basin are relatives of those homesteaders or even original entrants. An eighty-five-year old veteran filled the first fifty buckets of the 2001 protest against the headgate closing.

The Klamath Project was completed in the 1960s. Figure 6 shows its major facilities and the areas it irrigates today. Project irrigators in the Klamath Basin, unlike the beneficiaries of many other federal projects, have repaid their allotted share of project construction costs. Today, the project diverts about 1,345,000 acre-feet to irrigate approximately 240,000 acres in Oregon and California. An additional 175,000 acres in the Upper Klamath Basin are irrigated by private irrigation works upstream of the project.[49] (Because reliable figures are hard to come by, the actual privately irrigated acreage may be higher.)

The Klamath Project irrigates the best lands and highest-value crops in the Upper Basin.[50] Statistics are not available for the project or for the Upper Klamath Basin as a whole, but just over half of the irrigated acres in Klamath County, Oregon, produce harvestable crops, mainly hay and alfalfa. The rest of the irrigated land is livestock pasture. The most valuable cash crop is potatoes, but potato acreage in the basin has been declining. Potatoes are a thirsty crop, using 4.1 acre-feet of water per growing season compared to 3.6 acre-feet for other crops.[51] Water use in the Klamath Project is inefficient by western irrigation standards; 2 acre-feet are lost to evaporation for every acre-foot actually consumed by the crops.[52]

Although potatoes account for a relatively small percentage of irrigated acreage in the Upper Basin, the stresses that potato growers face provide a good illustration of the problems posed for the basin by modern economic trends, even without environmental regulation. Potato production is currently concentrated in three primary regions in Canada and the United

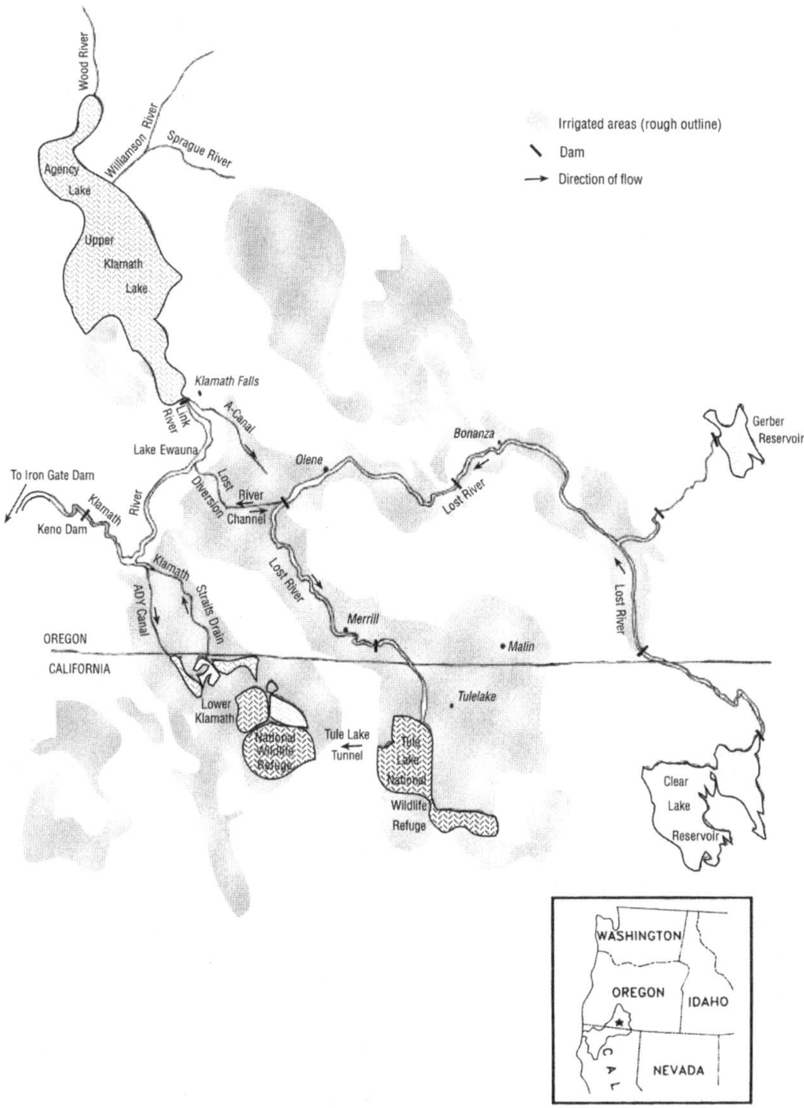

FIGURE 6

Water distribution in the Klamath irrigation project. This map shows the major facilities that make up the Klamath Irrigation project, and roughly indicates the lands the project irrigates. (Reprinted with the permission of the Oregon State University Extension Service from: Ron Hathaway and Theresa Welch, "Background," in William S. Braunworth Jr., Teresa Welch, and Ron Hathaway, eds., *Water Allocation in the Klamath Reclamation Project, 2001: An Assessment of Natural Resource, Economic, Social, and Institutional Issues with a Focus on the Upper Klamath Basin* [Oregon State University Extension Service, Special Report 1037, December 2002], 36).

States: the Columbia and Snake river basins in Washington, Oregon, and Idaho; the Red River Valley in North Dakota, Minnesota, and Manitoba; and northern Maine. The Upper Klamath Basin, like portions of the Midwest, is a secondary potato production area.[53] The basin has some natural advantages for potato growers, including exceptional soil quality and the absence of some major potato diseases. Nonetheless, it cannot compete effectively with the principal potato production regions. Potatoes today are primarily grown for the fast-food and processed-food industries; the promise of future market growth lies in Asian and other emerging markets that are developing a taste for American fast food. Modern practice in the fast-food and snack industries is to move potatoes seamlessly from the field to processing and freezing facilities. That cannot happen in the Upper Klamath Basin, which no longer has potato processing facilities.[54] Oregon has been called "Idaho with beaches" to describe its conservative leanings, but the potato-growing Klamath region could be called Idaho without the field-to-market advantages.

As a result, the vast majority of potatoes grown in the basin are sold for the fresh market rather than fast-food use.[55] A new variety, the Klamath Pearl, has been developed and is being marketed to high-end restaurants in the San Francisco Bay Area as well as to higher-end chain restaurants. Demand for fresh potatoes remains limited, however, and potato production is not directly supported by the federal farm welfare program. Klamath farmers have received some federal support, discussed in chapter 7, but they remain vulnerable to unfavorable world trends.

Ironically, the Klamath Project's adherence to the original reclamation vision contributes to its competitive disadvantages in today's global economy. The original Reclamation Act enshrined a populist vision of a landscape of small farms. At one time, large farms were seen as inconsistent with the "excess land" provisions of the Reclamation Act, which required that farmers whose holdings exceeded the 160- or 320-acre limit agree to sell their excess lands in order to be eligible to receive project water. From the beginning, these limits on landownership were intensely controversial and easy to avoid. The bureau disliked them because they conflicted with ideas of engineering and economic efficiency. Shortly after the Reclamation Service was organized, Frederick Newell provided Klamath farmers with a road map for avoiding the excess land provisions, suggesting that they deed "surplus land to their children or relatives. . . . And in ten years, when their water right was paid for, resume ownership."[56] Through the 1970s, enforcement of the excess land law had some passionate champions, but in 1982 Congress yielded to the long Interior practice of nonenforcement, bolstered by economic arguments that the acreage limitations were too small for efficient modern agriculture, and raised the size limit to 960 acres.

Unlike those benefiting from many other federal irrigation projects, most Klamath Project farms are under the legal size limit. In 2001, the average Upper Basin farm was 886 acres.[57] By contrast, Westlands Water District, on the west side of California's San Joaquin Valley, has between 200 and 2,500 farmers, depending on how agricultural partnerships are counted, farming 600,000 acres, three times the acreage watered by the Klamath Project.[58]

Furthermore, corporate agriculture plays virtually no role in the Klamath Basin, in stark contrast to more profitable agricultural regions such as California's Central Valley. Eighty-two percent of Upper Basin farms were sole proprietorships as of 2001, and 78 percent were operated by the person living on the farm.[59] At the other end of the spectrum, Westlands, irrigated by the last major reclamation project in California, has become the emblem of large, corporate farming and toxic drainage. The actual number of farmers is the subject of intense debate. The district claims that there are 600 farms,[60] but a study by an environmental organization claims that there are really only 50 different operations.[61]

A Contested, Flat Landscape

The roots of the current crisis lie both in the simple hydraulics of the Klamath Project and in the early decision to mix irrigation with waterfowl protection. The Klamath Project works basically by gravity. Upper Klamath Lake serves as the main storage facility for the Klamath Project, typically supplying between 350,000 and 450,000 acre-feet annually to irrigate project lands.[62] Because it is so shallow, Upper Klamath Lake is not capable of storing surplus water during wet years to buffer the system in critically dry years.[63] That means that, unlike many reclamation projects, the Klamath Project is at the mercy of the weather every year; a single dry year can put water supplies at risk.

The pre-project surface elevation of Upper Klamath Lake varied from a maximum of 4,143 feet above sea level to a minimum of about 4,140 feet. Operation of the project has brought Upper Klamath Lake as low as 4,137 feet.[64] That difference may seem small, but it drastically reduces the wetland habitat at the margins of the lake. At 4,140 feet, some 40 percent of the maximum potential wetland area is inundated, but at 4,137 feet all but 3 percent is dry.[65]

Link River Dam at the head of the Klamath River regulates flows out of Upper Klamath Lake. The A Canal is the major irrigation diversion, taking water from Upper Klamath Lake for delivery to the bulk of the project lands.[66] For a long time there were no fish screens at Link River Dam or A Canal, and those facilities entrained a large proportion of endangered sucker larvae and juveniles each year. Screens were finally added in 2003.[67]

The lack of carry-over storage in the Klamath Project increases the importance of return flows. Return flows from irrigation in the Tule Lake area flow to the Tule Lake National Wildlife Refuge, where they are used to irrigate refuge lands that are leased for farming. Return flows from those lands are passed on via the Tule Lake Tunnel to Lower Klamath Lake National Wildlife Refuge, where they again supply leased lands and finally refuge needs. Eventually, water that has not been consumed flows back into the Klamath River through the Straits Drain.[68]

The Klamath irrigation project is closely intertwined with a hydroelectric project, and that project may very well control the fate of agriculture in the basin. PacifiCorp operates a series of five hydropower dams on the Upper Klamath River, from Link River Dam in the north downstream to Iron Gate Dam, just below the California border. Link River Dam, although owned by the United States, is operated by PacifiCorp under contract with the Bureau of Reclamation and subject to minimum flow requirements imposed by the Federal Energy Regulatory Commission to protect fish in the lower Klamath River.[69] The remaining hydroelectric facilities are both owned and operated by PacifiCorp under federal license. As we explained in chapter 2, those dams impair downstream salmon runs. Historically, salmon ranged as far as Upper Klamath Lake, but the construction of the first hydropower dam on the Klamath River, called COPCO 1, in 1918 blocked salmon and steelhead access to the upper reaches of the Upper Klamath.[70]

Historically, Klamath Project irrigators have benefited from two major subsidies: cheap water and cheap power. The first is deeply rooted in history, but the second is an accident. In the United States, water has been virtually free. The states may own the water in trust for the public, but they have never charged for its use. Irrigators pay the costs of delivering water, which in the Klamath Project range from $12 to $70 per acre per year. They pay nothing for the water itself.[71] Electricity is a different matter, regardless of whether the power is public or private. Cheaper construction and operating costs allow public power providers to charge a bit less than investor-owned utilities, generally about 10 percent less, but the gap is closing. Major public power providers such as the Bonneville Power Authority and the Tennessee Valley Authority have had to impose large increases in recent years as energy costs have risen.

Power costs are crucial to the economics of irrigation, since they determine the amount of land that can be profitably planted. From the beginning, the Klamath irrigators got power rates that were not just below market but deeply subsidized. In 1917, the Bureau of Reclamation and COPCO, which was at that time the hydropower operator, reached an agreement. In return for the ability to regulate the outflow of Upper Klamath Lake, subject to existing irrigation rights, and construct the Link River dam, the company agreed to furnish cheap power to project irrigators. The original 1917 agreement between COPCO and the Bureau of Reclamation called for the utility to furnish power at 0.6¢ per kilowatt hour. The contract was renegotiated in 1956, but the irrigators have not faced a rate increase since 1917.

In 2004, PacifiCorp, the successor to California Oregon Power, sought permission from state regulators to raise rates in the Klamath Basin tenfold. That increase would end what has been in effect a long-term subsidy of Klamath farmers by other electricity customers by bringing costs to Klamath Basin irrigators to parity with those of other Oregon customers. Even so, the rates would remain low by most standards; Oregon enjoys some of the lowest rates in the country, thanks to the presence of the Bonneville Power Authority. Oregon's legislature responded quickly to PacifiCorp's proposal, in 2005 enacting a law that limited any increase in electric fees for Klamath irrigators to no more than 50 percent in any one year.[72] In the spring of 2006, Oregon's Public Utility Commission approved the first step of a phased increase expected to bring Klamath rates to parity with those of other agricultural pumpers within eight years.[73] Like virtually every proposed change to the status quo in the Klamath, this rate increase has been hotly contested. In addition to fighting it at the state commission, project irrigators tried to convince FERC that the federal license governing PacifiCorp's Klamath hydroelectric project forbade any rate increase before a new license was agreed upon. FERC rejected that argument.[74]

In the first year of the transition, electricity costs to project irrigators are scheduled to rise 36 percent. Although the irrigators will still enjoy a substantial subsidy for the short term, that is enough of an increase to impose a financial jolt. As farmers in the High Plains know, increased energy costs can force hard decisions, such as decisions to retire the land or invest in more efficient irrigation technology. Furthermore, rising power rates are not the only market pressure farmers are facing. In chapter 7 we look at the potential long-term impacts of the creation of water markets in the basin.

From the beginning, the Klamath Project was on an obvious potential collision course with the needs of wildlife. As is the case with many reclamation projects, the Klamath must share its space with waterfowl conservation areas; the Klamath Project sits squarely in the Pacific Flyway, the major migratory route for birds in western North America. For the first three-quarters of the twentieth century, as described in the next chapter, farmers routinely prevailed when the interests of wildlife ran up against those of irrigated agriculture. More recently, however, as we explain in chapter 5, the balance of power has shifted somewhat.

The Decline of Reclamation

From settlement of the West to the 1970s, the region's variable water supplies were shared relatively amicably among irrigated agriculture, grazers, urban users, public and private hydroelectric power generators, and the mining industry. Irrigated agriculture took the lion's share, and cities took most of the rest. Hydroelectric power generation is a nonconsumptive use, so much of the water that passed through the upstream turbines was ultimately consumed by downstream farms and cities. The federal government promoted this sharing by building storage reservoirs and financing reclamation districts to provide farmers with cheap, generally reliable subsidized water in the name of Jeffersonian democracy. The creation of this western Mesopotamia helped to settle a region that was originally thought to be inhospitable to large-scale human settlement. All benefits come with costs, though, and the reclamation era came, as we explain in the next chapter, at the expense of both environmental values and Native American tribes.

Today, the reclamation era has essentially passed. It was controversial from the start, but astute western political maneuvering, aided by the Great Depression, transformed it from an experiment in community building to a regional development program. Large dams were constructed on the Colorado, Columbia, and Missouri rivers, and excess water deliveries were permitted in powerful districts in California and Washington state. In the 1970s, historian Donald Worster compared the Bureau of Reclamation to the ancient hydrologic empires of China and Mesopotamia, but in fact the bureau began to lose power in the 1960s. The rapid rise of the environmental movement helped to destabilize the status quo by promoting a radical idea: a "new awareness of the environment as a living system—a 'web of life' or ecosystem—rather than just a storehouse of commodities to be extracted or a physical or chemical machine to be manipulated."[75] The rise of neo-economic theories of market superiority, such as cost-benefit analysis, and the idea that regulation was a way to perpetuate competitive advantages and inefficient subsidies rather than to serve the public interest ultimately led to a decline in federal water project construction. In short, economists questioned the need for subsidies, especially to large farmers, and environmentalists called for an accounting of the substantial environmental costs of the reclamation era.

Congress soon lost interest in dams as engines of regional development, especially as the West emerged as a modern service and tourism economy.

The reclamation era has been replaced by a less well-defined era of reallocation, restoration, and more modest "smart" new water projects. The new era is reflected in the Bureau of Reclamation's changed priorities and in a new competing vision of the ideal river. The Bureau still wields considerable power, but it is a shell of its former self. Today, it functions more as a water manager, facilitator, and ecosystem restorer than as a visionary regional developer. Rivers were once seen as commodities to be allocated among individual users to promote maximum human use, included diverting the entire flow in peak irrigation seasons. The ideal of such a "working river" was that no drop of water should flow to the sea unused. Today a new and not yet fully articulated vision of the "normative" river competes for dominance.[76] The normative river does not mean a return to predevelopment conditions, but it does mean that water is used in more environmentally sustainable ways and that efforts are made to restore and respect the river's natural hydrograph.[77] Rivers are now seen as integral parts of a natural landscape that can provide valuable ecosystem services along with irrigation water and hydroelectric power.[78]

The Klamath Project is struggling as the reclamation era ends. Changes in societal views of the roles that water should play in the Klamath landscape reflect the larger changing West. Many parts of the region have made the transition from a colonial commodity-production economy to one based on tourism, services, and finished-products export. In the intermountain West only 1.7 percent of the population now lives in completely rural counties, and only 4.2 percent of the region's economy depends on agriculture or natural resources.[79] The figures are only slightly higher for the Pacific Coast states.

These West-wide economic and social trends seem irreversible, but they fall on different areas and communities differently. In many western communities, farmers and ranchers have made the change to the new economy, but in others they either do not wish to change or cannot. Powerful vestiges of the former economy remain. Change generally requires a strong push from countervailing forces. The Klamath remains somewhat unique because it has not become one of the urban archipelagos of the new West. Irrigated agriculture in the Upper Klamath Basin has been somewhat isolated from national economic trends, but its isolation is becoming harder to maintain, despite the exceptionally generous support that the federal government has given the basin since the summer of 2001.

This does not mean that either the Klamath Project or irrigated agriculture will disappear from the basin. It does mean that irrigation will inevitably have to be scaled back. As a Tule Lake farmer told a group of Humboldt State University students, "We as project irrigators understand that there will never be certainty in our lives again."[80] The issues now are how much change will occur how quickly, and how all the cultures of the basin can adjust to the inevitable uncertainty that follows transition from one vision to another. Some in the agricultural community still cling to the idea of a revived reclamation era, and the hardening of the current consensus that global climate change means less water for arid areas fuels this dream. If climate change does bring a new era of dam and reservoir construction, however, the beneficiaries will be cities, not farmers.

CHAPTER 4

Those at the Margins: Indians and Wildlife

> The Yurok and their neighbors lived in a universe dominated by the Klamath. Their cardinal directions were upriver and downriver, high country and low. . . . Through this universe, each year at the same time, hordes of salmon appeared from somewhere in the ocean and madly forced their way into the mountains, dissipating their great strength and destroying their bodies as they made their determined way upstream. Upon these heroic animals the Indians' lives depended.
>
> Arthur McEvoy, "Aboriginal Fisheries"

From the time of their entry into the Klamath Basin, and continuing through the reclamation era, white settlers showed little regard for the interests of Indians or native fish and wildlife. For both groups, the net result was a marginalization that persists to this day, despite the intervening evolution of national values and the existence of legal regimes intended to protect the groups' interests.

The treatment of Indians is a sad story in the conquest and settlement of the United States. Even so, Indian tribes do enjoy a measure of legal rights, which make it possible for them to play a major role in the future of the basin. In brief, Indians were recognized as discrete populations from the beginning of British settlement and ultimately given a high degree of control over limited portions of their former territory, or of alternative lands less desired by white settlers.

Fish and wildlife were even worse off than Indians in the early days of white settlement. They lacked any legal rights; they were simply "things" to be captured. This idea began to break down in the late nineteenth century, as the notion that government should conserve wildlife and their habitats slowly took form. First, states began to claim that they owned all wildlife in trust for their citizens in order to limit hunting. In 1900, a broad coalition of "hunters, scientific naturalists, nature lovers, and humanitarians" succeeded in convincing Congress to pass the Lacey Act,[1] the first federal wildlife conservation statute.[2] The Lacey Act prohibited the interstate transportation of wildlife taken in violation of state law, but at the time states protected wildlife only if it had direct economic value. Even then, it was expendable if that was the price of progress. Environmental protection did not emerge as a broad policy objective until the 1960s. Modern environmentalism drew on the spiritual and aesthetic legacies of the progressive conservation era, but it adopted science as its foundation. Policy makers began to replace the malleable aesthetic notion of "nature" with the more scientific idea of protecting functioning ecosystems as the central organizing idea of environmentalism.

Today the two marginalized interests, Indians and the environment, are closely linked and enjoy a measure of real power. Proponents of tribal sovereignty and ecosystem restoration are at the forefront of efforts to reimagine and restore the Klamath Basin ecosystem. So far they have not been able to change fundamentally the allocation of water in the basin or the operation of the Klamath Project, but they have raised the possibility of alternative futures for this contested landscape, as well as questions about the legal basis of the irrigation economy. Actually implementing any alternative vision will require overcoming historical legacies that nearly wrote the Indians out of the basin's human communities and put fish and wildlife last in line for water.

Two late-twentieth-century innovations, the tribal sovereignty and environmental movements, provide momentum and tools to press for reversal of the legacies of the past. Such change never comes easily, however. Entrenched social patterns, cultural ties, economic dependence, and assumptions of entitlement all tend to maintain the trajectory established by history.

Marginalized People: The Indians

The distinctive legal feature of Indians in the United States is that their identity is tied to a specific land base. All Indian law flows from that characteristic. Weak, contested, and inconsistent as it is, Indian law provides a basis for tribal power that not all indigenous communities enjoy.[3] Unlike Australian aboriginals, who had no special legal personality until the late twentieth century, American Indians always had a group legal identity. Chief Justice John Marshall's paternal characterization of them as "domestic dependent nation[s]"[4] is the foundation of their claims to control over a portion of the basin's resources. Those claims had little practical effect in the Klamath Basin, however, until the Endangered Species Act added new political leverage.

The Upper Basin Tribes: Klamaths and Modocs

The manifold wrongs done to American Indians in the course of settling the country are well documented, but the wrongs done to the Upper Basin tribes are especially egregious. The majority community tried to eliminate not only their land base but their group identity. The Indians of the Upper Klamath Basin were less well equipped than other groups to defend their homelands or to survive the vicissitudes of American Indian policy. The basin tribes, the Klamath and Modoc, are members of the larger Snake Paiute Tribe. At one time, they used 22 million acres of what is now central Oregon and northern California. They subsisted primarily on suckers and yellow water lilies from the basin's shallow lakes. The fish were dried, the lilies ground into a flour. Indians in northern California and Oregon were more loosely organized than the eastern and Plains Indians and less impressive in the eyes of white settlers. Like other Indians, they were eventually "organized" by the federal government to promote settlement.

The federal government inherited from the British a tradition of dealing with Indian tribes as sovereign units. The United States also adopted the British colonial tradition of imposing artificial boundaries without regard to historic cultural distinctions. Following this pattern, federal officials often lumped together hostile tribes. It did that in the Upper Basin, creating a joint reservation for the Klamath Tribe and the feisty Modoc Indians of northern California. The 1864 Treaty of Council Grove, which settled many Indian land claims, gave the two groups 2.2 million acres, about one-tenth of the Klamath's historic territory. Later, the reservation was shrunk to about 1 million acres.

The pairing of Klamath and Modoc bands was not a happy one. Although the two groups shared a language bond, they had little else in common. The Klamaths regarded the Modocs, who subdued tribes farther south for slaves, as a historic oppressor and enemy.[5] Nonetheless, in order to satisfy white settlers along the Lost River, the Modocs were moved to the north and forced to share the Klamath reservation.[6] The result paralleled the much later experience of several of the republics created from the dissolving Yugoslavia—neither group was happy with their forced coexistence. The Klamaths disliked the Modocs, who only wanted to exact tribute from them. The Modocs wanted to remain in small bands, rather than living with the more numerous Klamaths.

The federal government's plan was to make both tribes take up irrigated agriculture. In the late nineteenth century, America was coming to the realization that Indians would not simply disappear in the face of superior white civilization. Few appreciated the tribal cultures that had evolved. Almost all enlightened thinkers concluded that the best hope for Indians was to assimilate them into white society through two major institutions: Christianity and irrigation.[7] Given the abundance of wildlife and plants in the Upper Basin, the region's tribes, unlike the desert tribes of Arizona, had never needed, and therefore had no tradition of, irrigation. In 1903, the Indian agent for the Klamath reservation announced plans to build a ditch at Modoc Point.[8] The government promised food while the tribes learned to farm but failed to provide more than a small amount of beef. As a result, in addition to intertribal conflict, the Indians faced near starvation on the reservation.

The federal government's ham-fisted attempts to force the region's Indians to adopt white ways led to a brief but bloody war.[9] In 1866, the Indian agent in Oregon had promised the Modocs a reservation at their home along the Lost River. Washington never acted on his suggestion, and his successor went along with the white settlers of the Lost River area, who preferred that the Modocs stay on the existing reservation. In 1872, led by Captain Jack Keintpoos, some 270 Modocs returned to their historic home, which abounded in game and edible plants and was free of the unwelcome Klamaths, against federal orders. Responding to pressure from white settlers, a party of 36 cavalrymen set out from Fort Klamath after them. The cavalry caught up with a group of about 70 Modocs along the Lost River. A battle followed, in which 8 soldiers and 15 Indians were killed. In retaliation for that attack, a band of Modocs killed 14 male white settlers, then fled into a maze of lava tubes, where other bands joined them. Thirty-five soldiers were killed when troops under the command of General Edward Canby tried to flush the Modocs out of this redoubt.

Another disaster followed. The Grant administration favored a policy of making peace with Indians. Over the objections of the War Department, General Canby was ordered to take a defensive position, and a peace commission was organized. Jawboning failed. A Modoc woman, known as Winema or Mrs. Toby Riddle, who was married to a white man, told the soldiers that Keintpoos would not negotiate and was violent. As often happens in war, however, good intelligence was ignored. Two of the 4 members of the commission argued that it was not safe to meet the Indians, but General Canby and a Methodist minister, Eleazer Thomas, overcame their objections. Supported by troops but unarmed, the 4-man peace commission went to negotiate with the Modocs on Good Friday, 1873. They were met by

8 armed Indians, who opened fire on a signal from Captain Jack.[10] General Canby and the Reverend Thomas were killed.

Captain Jack and his followers were flushed out but, fleeing south, succeeded in ambushing 85 soldiers. President Grant gave in to those who argued that the peace commission approach would not work with the Modocs and ordered their extermination. The outnumbered Indians began to surrender. Captain Jack was captured and publicly hanged after a trial that would never meet today's minimum standards of military justice. The end of the Modoc War removed Indian resistance to white settlement in the region. Some Modocs were allowed to remain on the Klamath reservation; others were sent to Oklahoma.

Notwithstanding the inauspicious beginning to their reservation life, the Klamath fared well compared to other reservation tribes. Some tribes, like the Navajo, were given spectacular but resource-poor landscapes. The Klamath reservation was both spectacular and resource rich. It included long stretches of the Williamson and Sprague rivers and the Klamath Marsh. Some portions were heavily timbered; others were good rangeland. The Klamaths managed to survive and even thrive on their homeland. By the 1950s, they had created a sustainable timber and grazing economy on the million-acre reservation; their incomes were almost the same as those of non-Indians in the region.

But the Klamaths barely survived prosperity and self-sufficiency. They are among the most prominent victims of a well-intended but mistaken shift in federal policy after World War II from supporting reservation culture to hastening assimilation by terminating reservations. Just as post–World War II declarations of universal human rights were lifting the spirits of colonial and indigenous peoples in Asia, Africa, and Australasia, the United States decided to solve the "Indian problem" once and for all by eliminating reservations and forcing Indians to become plain old Americans. In post-modern terms, the federal government wanted to make the Indians "white."

The architects of the termination policy believed it would provide real independence for Indians. They could not understand the support for reservation autonomy and the restoration of tribal culture that prevailed during the four administrations of Franklin Delano Roosevelt. In part, the divide was geographic. While easterners had come to appreciate the distinctive cultural identities of Indians, at least in the abstract, many westerners still saw the tribes as a nuisance at best, and in many cases as competitors for limited resources. There was also an element of the arrogant condescension of those who see themselves as conferring a superior way of life on the less fortunate. Senator Arthur V. Watkins of Utah, a leading architect of termination, cast himself in the mold of Abraham Lincoln when he declared that ninety-four years after the Emancipation Proclamation, "I see the following words emblazoned in letters above the heads of the Indians—These People Shall Be Free."[11] The freedom envisioned by Senator Watkins, of course, meant freedom to give up claims to ancient tribal lands and assimilate into white society.

The Klamaths suffered a common fate: Defeat generated discord.[12] Internal divisions began with the General Allotment Act of 1887,[13] which was intended to transform Indians into yeoman farmers in the mold of their white neighbors and to stamp out all vestiges of tribalism. Prior to the Allotment Act, Indian reservation lands could not be transferred out of tribal control without congressional consent. The Allotment Act changed that. It was premised on the universal consensus among scientifically enlightened white reformers that "private ownership of property was the principal instrument of social advantage in the natural order of progress . . . from a nomadic to agricultural state."[14] Following the pattern of the Homestead Act of 1866, tribal members were allotted 160 acres per household. Allotted lands were held in trust by the secretary of the interior for twenty-five years to preclude quick resale to exploitive whites. However, not all reservation land was allotted to tribal members. After each member received an allotment, the surplus lands were auctioned to white settlers and the proceeds used to finance Indian schools and other projects. About a quarter of the Klamath reservation was lost through allotment.

When the movement for termination came in the 1950s, a significant faction within the Klamath Tribe supported it.[15] Many other members objected, though, and a study by the new Stanford Research Institute concluded that termination would cause substantial social and economic disruption.[16] At a hearing on the termination proposal, an official of the Bureau of Indian Affairs predicted that after termination most tribal lands would pass out of Indian ownership.[17]

Nonetheless, Senator Watkins prevailed. In the exercise of its plenary power over Indians, in 1954 Congress enacted the Klamath Termination Act,[18] for the purpose of ending all "federal services furnished such Indians because of their *status as Indians*."[19] Once the termination process was complete, the Klamaths would essentially become non-Indians for legal purposes, ineligible for federal Indian benefits, and fully subject to state law.

In the name of progress, making Indians free and relieving the federal government from the welfare burdens of supporting the impoverished reservation, the Termination Act dismembered and disestablished the Klamath reservation. It authorized the sale of the Klamath Reservation Forest. Tribal members had the choice of either immediately selling their interests, which terminated tribal membership, or holding on to them. A leading Indian law scholar describes this as a Hobson's choice because "land not sold would be transferred from the federal administrative trustee to a private institutional trustee,"[20] a bank in Portland. With no other viable option, more than three-fourths of the Indians elected to cash out for $43,000 each. A few tried to join another tribe, but the Department of the Interior explained to them that the Termination Act foreclosed that option. Ten years later, the trust was terminated and most of the land that had not been sold was acquired by the United States for national forest purposes.

The reservation's valuable timberlands were opened for sale to finance the buyout of individual tribal interests. The original plan to benefit private timber interests was modified in one of the many western public lands fights in the 1950s, which helped to lay the foundation for the modern environmental movement a decade later. In 1958 the progressive U.S. senator from Oregon, Richard Newberger, succeeded in convincing Congress to pass legislation that guaranteed that the forestlands would be sold as larger sustained-yield units.[21] That may have helped keep alive the idea of national forests as sustainable forest reserves, but it did the Klamaths no good because they could not afford to bid on such large parcels. The paper company Crown-Zellerbach purchased 90,000 acres, but in the end the rest of the reservation became national forest. The United States took title to the lands that were not sold by 1961,[22] and today they form a majority of the Fremont-Winema National Forest.

The loss of tribal lands severely crippled the Klamaths. Most of the individual payments to former tribal members eventually found their way into white hands. The Klamaths incurred the wrath of their neighbors for their occasional crass displays of newly found wealth. Alcoholism, high school dropout rates, crime, and poverty—the litany of Indian ills—followed. Relations between Indians and their non-Indian neighbors have seldom been good in the West. The water conflicts in the Klamath Basin have been made more difficult by the enduring bitterness there between the tribe and the white community. Distrust and dislike run deep in the Upper Basin.

The Klamath Tribe has rebounded since the termination era. Beginning in the 1960s, tribes across the country began to organize to reassert their quasi-sovereign status, which had always been embedded in Indian law. They found a tool that could make tribal membership and reservation life a viable option. In 1986, the tribal status of the Klamath was restored,[23] albeit without the return of any land. Today, there are about seventeen hundred enrolled tribal members. All that remains of the Klamath reservation, though, is 372 acres shared by the Klamath, Modoc, and Yahooskin band of Snake Indian tribes. Its most prominent feature is a casino, which, because of its remote location, has never generated the revenues the tribes expected. The Klamath water conflicts, though, have revived talk of restoring a larger reservation. The Klamath Tribe has proposed to trade land for control of water, offering to subordinate its water rights to those of the irrigators in return for 695,000 acres of national forest.[24]

The Lower Basin Tribes: Yurok, Hoopa, and Karuk

The story of the Lower Basin tribes is similar in its broad outlines to that of the Upper Basin tribes. It lacks the excitement of a shooting war but features its own reservation confusion and controversy, spawning a dispute among tribes that still rages after fifty years.

California's Indians were decimated first by the Spanish and then by the Americans. They were not organized into large tribal groups like the Indians of the plains and the Southwest, nor did they build impressive structures or meet the stereotype of Rousseau's noble savage. In all ways, from their appearance to their level of social organization and culture, California Indians were considered vastly inferior by each successive wave of European conquerors. Today they are scattered in small groups, most without the benefits of tribal status or reservations.

Thanks to the abundance of salmon in the Lower Klamath River, the Lower Basin tribes were once "the wealthiest of all California Indians in terms of disposable resources."[25] Because of the remoteness of their location, they withstood the white settlement of California far better than most other tribes.[26] Today, though, that same remoteness poses a significant barrier to economic development.

Unlike the Klamaths, the Lower Basin tribes have managed to hold on to a land base, despite numerous termination attempts.[27] Currently, three tribes make their home in the vicinity of the lower Klamath River and the Trinity River, which joins the Klamath just before it empties into the ocean. The Yurok, whose name means "down the river," traditionally lived along the Klamath below its confluence with the Trinity. The Karuk, whose name means "up the river," lived farther up the Klamath, in an area centered around its confluence with the Salmon River. The Hoopas lived in the Hoopa Valley, through which the Trinity River flows to reach the Klamath.[28]

The California gold rush brought an influx of white settlers, dramatically increasing tensions with the native population. In response, federal authorities in northern California negotiated a series of treaties with bands in the region, but the Senate, not wanting to constrain the search for gold, refused to ratify them. Finally, in 1853, Congress authorized the president to create Indian reservations from the public domain.[29] Under that direction, the Klamath River Reservation, running a mile on either side of the river from its mouth to about 20 miles upstream, was created in 1855 by executive order.

The Yurok did not need much convincing to settle on this reservation, which was within their traditional lands and straddled their river with its abundant salmon. The Hoopa, however, were not willing to leave their Trinity River valley for the canyon of the Klamath. Government was chaotic and informal in those frontier days. In 1864 Austin Wiley, the U.S. superintendent of Indian affairs for California took it upon himself to sign a treaty with the Hoopa. Pursuant to that treaty, he proclaimed the creation of the Hoopa Valley Reservation,[30] a square of land roughly 12 miles long on each side centered on the lower end of the Trinity River, ending at the confluence of the Trinity and Klamath rivers about 50 miles upstream from the mouth of the Klamath. Congress was never presented with Wiley's treaty but nevertheless provided funding for the reservation. Thirteen years later President Grant issued an executive order essentially confirming Wiley's proclamation, formally establishing the Hoopa Valley Reservation.

Meanwhile, Congress had sown additional confusion by enacting an 1864 law authorizing the president to create no more than four Indian reservations within the state and providing that any existing Indian reservations that were not to be retained should be offered for public sale. Two of the three reservations created prior to 1864, along the Smith River and in Mendocino, were subsequently abolished by Congress, but no action was taken with respect to the Klamath River Reservation. The Yuroks remained there, and the Department of the Interior continued to treat it as a reservation. The federal courts threw its status into doubt, however, when they ruled in 1888 and 1889 that, because it had not been expressly retained after the 1864 law, the reservation had lost its status as Indian country.[31] President Benjamin Harrison temporarily resolved the confusion with an 1891 executive order. Because the 1864 law limited the number of reservations in California to no more than four and that number had already been reached, Harrison extended the Hoopa Valley Reservation to include a tract extending a mile on each side of the Klamath River from the existing reservation to the Pacific Ocean.[32] The expanded reservation encompassed the Yurok's Klamath River Reservation.

The Karuk were also supposed to occupy this joint reservation, but most of them instead retreated first to the high country nearby and then back to their traditional homelands along the middle Klamath River. They never got their own reservation. They now occupy scattered "trust lands," parcels held in trust for the tribe or individual Karuk by the United States. The Karuk trust lands total roughly 750 acres, compared to a historic territory of well over a million acres along the Klamath between Iron Gate Dam and the confluence with the Trinity River.

President Harrison's executive order did not end the controversy over the status of reservation lands in the Lower Basin for long. Starting in 1879, bills to formally abolish the Klamath River Reservation had been repeatedly but unsuccessfully introduced in Congress. Finally, in 1892, Congress passed a law that, while not explicitly terminating the reservation, declared the lands of the original Klamath River Reservation open to settlement under the homestead laws, subject to the Secretary of the Interior's power to allot lands to individual Indians or to reserve them for permanent Indian use.[33] Both Congress and the Department of the Interior continued to treat the area as a reservation, but it was not until 1973 that its continuing vitality was put beyond question. California's courts had upheld application of the state's gillnet ban within the boundaries of the reservation on the grounds that it had been terminated by the 1892 act. The U.S. Supreme Court overruled, concluding that while the law allowed the Secretary of the Interior to allot lands within the reservation for sale, it did not abolish the reservation.

The union of Hoopa and Yurok reservations produced a dispute about who was entitled to revenues from the timber harvested in the Hoopa Valley that lingers today. Since 1950, when it first recognized the Hoopa Valley Tribe, the Bureau of Indian Affairs had distributed timber income only to members of that tribe. A number of Yuroks who lived outside the original square of the Hoopa Valley Reservation but within the extended 1891 boundaries brought suit, claiming that they were entitled to a share of the revenues. In a series of rulings between 1973 and 1981, the court of claims agreed, deciding that all Indians who lived within the extended reservation were entitled to an equal share of the timber revenues.

Congress responded to that ruling by partitioning the reservation into two pieces, restoring the Hoopa Valley Reservation to its original square dimensions and creating a separate Yurok Reservation consisting of the lands added in the 1891 executive order.[34] Indians currently living in the reservation but not enrolled in the Hoopa or Yurok tribes were given the choice of applying for membership in one of the tribes or taking a lump-sum cash-out of $15,000.[35] The Settlement Act made the partition contingent on both tribes waiving any claims arising from it against the United States. The Hoopa accepted that condition and waived their rights, but the Yurok did not. Yurok and Karuk who had been living within the Hoopa "square" filed complaints claiming that the Settlement Act effected a taking of their property interests. They lost when the courts ruled that Congress had never clearly given them permanent property rights in the area.[36] Since the 1823 landmark decision *Johnson v. M'Intosh*,[37] the Supreme Court has recognized a distinct form of Indian aboriginal title, a "right of occupancy" that may be terminated at any time without compensation.[38] Indians gain conventional, permanent property rights protected against government intrusion only by congressional action; the displaced Yurok and Karuk could not show that they had been granted any such rights.

Although the property rights litigation has now run its course, controversy over the settlement fund, which escrowed timber money pending resolution of the claims, has not. The fund was to be divided equally between the Hoopa and Yurok if both waived their rights to sue. The Hoopa received their share, $34 million, in 1991, based on their waiver. The share that would have gone to the Yurok was not distributed; it has grown to some $90 million. The Yurok claim they are now entitled to that money, because they are now (after losing in court) willing to waive their claims. The Hoopa argue that the Yurok, having resorted to litigation, are entitled to nothing. After unsuccessfully seeking advice from Congress, the Department of the Interior in 2007 announced that it would give all the remaining money to the Yurok. The Hoopa's attempt to get that decision administratively overturned was unsuccessful.[39]

Despite the lingering confusion and controversy over their reservation boundaries, the Lower Basin tribes have maintained their tribal culture better than bands located in closer proximity to California's urban areas. Nonetheless, today both the economies and the cultures of the Lower Basin tribes are in disarray. The vast majority of the Yurok, for example, live below the poverty level; four-fifths are unemployed, and nearly half of the homes lack electricity and phone service.[40]

The Hoopa have fared little better. The remoteness that saved them in the past now stands as a barrier to economic vitality. To reach the Hoopa reservation along the Trinity River requires a drive of an hour and a half from Weaverville, itself remote from any population center. The highway runs alongside the Trinity River, which in some places is wide and placid, flowing over a series of low gravel bars, and in other places is a narrow white-water torrent rushing through deep canyons. There is little traffic other than chip trucks taking the remnants of local forests to California's last pulp mill, on the coast just outside of Eureka. The river turns north toward the Hoopa Valley Reservation at Willow Creek, population 1,700. Nature has supplied the reservation with spectacular scenery—forested mountains look over a wide riparian valley. But economic prosperity has not followed. There is a large new firehouse, and the schools and cemetery are well kept. But the homes lining the highway are mostly trailers. The casino, called the Lucky Bear, is a dilapidated building perched at a bend of the river next to a run-down motel, sharing a parking lot with the grocery store, tribal police station, and courthouse.

Gaming is not the economic answer here—the reservation is an hour away from Eureka, the closest population center of any size, and several competing casinos are closer, on the more heavily traveled coast highway.

The Karuk are even worse off in that sense; they do not yet have a casino, although they are seeking to establish one near Yreka, with access to Interstate 5. Although they lack any significant economic engine, they keep their culture alive, in significant part by continuing their traditional dip-net fishing for salmon at Ishi Pishi Falls. Other traditional fishing areas have been abandoned due to declining runs and increasing state regulation.

Indian Water and Fishing Rights: The Basis of Power

Based on a one-hundred-year-old U.S. Supreme Court case, the Klamaths, like many other reservation tribes, have a unique species of federal water right. Aboriginal peoples maintain their group identity through historical and spiritual connections to a specific land base.[41] In the United States, a special class of water rights, first articulated in the celebrated and still surprising *Winters* decision of 1908, recognizes that connection.[42]

The dispute in *Winters* arose after much of what had been the Great Blackfeet Indian Reservation in Montana was opened to white settlement. In the 1890s, settlers arrived on the new Great Northern Railroad and began to irrigate along the Milk River. The federal government built a small irrigation project on what remained of the reservation, but during a drought upstream white irrigators claimed the entire flow of the river based on appropriative rights they had acquired under state law. The local U.S. attorney decided to challenge the upstream diversions and received permission from the Justice Department in Washington to file suit.[43] He asserted that the tribes had superior water rights.

The Supreme Court agreed. The Court's surprising sympathy toward the Indians at a time when large segments of society viewed tribes as either an anachronism or an impediment to progress can probably best be explained as a judicial complement to the then dominant federal policy of assimilation. As Justice Joseph McKenna pointed out, without a guarantee of water Indians would not have agreed to abandon their nomadic ways to become pastoralists and farmers.[44] Two alternative legal theories underpin the *Winters* decision: Either the Indians had water rights predating white settlement that were preserved by their treaty with the United States, or the United States effectively reserved water, making it unavailable for later state appropriation, when the reservation was created. The first theory rests on the treaty power of the Constitution; it would compel the conclusion that Indian water rights precede any white settlement. The second theory rests on the federal government's property clause power over the public domain; it would allow for the possibility that non-Indians could hold superior water rights if settlement preceded creation of the reservation.

The type of federal water rights recognized by the Supreme Court in *Winters* have become known as "reserved" or "*Winters*" rights. They combine elements of the eastern riparian and western prior appropriation systems. Like riparian rights, *Winters* rights arise by virtue of landownership alone; water does not have to be removed from the stream or put to beneficial use to perfect the right. Like appropriative water rights, federal reserved rights have priority dates. Usually, Indian reserved rights are thought to date from the creation of the reservation. In some cases, however, they have been considered to arise from a treaty, dating "from time immemorial," holding absolute priority over all other water rights.

The benefits of the *Winters* decision proved elusive for many tribes until the late twentieth century. Indians were expected to use their reserved water rights to become irrigators like their non-Indian neighbors. Ultimately, the Supreme Court ruled that Indian tribes were entitled to sufficient water to serve the practicably irrigable acreage on the reservation. On the assumption that Indian reserved rights could be used only for irrigation, not for instream uses such as fisheries maintenance, western states could cheerfully embrace this standard. A shameful lack of federal support for Indian irrigation projects ensured that irrigation on the reservations lagged far behind other projects. Thus, there was little fear that Indian water rights would actually compete with white uses, or for that matter provide any real benefit to the tribes.

Of course, such a cramped reading of *Winters* is inconsistent with its treaty rationale. There need be no limit on the purposes of a reservation, or on the possible uses of reservation waters. Over time, a few courts expanded the interpretation of *Winters* rights to include support of hunting and fishing. In 2001, the Arizona Supreme Court ruled that the purpose of reserved rights was not to confine Indians to an increasingly unsustainable future but to support viable homelands for them.[45] It remains to be seen, though, whether this standard will in the end result in more or less water for tribes.

The Scope of Indian Reserved Rights in the Klamath Basin

So far, the *Winters* decision has had little practical impact on water allocation in the Klamath Basin. Neither Upper nor Lower Basin tribes seek water for irrigation. Both do seek water for fish, and the courts have confirmed that both have rights to water needed to support those fish. Practical problems and political resistance, however, have so far kept the tribes' water rights from producing higher lake levels or increased stream flows.

Upstream: Water Rights for a Landless Tribe

The Klamath's ability to claim any Indian water rights has been complicated by their "irregular" status as a tribe with no reservation. After the reservation had been "essentially extinguished" by the Klamath Termination Act,[46] the federal government sought a determination of the tribe's water rights in the Williamson River, which feeds Upper Klamath Lake. The United States, on behalf of and joined by the Klamath Tribe, argued that the treaty reserved the right to fish, hunt, trap, and gather edible plants on the reservation. Oregon countered that the Termination Act extinguished any tribal water rights. The Ninth Circuit agreed with the United States. In *United States v. Adair*,[47] it held that the Termination Act expressly preserved preexisting water rights, including the right to instream flows needed to make treaty hunting and fishing rights effective.[48] Those rights, the court ruled, dated not merely to the 1864 treaty but to time immemorial. Under *Adair*, Indian successors to lands parceled out of the reservation enjoy a portion of the tribal reserved right. Non-Indian successors got a bit less; they hold an 1864 priority to water sufficient to supply their reasonably irrigable acreage.[49]

United States v. Adair was a significant and lasting tactical victory for the Klamath Tribe, but it did not quantify the tribe's reserved rights, and it left many questions hanging. The instream flow right allows the tribe to enjoin depletions of the river that threaten to interfere with protected hunting and fishing rights. This is an important modification of prior appropriation, but the basic practice of prior appropriation—use until someone objects—remains the real rule of the river.[50] The district court subsequently interpreted *Adair* to give the tribe the right to sufficient water to support aquatic habitat, but only currently productive habitat, not the much larger habitat found in the basin in 1864. Subsequently, the Oregon Water Resources Department, in the course of the Klamath Basin adjudication, read *Adair* to limit Indian water use to that sufficient to provide for a moderate living, capped by the level of hunting, fishing, and gathering activity in 1979. This crabbed interpretation of the tribe's treaty entitlement was rejected by the federal district court. Instead, the court said that the tribe has the right to whatever water is necessary "to support productive habitat so there may be game to hunt, and fish to fish, as well as edible plants to gather."[51]

The precise extent of the Klamath Tribe's rights will be determined in an adjudication controlled by the state of Oregon. The legal doctrine of sovereign immunity protects the federal government against most lawsuits, but Congress can choose to waive that immunity, and it has done so with respect to certain state water right determinations. A 1952 law known as the McCarran Amendment allows states to compel the United States to assert its claims in state water right adjudications.[52] That law, bolstered by two Supreme Court decisions—one broadening the definition of a qualifying "general stream adjudication" [53] and the other holding that federal claims on behalf of Indian tribes were included in the sovereignty immunity waiver[54]—has created strong incentives for western states to invest in the considerable costs of comprehensive adjudications.

A wave of large-scale adjudications began in the 1970s. Many, including that of the Klamath Basin, are not yet finished. While they proceed, all unquantified federal rights remain effectively in abeyance, at the mercy of a process conducted by state institutions that are frequently hostile to Indian rights. As the authors of a recent study conclude:

> In short, by authorizing state courts to interpret federally-reserved water rights, the McCarran Amendment has forced tribes into hostile forums in which tribes must be prepared to compromise their claims for streamflows that fully support the purposes of the reserved rights, perhaps settling for stream improvements that can partially restore river ecosystems. Although tribal reserved water rights claims may open the door to discussions about streamflow restoration, in practice the McCarran Amendment Era has reduced these claims to mere bargaining chips rather than vehicles for achieving the purpose of reservations through streamflow restoration.[55]

In the Upper Klamath Basin, the net result is that for the moment Indian water uses remain effectively subordinate to water uses by Klamath Project beneficiaries. Because they hold the potential to drastically reshape the existing water order, however, the Klamath Tribe's water rights are a powerful bargaining chip. Tribal reserved rights potentially allow the Klamath to claim enough water to maintain flows at a level not seen since white settlement. But they are only a bargaining chip. Until they are quantified, the tribe's water rights do not fundamentally change the status quo. While the adjudication process drags on, irrigators continue to use much of the basin's water, including water to which the tribes may have a legally superior right.

The tribe would like to see its water rights not only quantified but reunified with a portion of the former tribal land. Both of those could happen in the relatively near future. The Oregon adjudication is winding its way to eventual completion, and there is talk that the federal government might return 690,000 acres of the national forestlands carved out of the old reservation.

Even so, the question remains of how much benefit the tribe will ever get from its water rights. Vindication of those rights will not necessarily maintain traditional fisheries. The Klamath have been forced to assimilate more than other tribes over the past 150 years; at this point it is not clear that a traditional culture can be revived, let alone sustained. Nor will legal victory bring economic prosperity. Some tribes—with lands close to growing, thirsty cities—have been able to realize substantial revenues by selling or leasing water rights,[56] but that strategy is unlikely to succeed for the isolated Klamath.

Downstream: Rights without a Remedy

In the Lower Basin, the Yurok and Hoopa have federally recognized treaty fishing rights, with accompanying water rights as necessary to support the fisheries. The Karuk do not yet have any federally recognized fishing rights, although they believe they are entitled to the same rights held by other tribes in the region.

Nothing comes easily, of course, in the Klamath Basin. The Pacific Fishery Management Council, the commercial fishing–dominated body that sets ocean salmon quotas for the region, "consistently failed to set harvest regulations sufficient to meet conservation requirements, forcing the Interior Department to severely curtail Indian salmon harvesting in the Klamath River."[57] Finally, in 1993, the Secretary of the Interior managed to convince the Secretary of Commerce, who oversees council fishing regulations, that the tribes were entitled to a 50 percent share of the available harvest. The Secretary of Commerce reduced the council's quota, on the grounds that it did not leave enough fish for the tribes. Under the federal fishing statutes, regulations can properly be adopted to protect Indian fishing rights. Commercial fishermen contested the decision, arguing that the Yurok and Hoopa had no such rights.

The Ninth Circuit sharply disagreed. In *Parravano v. Babbitt*,[58] it endorsed the continuing vitality of the tribes' hunting and fishing rights. That those rights originated in executive orders rather than treaties does not, the court emphasized, reduce their legitimacy. Indian water law has never distinguished between the early treaty reservations and the later ones created by executive orders after Congress ended treaty negotiations in 1871. Moreover, although the relevant executive orders did not explicitly mention salmon, they set aside lands "for Indian purposes." The court had no doubt that those purposes included traditional salmon fishing. Under the Ninth Circuit's *Adair* decision, the Yurok and Hoopa fishing rights would presumably incorporate instream water rights as necessary to support the fishery. *Adair* suggests that those rights would carry a priority date of time immemorial, although the irrigators believe the priority date could not be earlier than 1891.

The Karuk are convinced they, too, have fishing rights, but their position is legally more difficult. Certainly, they traditionally relied on fishing in the middle Klamath region for their livelihood. The drastic decline of salmon in the Karuk diet, from as much as a pound per day traditionally to less than 5 pounds per year today, has been linked to a surge in diabetes and heart disease.[59] The Karuk do not, however, have a ratified treaty. Nor, although they probably were intended to share in the Hoopa Valley Reservation, were they explicitly mentioned in the executive orders creating it. Indeed, none of the tribes—all of which traditionally lacked the kind of clear political structure that made sense to Anglo-European observers—was explicitly recognized until 1950, when the Hoopa Valley Tribe was formally organized under federal law. History has left the Karuk in a kind of legal limbo, with minimal land and uncertain hunting and fishing rights.

While the recognition of Yurok and Hoopa fishing rights has encouraged stronger control of ocean salmon fisheries, it has had negligible effect on river conditions or water allocation. There are two potential paths for converting fishing rights to improved river flows: through the Oregon adjudication and through operation of the Klamath Project. The tribes have tried both, but so far neither has led to the desired result. Oregon's adjudication of water rights in the Upper Klamath Basin has obvious implications for the instream flow rights of the Lower Basin tribes, because it will effectively determine how much water flows to the California border. Yet in that adjudication the United States has not asserted any claims on behalf of the Lower Basin tribes, and the tribes themselves have been rebuffed by the state. Oregon's position is essentially the same as that of a University of Chicago law professor who argues that the government has no duty to consider the needs of future generations because future people are foreigners to the present generation and thus "the future is another country."[60]

As for the operation of the Klamath Project, as a federal actor the Bureau of Reclamation must protect tribal fishing (and other) rights. The Department of the Interior has recognized that fulfilling the trust responsibility of the United States to protect tribal fishing rights may call for increasing river flows: "Protection of the fishery itself is necessary to make the tribal fishing right meaningful."[61] Nonetheless, it is difficult to force federal agencies to take specific measures to protect fish and their habitat. The Yurok tried to do that in 2002. They filed suit after a massive salmon die-off in the Lower Klamath, caused in part by Klamath Project operations, seeking a court order requiring the bureau to operate the Klamath Project in a manner consistent with the Yurok's fishing rights. The court dismissed the claim, ruling that the tribe had failed to show that another fish kill was likely, and that in any case it could not bring a generalized challenge to Klamath Project operations.[62] Despite acknowledging the United States' obligations as trustee for the tribes to protect tribal fishing interests, the court made it clear that it would not tell the bureau how to execute those obligations.

Unrealized Tribal Power

The control of water in the Klamath is the key to the basin's destiny. Water entitlements are both a source and a manifestation of political power. The Klamath farmers derive much of their political power from their water entitlements, water rights perfected by hard work under the doctrine of prior appropriation and protected by state and federal law. By contrast, the tribes' rights are at best negative and have so far carried little political power. As the Ninth Circuit said in *Adair*, "The entitlement consists of the right to prevent other appropriators from depleting the stream's waters below a protected area in any area where the non-consumptive right applies." Although water rights doctrine continues to evolve, it remains biased in favor of the status quo, and less protective of Indian rights than it appears. Much the same story could be told about the interests of wildlife. The law, which has long nominally protected at least some of the Klamath Basin's wildlife, has until recently been regularly subordinated to irrigation interests.

The Marginalized Environment

Historically, in the Klamath Basin and throughout the West, the interests of fish and wildlife were routinely subordinated to those of the economy. While some attention was paid to the conservation of fish stocks during the reclamation era, that concern was closely connected to the fisheries' economic value. As water projects proliferated, the decline of even commercially valuable fish was considered an inevitable by-product of progress. There was no concern for nature on its own terms and precious little for its aesthetic or spiritual values. One by one, the West's streams were dammed and diverted, converted from rivers that worked to working rivers. It was not just fish that declined, of course. Birds and other wildlife suffered a similar fate as their natural habitat was replaced by cultivated and urban land.

Fish Lose Out

The history of water development in the United States has been intimately intertwined with the decline of native fish. Early on, the effects of small diversions and dams may simply not have been noticed. But as the scale of water projects increased, their impacts on sport and commercial fisheries became obvious. Efforts to limit those impacts, however, were for many years more symbolic than real. Federal lawmakers demanded consideration of wildlife in water development decisions but did not impose any substantive standards or authorize citizen oversight. Fueled by optimistic assumptions about the tenacity of fish runs and the efficacy of hatcheries, water development continued apace as fisheries dwindled.

Attempts to bring wildlife interests into water project planning began in 1934, when Congress enacted the Fish and Wildlife Coordination Act.[63] The Coordination Act broadly encouraged cooperation among federal agencies and between federal and state governments for wildlife conservation purposes. It focused special attention on federal water projects, which were already recognized as tied to fisheries declines. The new law required consultation with federal fisheries experts before new dams were authorized or constructed. Read literally, it also appeared to impose a substantive requirement that new dams include provisions for fish passage if economically practicable.[64] The law's seemingly strong language was tempered, however, by statements in the legislative history denying that it was intended to be mandatory.[65] In light of those comments, the Bureau of Reclamation and the courts treated the Coordination Act as nonbinding.

In a pattern that is familiar in the history of federal environmental law, the Coordination Act was amended a dozen years after its passage,[66] and again a dozen years after that,[67] because it had failed to achieve its stated goals. The consultation requirement was widened to encompass all water projects with a federal nexus and extended to state as well as federal wildlife agencies. Conservation recommendations emerging from consultation were required to be included in project reports. Eventually, Congress declared that a purpose of the Coordination Act was "to provide that wildlife conservation shall receive equal consideration" with other factors in water development,[68] and ordered water development agencies to include wildlife protection measures they found "should be adopted to obtain maximum overall project benefits."[69]

Still, the substantive effect of the Coordination Act remained minimal. The Bureau of Reclamation and the Army Corps of Engineers paid scant attention to the effects of their projects on the fish of the fast-flowing streams they impounded, except to claim increases in flatwater fishing opportunities as benefits in economic analyses of proposed projects. Federal courts declined to allow outside challenges, either to force consultation or to require project modifications. Dams continued to be built and water to be diverted to agriculture with little regard for the ecosystems altered.

Other federal efforts in this era suffered from the same shortcomings. In 1965, the Anadromous Fish Conservation Act,[70] passed in response to the depletion of anadromous fish by water projects, simply followed the Coordination Act in authorizing the Department of the Interior to cooperate with states for conservation purposes. Since its enactment in 1920, the Federal Power Act (FPA), which regulates hydropower development, had required that federal authorities find proposed projects "justified in the public interest" before issuing licenses.[71] It was not until the 1960s, however, that the federal courts began to notice that the public interest might actually call for protection of at least commercial and sport fisheries. A Supreme Court decision in 1967 mandated that effects on salmon be considered in the decision to license a private power project on the Snake River.[72] That particular project eventually died when Congress decided to include the site in the Hells Canyon National Recreation Area,[73] but the case had little effect on hydropower licensing practice. For many years, dam operators and federal licensing authorities simply asserted that projects could be operated consistent with fish conservation.

California made some early efforts of its own to protect commercially important fish from the impacts of water projects, but those dwindled as large federal projects succeeded small private ones. In 1852, the state passed a measure outlawing obstructions in rivers that interfered with salmon passage but providing exemptions for mining, milling, and agricultural dams. By 1870, the law had been broadened to cover all obstructions but also softened to require only that fishways be provided to the extent practicable. In 1937, the law was strengthened again, to require release of sufficient water from dams to keep the fish below "in good condition."[74] Notwithstanding these state laws, farmers mostly retained the upper hand. When wildlife officials tried to force farmers to screen irrigation ditches, the legislature ordered the state to pay half the costs. Enforcement of screening and fishway requirements was difficult, at best. There were some notable fish conservation successes, however. After a protracted battle, the California Fish and Game Commission managed to force the Anderson-Cottonwood Irrigation District to build a fishway around a dam that had blocked the main stem of the Sacramento River.[75]

Water Projects and Fish in the Klamath Basin

In the Klamath Basin, early water resources development included some measures intended to protect downstream salmon fisheries, but those measures proved ineffectual. When COPCO Dam was completed in 1918, the power company offered to install a fish ladder but refused to put in more than one. The California Fish and Game Commission decided that a fishway would not be effective, given the height of the dam, and in any case that young fish moving seaward would be destroyed by the turbines. At the commission's request, therefore, the company created a hatchery below the dam instead, to replace the salmon spawning grounds made unavailable by the dam.[76]

About the same time, two other hydropower dams were proposed much lower on the Klamath River. The Fish and Game Commission mounted an intense campaign against those dams, which it believed would wipe out the Klamath salmon run. The commission spearheaded a successful initiative drive to protect the river. In 1924, the people of California voted to forbid the construction or maintenance of any dam or obstruction on the Klamath River below its confluence with the Shasta River near Yreka.[77]

Despite the hatchery, Klamath River salmon and steelhead declined after COPCO Dam began commercial operation. Part of the problem was dramatic fluctuations in river levels. Demand for hydropower is high during the day and low at night. Operating COPCO Dam in response to that fluctuating demand produced dramatic fluctuations in river levels below the dam, drying out the river for miles daily and then inundating it. Fish were stranded, spawning beds disrupted, and fishermen inconvenienced. In response to a state lawsuit, the company agreed in 1959 to build Iron Gate Dam to dampen water level fluctuations. It also agreed to construct a new hatchery, both to compensate for spawning habitat newly inundated by Iron Gate Reservoir and to replace the hatchery at COPCO Dam, which had been closed in 1948.[78]

Anglers argued that high temperatures and poor water quality attributable to COPCO and upstream dams were also causing problems for Klamath salmon, but they did not find a sympathetic audience. The state Fish and Game Commission refused to seek temperature improvements because the costs would be very high and it would be difficult to prove that the changes would measurably increase spawning success.[79] The FWS was even more dismissive of temperature concerns.[80]

The Klamath Project and the expansion of agriculture in the Upper Basin are also closely linked with declines of the Lost River and shortnose suckers, as well as other Upper Basin fish species. As we have previously detailed, the Lost River and shortnose suckers once inhabited all the major lakes of the Upper Basin and their tributaries,[81] supporting multiple canneries.[82] They remained the target of a recreational as well as a tribal fishery until catches sharply declined in the 1980s. The draining of Lower Klamath Lake for conversion to agriculture essentially eliminated its sucker population.[83] Draining also eliminated the sucker populations of Tule Lake; with its partial reinundation, suckers have returned but apparently still do not reproduce there. Dam construction throughout the basin has sharply limited the availability of spawning habitat. Today, self-sustaining populations of the suckers are limited to Upper Klamath and Clear lakes and their tributaries. Those populations fell off sharply in the 1980s, leading to closure of the fisheries and eventually to listing under the ESA. Tributary channelization, accumulation of sediment, and high nutrient loads, from agricultural runoff and the decomposition of drained wetland soils, are among the agriculture-related threats to the remaining sucker populations.

"Protected" Areas Give Way to Agriculture

At the end of the nineteenth century, attitudes toward the "public domain," as it was then called, began to change. The dominant idea had been that the federal government should dispose of its lands, transferring them to the states and individual settlers, so that they could be pressed into productive use. For a variety of reasons, by the end of the nineteenth century the idea that the federal government should retain and manage some lands in perpetuity took root. Lands were gradually withdrawn from entry under the homestead laws and reserved for permanent public ownership. At first, only military forts and Indian reservations were retained. Soon, though, retention expanded to include striking natural areas; the creation of Yellowstone National Park in 1872 set the precedent for the national park system. The progressive conservation movement contributed the idea that the federal government could manage lands more efficiently for resource extraction than, in Gifford Pinchot's words, the "big money" that was gaining control of large tracts of land as the United States disposed of it. That idea justified keeping forest and grazing lands, not just parks, in long-term federal ownership.

Two related ideas emerged from this foundational era in United States resources and environmental policy: concern over the rapid exhaustion of economically valuable natural resources[84] and recognition of the value of public lands for their aesthetic and recreational values. The first we call conservation. Conservation posited that the government should retain large parts of the public domain, especially areas not suitable for agriculture, in order to manage the exploitation of natural resources in the public interest. The second we call preservation. That led to the idea that certain public lands should be set aside for nonextractive uses.

At the turn of the century, the distinction between multiple use, which became the dominant conservation standard, and preservation was not as sharply drawn as it is today. The protection of wildlife was influenced by the conservation movement's notion that public lands should be used efficiently.

Wildlife were seen not as inherently valuable, but as an exhaustible resource to be managed and conserved for sustainable human exploitation. Concern over the decline of game species led to a number of late-nineteenth-century conservation initiatives.

The creation of national wildlife refuges (NWRs) was one of these initiatives. Today, wildlife refuges are something of an intermediary between the limited-use national park system and the expansive, open-ended multiple-use management of forests and grazing lands, but it took decades for that view to crystallize. The national wildlife refuge system grew on an ad hoc basis, one unit at a time. Each unit's purposes were separately defined in the legislation or executive order creating it. Local interests had ample opportunity to influence those definitions, which often included commodity uses. The refuges were finally united in a single system in 1966, under the stewardship of Secretary of the Interior Stewart Udall. It was not until 1997 that Congress passed legislation establishing a single dominant purpose for the system, the restoration and maintenance of biotic systems.[85] Even then, the new organic legislation for the refuge system left the purposes of individual refuges, as defined in their enabling documents, undisturbed. As a result, even though they are nominally devoted to wildlife protection, many refuges retain the scars of the multipurpose era.

The first wildlife refuge may have been created in 1882 in Alaska, but the foundations of the present system date from 1903, when, in typically unabashed style, President Theodore Roosevelt issued an unprecedented executive order dedicating Pelican Island in Florida to the preservation of breeding habitat for native birds. For the first time, wildlife were being protected for something other than their commercial value.[86]

Farming versus Waterfowl in the Klamath Basin

Just five years later, inspired by a collection of wildlife photographs from the area, Roosevelt created the Lower Klamath Lake National Wildlife Refuge. Other refuges were soon established nearby: Clear Lake National Wildlife Refuge in 1911, Tule Lake and Upper Klamath Lake in 1928. The Upper Klamath Basin refuge complex was completed with the addition of Klamath Marsh in 1958 and Bear Valley, a bald eagle roosting site, in 1978.

The Klamath Basin refuges were the first to be superimposed on "a watershed being revamped by the Reclamation Service."[87] It may have seemed at the time that agriculture and wildlife protection could coexist, but the two have often conflicted, and farming has always had the upper hand. The fate of Lower Klamath Lake provides one illustration. Although federal botanists concluded that the soils beneath it were too alkaline for crops, pressures for settlement could not be denied. In 1915, President Wilson reduced the size of the Lower Klamath Lake refuge by more than half. A drainage district organized with the help of federal reclamation officials then closed the hydrologic connection between Lower Klamath Lake and the Klamath River, reducing the lake to a 365-acre pond.[88] The environmental consequences were clear. The area turned into a "desert waste of peat and alkali" that periodically burned.[89] Restoration began in 1941, when a tunnel was constructed to bring irrigation return flows from Tule Lake back into Lower Klamath Lake. Some marsh was restored, and the birds returned.

The dominance of farming is also apparent in refuge management. A 1946 incident is illustrative. When farmers in the Tule Lake area complained about waterfowl eating their crops, the Fish and Wildlife Service stepped in to practice what might now be called adaptive management, trying a number of methods to help the farmers clear birds out of their fields. Using military surplus equipment, including smoke grenades, searchlights, and small airplanes, the FWS herded the birds back into the refuges. It also issued permits that allowed local farmers to scare birds from the fields with shotguns and flares. The combined efforts contained the birds on the refuge until farmers completed their harvest.[90]

Special legislation has cemented the place of agriculture even on the Klamath refuges themselves. Pressure to open refuge lands to farming is a product of post–World War II development in the Upper Basin. Homesteading began in the Tule Lake area in 1916 and did not end until 1949. The final distribution of Klamath Basin lands was one of the last gasps of the great project of public land disposition and one of the last examples of use of the public lands to repay veterans for their service to the nation. More than two thousand applications were filed for the 7,528 acres to be distributed. Some 2,300 acres of refuge land were released for homesteading in 1948 and an additional 22,000 acres were leased for farming. Local area farmers appealed to Secretary of the Interior Douglas McKay, a former governor of Oregon, to release more lands but to no avail.

Finally, the 1964 Kuchel Act closed the refuge lands to any further homesteading, declaring those lands "dedicated to wildlife conservation." The price of that declaration was a provision calling for continued agricultural use of refuge lands "consistent with proper waterfowl management."[91] The Kuchel Act authorizes the federal government to lease Klamath Basin refuge lands for crop production. By agreement with FWS, the Bureau of Reclamation administers the agricultural leasing program. More than 25,000 acres are farmed under the authority of the Kuchel Act; crops on the refuges are irrigated with more than 50,000 acre-feet of water each year. The bulk of the farmed acreage is planted to grain crops, but some is used for others, such as potatoes and onions.[92] Some Kuchel Act lands are leased; on others farmers "pay" the refuge by leaving a share of their grain crops standing in the field when they ripen to feed the migratory birds that arrive in the fall.

The Fish and Wildlife Service never made a formal determination that farming on the refuges was consistent with waterfowl conservation until forced by litigation to do so in the mid-1990s. Since then, environmental groups have sought to force FWS to put the water needs of refuge wetlands ahead of those of farmers. They won a paper victory in 1999, when FWS concluded that leasing land for agriculture was compatible with the conservation purposes of the refuges only if the water needs of refuge wetlands were given priority. That decision, which was hotly contested by lessee farmers, was never implemented, however, and was withdrawn in 2002.

Although refuge-based farming still enjoys strong local support, today it may not be a net economic plus for the area. In 2002, a study conducted by FWS found that expenditures by recreational visitors to the remote Tule Lake NWR slightly exceeded the revenues from leasing refuge land for crop production.[93] This sort of "ecotourism" revenue is expected to increase in the future. Nonetheless, FWS has implemented a pilot "walking wetlands" program in the refuge. Lands are alternately drained, put into potato production, and then flooded.

It is not just Kuchel Act farming that is problematic for the refuges. In one sense, the refuges are in competition for water with all irrigators in the Upper Basin. In another sense, though, a series of past decisions have left the refuges dependent on Klamath Project irrigators. Both Lower Klamath Lake and Tule Lake NWRs rely on return flows from upstream Klamath Project irrigation to maintain their waters and wetlands, the features essential to the waterfowl and other migratory birds for which the refuges were established. In 2001, therefore, Tule Lake was essentially dry

Federal Reserved Water Rights for Refuges

Like the tribes, the refuges have federal reserved water rights but have not found it easy to turn those rights into wet water. We have already explained that Indian reserved water rights were first recognized in 1908, in *Winters v. United States*. For more than fifty years, westerners assumed that *Winters* applied only to claims for Indian reservations. But in 1963 the Supreme Court decided *Arizona v. California* and, in the course of resolving epic litigation to divide the Lower Colorado River, declared that federal reserved rights could be claimed to fulfill the purposes of any public land withdrawal. A few years later, though, the Court took back some of what it had given. In *United States v. New Mexico*,[94] it limited non-Indian federal reserved rights to the minimum amount of water necessary to fulfill the primary (not secondary) purposes of the reservation.

New Mexico has made it difficult but not impossible for the federal government to assert non-Indian reserved water rights for public lands such as national wildlife refuges. In *New Mexico*, the Court read the relevant statutes narrowly to reach the result that national forests could claim reserved rights only for their primary purposes, as declared in the 1897 Organic Act, of "securing favorable conditions of water flows" for downstream users and ensuring "a continuous supply of timber."[95] Even when instream flows are clearly related to a reservation purpose, it may be difficult to prove that a specific flow is necessary to achieve that purpose. In one case, for instance, the Forest Service tried to assert reserved water rights for flows needed for sediment transport. A federal district court agreed that maintaining stream integrity fell within the bounds of "securing favorable conditions of water flows" but held that the instream flows sought by the Forest Service were not necessary to support that hydrologic function.[96]

Where federal reserved rights are not available or the federal government is reluctant to seek them, water rights can sometimes be obtained under state law. The federal government has filed many such claims, but their usefulness is sharply limited. In Colorado and Idaho, for example, attempts by the Forest Service to acquire instream flow rights were rebuffed because, by state law, those rights may be held only by a state agency.[97] At best, new filings for instream flow rights carry a recent priority date. Given the overappropriated state of the West's rivers, such junior rights are often not very useful.

Refuge Water Rights Claims in the Klamath

In the Klamath adjudication, the United States filed a total of twenty-one claims for the Upper Basin's complex of NWRs. Seven are based on succession to the irrigation rights of Indian allottees who once owned land now located within the newest of the refuges, Klamath Marsh. Twelve are typical federal reserved rights claims, with a claimed priority as of the date the refuge was established or additional lands were added to it. All claim water only for out-of-stream uses.

The two 1905 claims are, understandably, the most hotly contested. All of the refuges were established after appropriation of the basin's waters for the Klamath Project in 1905; their federal reserved rights would therefore be junior to the rights of project irrigators. For Lower Klamath and Tule Lake NWRs, however, the United States asserts that it also holds rights based on the 1905 Klamath Project appropriations for lands within the refuges that were ceded by the state to the federal government as a condition of project construction. Under those two claims, the United States asserts the right to more than 125,000 acre-feet. A preliminary state evaluation of the claims acknowledges the 1905 priority but concludes that the United States has not established the quantity of water used.

With respect to the more traditional reserved rights claims, the United States has not been notably aggressive. Oregon has been willing to treat claims with recent priority dates generously but has worked to narrow the more senior possible claims. In the *Adair* litigation, the United States agreed to take a 1985 priority date for the Klamath Marsh National Wildlife Refuge in Oregon, although the refuge was created in 1960. In return for that concession, Oregon has agreed that the primary purpose of the refuge is migratory bird conservation and thus the United States is entitled to the minimum amount of water necessary to prevent frustration of that objective. The state takes a harder line on rights claimed by the United States in the Upper Klamath NWR, which would carry a 1928 priority date. President Hoover's original executive order[98] described the purpose of the refuge as "a breeding ground for birds and wild animals," but Congress later described the purpose as "to preserve intact the existing habitat for migratory waterfowl in this vital area of the Pacific flyway."[99] Following the letter of the *New Mexico* decision, Oregon claims that any water rights the Upper Klamath refuge may have can be used only to manage migrating waterfowl.[100]

Whatever rights the Oregon adjudication ultimately confirms for the Klamath refuges will be of only limited use, because they are not instream rights. The refuges lack firm water rights capable of protecting aquatic ecosystems. Their water comes, to a large extent, in the form of return flows from project irrigation. In the drought summer of 2001, when irrigation was cut off, the refuges were left begging for water. FWS's 2001 biological opinion (BiOp) had called for the refuges to receive 32,255 acre-feet of water, an amount FWS considered sufficient to support about 1,000 bald eagles and 6 percent of the usual population of 1.8 million other birds. Small donations from PacifiCorp, a 2,600 acre-foot release from Clear Lake, timely rainfall, and spot purchases ultimately got the refuges to nearly three-quarters of the amount recommended in the BiOp.

There are alternatives to a federal reserved right that might work in the Klamath. During the Clinton administration, Secretary of the Interior Bruce Babbitt was able to secure several important reserved rights through negotiation. Utah water users agreed to recognize an unquantified federal reserved right on the Virgin River above Zion National Park.[101] A federal nonreserved right was created for the Great Sand Dunes National Park in Colorado. The federal government appropriated surface and groundwater under Colorado state law, but the National Park Service is the holder of the right and the right is defined by federal law.[102] There is unlikely to be any new water up for grabs in the Klamath Basin, but Oregon's water conservation law could perhaps be used to create that kind of opportunity.

CHAPTER 5

Bringing Marginal Interests toward the Center

> The plain intent of Congress in enacting this statute was to halt and reverse the trend toward species extinction, whatever the cost.
>
> *Tennessee Valley Authority v. Hill* (1978)

The process for allocating the basin's water resources and the factors considered in that process have changed dramatically since the early days of the Klamath Project. In the early twentieth century, the newly developed system of appropriative water rights was in full swing in the West, encouraging removal of water from its native streams to places where it could be put to work in the ways white settlers deemed useful. Gradually, society has come to recognize that the West's water was already working to support ecosystems before irrigation ditches were dug and power plants built. Values have changed, but, by and large, the laws put in place to settle the West, which distributed property rights to those who put resources to use, remain in place.

Congress and the courts have nibbled around the edges of old doctrines, modifying them here and there and adding new layers to reflect new societal interests, but have not fundamentally reformed them. The law has simply grown by accretion, with little attempt at harmonization. The result is an uncomfortably divided governance structure that puts private interests at odds with public ones; state and local government at odds with federal authorities; and, within the federal government, conservation-oriented agencies at odds with development-oriented agencies.

Changing the Power Structure

As described in the preceding chapter, until recently the law strongly favored water development, providing little protection for the interests of either Indian tribes or the environment. Reserved water rights provide some benefits to the tribes but do not automatically ensure that species or resources important to the tribes (let alone to others) are protected. Many tribes, especially those with reservations near urban areas, have been able to negotiate congressional settlements that enable them to profit from quantified water rights through leasing those rights. Tribes like the Klamaths, though, with little political power and only inchoate water rights, are easily ignored in favor of the status quo.

Over the course of a century, the development of environmental law has gradually increased the power of environmental interests to contest the water allocation status quo, and some tribes have become sophisticated in using the new laws to advance their interests. The path has hardly been an easy one. It has proven relatively simple to enact laws that offer the promise of conservation but far more difficult to bring that promise to fruition on the landscape. Chapter 4 explained how both federal and state conservation efforts, including the establishment of wildlife refuges and restrictions on water development, have provided only marginal protection, leaving irrigated agriculture firmly in control of the basin's waters. In this chapter, we focus on the Endangered Species Act, the law that may finally have tipped the balance, but not before the basin's fish slipped into a steep decline.

The Environmental Era

As we have explained, the early development of water resources, in the Klamath Basin as throughout the West, essentially ignored both the nonhuman environment and those human interests that conflicted with water diversion and resource extraction. The first wave of legal reform through the conservation movement brought greater attention to living resources, leading in the Klamath Basin to the creation of a complex of wildlife refuges and some concern for the impacts of dams on fisheries. Those reforms, though, did not fundamentally challenge the need to exploit resources. Extractive interests continued to dominate through the first half of the twentieth century.

The environmental movement of the 1960s and 1970s promised to change that by establishing a new balance between people and nature.[1] A host of laws from the environmental era called for greater attention to the environmental impacts of extractive activities. The National Environmental Policy Act (NEPA) brought the environmental consequences of federal activities into the open by requiring the preparation and public disclosure of environmental impact statements.[2] The Clean Water Act (CWA) established a national goal of restoring and maintaining the physical, chemical, and biological integrity of the nation's waters.[3] New organic acts for the Bureau of Land Management and the Forest Service, managers of the largest federal land systems, called for planning, increased public participation, and greater consideration of wildlife and recreational resources.[4]

While each of these laws has had some impact on resource management in the basin, the power structure did not change noticeably until three species of fish in the basin were listed under the ESA. NEPA is strictly procedural. It does not place any substantive limits on environmental impacts, requiring only that they be acknowledged. In the absence of a strong local pro-environment political constituency, NEPA alone is not likely to change decisions. As for the Clean Water Act, its regulatory provisions are much narrower than its sweeping goals. It regulates only the addition of pollutants to water from industrial point sources, which contribute minimally to the environmental problems of the Klamath Basin. Finally, the federal land management laws call for consideration of the nonhuman environment in the course of preparing the plans that effectively zone public lands, but the overall framework of multiple-use management leaves the land management agencies with wide discretion, which they have continued to exercise primarily for the benefit of their traditional constituencies, extractive resource users (especially during Republican administrations).

The Endangered Species Act

Passage in 1973 of the Endangered Species Act tilted the balance of power more strongly toward fish and wildlife and the ecosystems they inhabit. Before 1973, federal wildlife agencies had the power to comment on water projects, but about all that typically produced was a sop—maybe a fish ladder around a dam or a hatchery below it. After 1973, suddenly wildlife protection was a substantive requirement, not just a luxury to be provided if consistent with resource development.

On paper, the ESA sets virtually absolute minimum conservation thresholds.[5] The law is only as strong as its implementation, however, and implementation of the ESA faces political hurdles at every step. In some cases, strong enforcement of a "macho" statute like the ESA may catalyze creative political solutions to thorny environmental conflicts. So far in the Klamath Basin, however, ESA enforcement has only spurred more conflict and increased pressure on the wildlife agencies to make the law more "user friendly," which tends to mean less protective of listed species.

The ESA in Context

Although the ESA is often thought of as the apex of twentieth-century environmental law, its roots lie firmly in the nineteenth century. Dramatic declines of commercially valuable and charismatic species such as bison, passenger pigeons, and songbirds as the frontier marched westward triggered the modern wildlife conservation movement. The emphasis of that movement remains on preventing individual species extinction rather than on protecting ecosystems or biodiversity. In many respects, the story of the ESA today, in the Klamath and other areas, is one of trying to use a tool designed for species preservation to achieve the modern goal of biodiversity conservation.

How the ESA Works

Two federal agencies located in different cabinet departments share primary responsibility for implementing the ESA. The Department of the Interior's Fish and Wildlife Service looks after terrestrial species and freshwater fish, including the Upper Basin's Lost River and shortnose suckers. The Department of Commerce's National Marine Fisheries Service (also known as NOAA Fisheries) is responsible for marine species and anadromous fish such as the Lower Basin's coho salmon. The ESA directs these two services to list species as "endangered" if they are in danger of extinction throughout all or a significant part of their range,[6] or as "threatened" if they are likely to become endangered in the foreseeable future.[7] For ESA purposes, the word *species* encompasses more than the taxonomic species recognized by biologists. The law defines species to include subspecies and, for vertebrate groups such as fish, "distinct population segments" that interbreed when mature. These subsets of biological species are entitled to the ESA's protection if they are disappearing.

Listing decisions are supposed to be entirely scientific. The ESA originally directed the regulatory agencies to consider the best scientific data available when making listing decisions.[8] In the early 1980s, the Reagan administration essentially halted listing activity because it thought the economic impacts of endangered species protection were unjustifiably high. In response, Congress amended the ESA to require that listing decisions rest *solely* on the best scientific data—that is, that nothing else be considered.[9] That change was intended to prevent "non-biological considerations" in general, and the costs of species protection in particular, from affecting listing decisions.[10] It has not eliminated controversy or the suspicion (from both sides of the aisle) that political factors strongly influence listing decisions.

There is an ecosystem component to the ESA, but it is a limited one. At the time of listing, the law directs the FWS and the NMFS to designate "critical habitat," those areas requiring special protection where physical or biological features essential to the species are found.[11] Until recently, that obligation was almost always ignored. As of 1999, critical habitat had been designated for less than 10 percent of listed species.[12] Critical habitat designation tends to incite local political opposition, and the federal services regard it as providing little in the way of conservation benefits.[13] Under the pressure of litigation from environmental groups, however, they have recently been forced to designate critical habitat for more listed species.[14]

Successfully running the listing gauntlet is strong evidence that a species is in dire trouble; barriers typically prevent species from reaching the protected list until their numbers are drastically reduced or declining with frightening rapidity. At that point, one might suppose that the law would aggressively protect them against any further harm. The ESA has never worked that way, however. In typical American fashion, it tries to let us have it both ways, providing just enough protection to stave off extinction while allowing as much human use of the species' habitat as possible.

The ESA protects listed species in two major ways. First, section 9 restricts the "take" of listed species by any person for any reason. This seemingly absolute prohibition is responsible for the ESA's reputation as the pit bull of environmental laws. The statute, together with the services' implementing regulations, defines "take" broadly, so that prohibited activities include not only capturing or killing a protected animal but also altering its habitat in any way that causes injury.[15]

When the ESA was first enacted, its prohibition on take by nonfederal actors was absolute. Today it is much more flexible. In 1982, concerned that private actors were being held to a standard the federal government did not have to meet, and convinced that development could at least sometimes be compatible with conservation, Congress authorized the services to issue permits allowing the take of any listed species.[16] Permits can be issued only for take that is "incidental" to some other activity; they cannot authorize the deliberate taking of a listed species. Permit applicants must agree to minimize and mitigate the impacts of their activities to the extent feasible, and must persuade the permitting agencies that their actions will not substantially increase the likelihood of extinction. Typically, incidental take permits for terrestrial development require that developers dedicate some land to conservation or pay into a fund that is used to buy land for conservation in return for the right to develop. The process is not much different from other sorts of bargains developers know they must strike with zoning authorities to get their projects approved. How well it works for the species it is supposed to protect is an open question, but at least it makes conceptual sense to both landowners and conservationists.

The incidental take permit process is more difficult to fit to the aquatic context, however. Rivers cannot be neatly divided into wet sections for fish and other sections for irrigators to dry up. In addition, unlike land developers, water users are typically trying to continue a historic use rather than start a new one. They tend to resist the idea that they should negotiate with regulators in order to continue using water. We are not aware of any use of sections 9 or 10 in the Klamath Basin. The take provision, even tempered by the possibility of permits, may be simply too big a club to wield against water users because going after one almost requires going after all.

The ESA's other regulatory requirement applies only to federal actors. Under section 7, actions taken, authorized, or funded by federal agencies must not be likely to jeopardize the continued existence of any listed species or adversely modify any formally designated critical habitat.[17] Federal actors can get permission to cross the jeopardy threshold only by a supermajority vote of a cabinet-level committee popularly known as the God Squad. The God Squad is rarely invoked and even more rarely allows an exemption. Indeed, it has done so only once, when the Bush I administration sought permission to conduct timber sales in the Pacific Northwest that might have driven the northern spotted owl to extinction. Although the exemption was granted, it was never used because the election of Bill Clinton intervened, and the new administration decided that the nation and region could live without those timber sales.

The statute does not further explain what it means to cause jeopardy or adverse modification. Those are not terms of art that were in common use by scientists or resource managers prior to their incorporation into law. Regulatory agencies enjoy some discretion to give content to vague terms like these in statutes they implement. In general, the federal courts have the job of interpreting statutes when Congress has not made its intentions crystal clear. But where Congress has delegated regulatory authority to an agency, that agency shares interpretive power with the courts. The Supreme Court, in a 1984 case entitled *Chevron USA v. Natural Resources Defense Council*,[18] recognized that Congress delegates regulatory authority in part to take advantage of agencies' special expertise and ongoing experience with the details of particular policy problems. The legislature, therefore, often intends to give regulatory agencies some room to define the specifics of their programs. The *Chevron* doctrine requires that federal courts defer to those agency interpretations if Congress has not been specific and the agency's position is a reasonable one. In practice, where *Chevron* applies, it complicates efforts to persuade courts to look beyond an agency's interpretation of its authority.

Because "jeopardize the continued existence of" and "adversely modify," the terms used by Congress in section 7 of the ESA, are not clear, the services enjoy some discretion to define them. They have done so through joint regulations that, at first glance, appear highly protective. They define the jeopardy limit as forbidding actions "that reasonably would be expected, directly or indirectly, to reduce appreciably the likelihood of both the survival and recovery" of the species in the wild.[19] Appearances can be deceiving, however. This definition is neither as specific nor as demanding as it looks. Because it requires that the proposed action reduce the likelihood of *both* survival and recovery, the services typically do not worry about impacts on recovery alone. The agencies do not view actions likely to merely slow or complicate the recovery of a listed species to the point that it can be removed from the protected list as causing prohibited jeopardy. In practice, therefore, avoiding jeopardy typically means modifying the project or mitigating its impacts only to the extent needed to maintain the smallest population that might plausibly be considered viable.

The wildlife agencies have defined adverse modification of critical habitat in terms nearly identical to the definition of jeopardy,[20] essentially collapsing the two duties of section 7 into one. Two federal courts of appeals have ruled that the agencies' definition of adverse modification is too limited, reasoning that Congress would not have enumerated two separate duties if it intended them to be identical.[21] Within those circuits, which cover much of the western United States, federal actions may not affect critical habitat in ways likely to appreciably reduce the likelihood of recovery. Beyond those circuits, though, FWS has made no move to modify its definitions.

An elaborate procedure has been developed to satisfy the requirements of section 7(a)(2). A federal agency contemplating action must first request from FWS and NMFS lists of species that may be in the action area. The action agency then prepares a "biological assessment" to determine whether the action is likely to affect those species, and if so to what extent. If the biological assessment finds that an adverse effect is likely, the action agency must enter into formal consultation with the appropriate service.[22] Consultation culminates in issuance by the service of a formal biological opinion stating that the action either is or is not likely to jeopardize the continued existence of the species or adversely modify its critical habitat.[23] Consultation is something of a negotiation process between the action agency and the wildlife agency. Drafts are shared and comments solicited before the opinion is finalized. The process is not open to public participation or comment, however.

BiOps include "incidental take statements" detailing the expected level of take and "reasonable and prudent measures" (RPMs) consistent with the basic design of the action that must be taken to minimize and mitigate the impacts of that take.[24] Actions in compliance with an incidental take statement are insulated from liability for take under section 9.[25] That protection extends not only to the action agency but also to any other entities whose actions fall within the scope of the BiOp,[26] such as irrigators in the case of consultation on a reclamation water project. A BiOp that finds that the proposed action would exceed the thresholds of jeopardy or adverse modification must also offer "reasonable and prudent alternatives" that will reduce the impacts sufficiently to allow the action to proceed.[27] Reasonable and prudent alternatives must be consistent with the intended purpose of the action, within the scope of the agency's authority, and economically feasible.[28]

BiOps issued by FWS and NMFS are not technically binding on action agencies, which retain the ultimate responsibility for compliance with the standards of the ESA. But the opinion of the wildlife agencies is undeniably influential. At a minimum, a federal agency that decides to proceed with an action in the face of an unfavorable BiOp must be prepared to defend its decision against vigorous challenge. Interested citizens and environmental groups can challenge in court any agency actions they believe violate the ESA. An unfavorable BiOp would not only invite such a suit but also provide the evidence needed to pursue it. Courts, which recognize the wildlife agencies as experts on the needs of listed species, might be expected to defer to their views as opposed to those of the action agency.[29] Persons acting under the authority of or in connection with the federal action also might find themselves in violation of the prohibition on take. Not surprisingly, until recently action agencies routinely accepted BiOps as effectively binding.

The ESA requires that the benefit of the doubt go to listed species in a close case, but it is not specific about what that means. It says only that agencies "must ensure" that their actions are "not likely" to jeopardize listed species or adversely modify critical habitat. The two services have issued a joint handbook that directs their personnel, in preparing BiOps, to give the benefit of the doubt to species if faced with "significant data gaps."[30] In practice, because the courts are inclined to defer to the "scientific" conclusions of expert agencies, the services enjoy substantial discretion in determining both the extent of risk and the degree of confidence in the available information needed to justify a jeopardy (or for that matter a no-jeopardy) opinion.[31]

The duty to consult under section 7 applies so long as "discretionary federal involvement or control" remains.[32] Following the lead of the Supreme Court in *Tennessee Valley Authority v. Hill*,[33] the federal courts have construed section 7 broadly. If the action agency has any authority to make or require changes that might alter the action's effects on listed species, the duty to consult continues.[34] Whether and to what extent the ESA's consultation requirement applies to the simple presence of dams, as opposed to their operation, are hotly contested. The current administration believes that the presence of dams, because it cannot be changed by the operating agency control, is outside the scope of consultation. In a case challenging operations plans for the Columbia River dam system, the Ninth Circuit rejected that view, ruling that where there is *some* federal discretion, listed species must be protected, even if part of the danger comes from actions the agency cannot now reverse.[35]

Section 7 also imposes another, less well-defined, duty on federal agencies. It directs the Department of the Interior to use the programs it administers in furtherance of the purposes of the ESA. Other federal agencies are told to use their authorities to carry out programs for the conservation of listed species.[36] The FWS has taken the position that this duty does not mandate any particular action, instead leaving considerable discretion to each agency.[37] The federal courts have deferred to this view,[38] essentially turning this provision into a procedural requirement mandating consideration and planning for the needs of listed species but not specifying particular substantive steps.[39] It has not proven useful to outsiders seeking to force conservation measures on reluctant agencies. Nonetheless, it carries some power as a justification for conservation actions by agencies that are so inclined. It permits the agencies to take any and all steps they choose, within the limits of their existing statutory authorities, to protect or aid listed species.[40]

The ESA and State Water Rights

Water project operations tend to harm aquatic species in two different ways: through depletion of water and through entrainment. Not surprisingly, the survival of aquatic species is often a function of the amount of water in a stream or lake, either directly or because the quantity of water is closely related to temperature and other important water quality characteristics. To protect listed species against excessive depletions, it may be necessary either to limit diversions during crucial times of the year or to require the release of water from upstream reservoirs. Entrainment refers to the trapping of fish in project facilities, such as irrigation canals or hydropower turbines. Entrainment can harm fish directly, by subjecting them to mechanical insults (such as grinding by turbines or pumps or battering against screens), or indirectly, by channeling them to areas unsuitable for spawning or too dry support aquatic life (such as the crop fields to which irrigation canals lead). Entrainment can sometimes be reduced by installing protective screens, or by changing the amount or timing of pump operations.

The imposition of conservation requirements can directly or indirectly limit the enjoyment of state-created and federal water rights, as well as less defined entitlements to water. The scope of federal discretion to impose such regulatory limits on those rights through the ESA remains murky and hotly contested. Congress has repeatedly indicated a vague intent to give some deference to state authority over water allocation, but it has not exempted the creation or exercise of water rights from federal environmental laws. Nor has it expressly created a federal "conservation water right" that could be integrated into state allocation systems. Instead, it has tried to have it both ways, superficially endorsing a commitment to state control of water allocation without really giving the states (or state water right holders) strong leverage to avoid federal regulation. The result has been that water right holders generally lose in the courts when their water use comes into conflict with federal environmental laws, but they consistently feel wronged by that outcome.

A section of the Clean Water Act known as the Wallop Amendment, for example, states, "It is the policy of Congress that the authority of each state to allocate water within its jurisdiction shall not be superseded, abrogated, or otherwise impaired . . . [and] that nothing in the Act shall be construed to supersede or abrogate rights to quantities of water which have been established by any state."[41] To paraphrase Justice Oliver Wendell Holmes, this vague amendment, a sop to western water interests, has proved too "slender a reed" to support state supremacy.[42] In *Riverside Irrigation District v. Andrews*,[43] irrigators in Colorado challenged the Army Corps of Engineers' requirement that they seek a permit to build a small dam and reservoir on a tributary of the Platte River. Although other dams of the same size were authorized under a nationwide permit without individual review, the Corps reasoned that this dam would facilitate irrigation diversions that in turn would decrease flows several hundred miles downstream, thereby putting endangered whooping cranes at risk. The irrigation district argued that the Wallop Amendment and an interstate compact prevented the Corps from interfering with state-created water rights. The court rejected that argument, holding that the clear declaration of agency duties in ESA section 7 trumped the general policy statement of the Wallop Amendment. It made the following observation, however:

> A fair reading of the statute as a whole makes clear that, where both the state's interest in allocating water and the federal government's interest in protecting the environment are implicated, Congress intended an accommodation.[44]

In this case, the court thought such an accommodation could best be "reached in the individual permit process."[45]

The ESA itself contains a policy statement even weaker than that in the Wallop Amendment, providing simply that it is "the policy of Congress that Federal agencies shall cooperate with State and local agencies to resolve water resource issues in concert with conservation of endangered species."[46] Congress adopted this provision in lieu of proposed language directly modeled on the Wallop Amendment that would have stated that the ESA did not supersede or abrogate either state authority to allocate water or existing state water rights.[47] Only one court has directly addressed the effect of this provision, rejecting a claim by irrigators that it precluded enforcement of the ESA to limit entrainment of protected fish by irrigation pumps. The court wrote,

> This provision does not require, however, that state water rights should prevail over the restrictions set forth in the Act. Such an interpretation would render the Act a nullity. The Act provides no exemption from compliance to persons possessing state water rights, and thus . . . state water rights do not provide . . . a special privilege to ignore the Endangered Species Act.[48]

The ESA, because it is not subservient to state water law, can provide leverage to change the status quo of water allocation. The Pyramid Lake Paiute Tribe of Nevada, for example, has been able to use the combination of the ESA and federal trust obligations to force such a change. Located around Pyramid Lake, a remnant of ancient Lake Lahontan in Nevada, the tribe has sought to sustain its traditional unity among people, lake, and fish.[49] The listing of two endangered fish species, the cui-ui, which has been extirpated from all of its former habitats except Pyramid Lake, and the Lahontan cutthroat trout, which persists in a handful of rivers and lakes in the region, has helped to transform the tribe from a marginal to a major stakeholder in the basin.

The Pyramid Lake Paiute Tribe's troubles go back to 1905, when about half the flow of the lower Truckee River, which supports the fish vital to the tribe, was diverted to the Carson Basin to provide carryover storage for the Newlands Reclamation Project.[50] The federal government intervened in the Truckee River adjudication that followed, but it claimed reserved rights only for farming, not for maintenance of the lake's fishery, on behalf of the tribe. The 1944 Orr Ditch Decree confirmed only those limited tribal rights, and in 1983 the Supreme Court held that there was no compelling reason to reopen the decree, on which many non-Indians, notably including irrigators served by the Truckee-Carson Irrigation District (TCID), had relied.[51]

Although it was unable to force the state to recognize water rights to provide for the needs of the fish, the tribe was nonetheless able to use federal law to increase instream flows. It first obtained a ruling that the Department of the Interior's trust duties required it to operate the Lahontan Reservoir, located behind Stampede Dam on the Little Truckee River in California and the source of water for TCID, more efficiently.[52] The resulting Operating Criteria and Procedures forced the progressively more efficient operation of TCID.[53] Also, the Secretary of the Interior refused to sell additional water, which the district regarded as excess but the tribe saw as vital for the fish, to the district for municipal and irrigation use. Water users challenged the decision, arguing that reclamation law required that all project water be made available to them. The district court held that Interior was "required to give the [endangered species] priority over all other purposes" of the project until they were no longer listed, but that any water "not required under the Endangered Species Act" must be offered to the water users.

On appeal, that holding was somewhat modified. All parties conceded that preventing jeopardy under the ESA took priority over the Bureau of Reclamation's obligations under the reclamation laws.[54] The water users argued that once the "no jeopardy" requirement was satisfied, Interior had no further authority to provide water to the fish. The Ninth Circuit disagreed, holding that the ESA allowed Interior to direct the water to conservation purposes rather than selling it to the water users. That conclusion rested on the court's determination that the project's enabling legislation did not require sale of all available water to recoup construction costs.[55] Nor did any long-term contracts require the sale of water. Essentially, the case stands for the proposition that the Bureau of Reclamation, like other federal agencies, can choose to devote any resources within its discretionary control to endangered species protection.

The decision left some key questions unanswered about the relationship of the ESA to water project operations. It expressly did not reach the question of whether, if the project legislation had required sale of all project water, the ESA would have superseded that requirement, either permitting or requiring devotion of water to conservation purposes.[56] Subsequent cases suggest that it would not. The ESA's generalized duty to conserve listed species has been held to operate only within the limits of the agency's preexisting statutory authority,[57] and, as explained above, to leave substantial discretion to the agency within that authority. Short of a jeopardy determination, therefore, it is unlikely that the Bureau of Reclamation could withhold water it was bound by statute or contract to deliver, or that it could be forced to withhold water it chose to deliver.

If project water deliveries would fail the jeopardy test, however, the ESA requires that they be withheld, notwithstanding the existence of water contracts. The first decision to that effect came in 1995, in *O'Neill v. United States*.[58] Westlands Water District held a long-term water contract obligating the United States to furnish it with 900,000 acre-feet of water annually from the Central Valley Project in California, subject to shortages arising from drought or any other causes. After NMFS issued a BiOp concluding that operation of the Central Valley Project would jeopardize the Sacramento winter-run chinook, Reclamation cut delivery to Westlands by 50 percent.

Westlands sued, but the Ninth Circuit held that a liability disclaimer in the contract, combined with the requirements of the ESA, excused compliance with the delivery contract. The Ninth Circuit later reiterated that view in *Klamath Water Users Protective Association v. Patterson*,[59] in response to a challenge to operation of the Link River Dam in accordance with Reclamation's ESA-based operating plan. In affirming the district court's holding that irrigator's water rights were subservient to the ESA, the court in *Klamath Water Users* wrote the following:

> It is well settled that contractual arrangements can be altered by subsequent Congressional legislation. The ESA was enacted in 1973 to halt and reverse the trend toward species extinction, whatever the cost. Even in circumstances where the ESA was passed well after the agreement, the legislation still applies as long as the federal agency retains some measure of control over the activity. Therefore, when an agency, such as Reclamation, decides to take action, the ESA generally applies to the contract.[60]

In a 1995 memorandum dealing specifically with the Klamath Project, the regional solicitor of the Department of the Interior had expressed the same view:

> Reclamation has an obligation to deliver water to the project water users . . . subject to the availability of water. . . . Water would not be available, for example, due to drought, a need to forego [sic] diversions to satisfy prior existing rights, or *compliance with other federal laws such as the Endangered Species Act*.[61]

O'Neill and *Klamath Water Users* leave open the possibility that some Reclamation project authorizations could preclude adjustment of deliveries for ESA purposes. *Klamath Water Users* depended in part on the court's determination that Reclamation had authority to manage the dam as required by the ESA.[62] Because ESA section 7 applies only to federal "actions," Reclamation might claim that authorizing legislation leaves it no discretion to adjust deliveries for conservation purposes, and that therefore section 7 does not apply. Indeed, Reclamation took that position in disputes over irrigation on the Rio Grande.[63] It has been strengthened by the Supreme Court's most recent ESA decision, *National Association of Home Builders v. Defenders of Wildlife*,[64] which endorsed the FWS's view that only discretionary federal actions are subject to the consultation requirement. Undoubtedly, the extent of agency discretion over current operation of established water projects, and therefore the extent to which the ESA applies to current operations, will continue to be disputed for some years. In the Klamath Basin, however, the *Klamath Water Users* decision establishes that the ESA applies to annual operational decisions.[65]

"Takings" Claims

The Bureau of Reclamation is required to withhold water when necessary to protect endangered species, even from those holding valid water rights and water delivery contracts. Water rights holders understandably regard it as unfair to deprive them of rights on which they have come to rely. If they must give up their water, they argue, at least they should be compensated for its financial value to them. The law, however, does not currently support that claim. In the Klamath Basin, in fact, arguments for compensation have been directly rejected.

Water users base their claim on the Fifth Amendment to the U.S. Constitution, which requires government to pay compensation if it takes private property for public use. The law of takings is notoriously complex. The Supreme Court has held that the government must compensate property owners in three situations: if it permanently physically occupies property; if it denies all economically viable use of property; or if it unfairly singles out some persons to bear burdens that should be shared by the public as a whole. Those principles are tough enough to apply to restrictions on land use. The challenge is magnified for restrictions on water delivery, because it is unclear what it means to "physically occupy" or deny all economically viable use of a water right.

Students of water law have long noted that water is not like other resources. One important difference means that water users necessarily have weaker takings claims than landowners. A water right is only a contingent entitlement to use a specific source of water; all users are subject to a variety of risks from drought, competing claims from other users, and the power of the state to decide which uses are in the public interest. A key factor in the Supreme Court's evaluation of the fairness of regulations is their impact on "reasonable investment-backed expectations." All property owners have to anticipate that changes in public values will limit the enjoyment of their rights. The Constitution does not prohibit such changes, but it does require that they be effectuated fairly. While they must anticipate some degree of social transformation, most landowners are entitled to assume that the physical form of their land and the corresponding ability to occupy it will remain relatively constant over time. The vagaries of climate, especially in the West, mean that water users are not entitled to make the same assumption. Their expectations must take into account the likelihood that water supply will vary considerably from year to year. The priority system for appropriative rights was developed precisely in response to that kind of variability.

Standard contracts for water delivery from Bureau of Reclamation projects not only explicitly incorporate the prospect of shortfalls, they specify that irrigators, rather than the federal government, must bear that risk. The contracts typically speak to shortages from "drought or any other causes." The federal courts have generally agreed that such contracts protect the United States from monetary liability for water restrictions required by the ESA. In *O'Neill v. United States*,[66] for example, water contractors sought damages from the United States after deliveries from the Central Valley Project were reduced in order to protect the delta smelt. The Ninth Circuit ruled that a typical shortage clause, which absolved the United States of liability for water shortages "on account of errors in operation, drought, or any other causes" applied. Most Klamath Project contracts include similar shortage clauses.[67]

Although the U.S. Supreme Court has not yet weighed in, it appears likely to agree with the Ninth Circuit that the United States would not be liable for ESA-induced reductions in Klamath Project deliveries. In general, parties to a contract are not required to meet their obligations when doing so would violate the law. Suppose, for example, that an importer entered into a contract in 2003 to supply specified amounts of Beluga caviar to a restaurant for five years. In 2004, the listing of the Beluga sturgeon as a threatened species made it unlawful to import Beluga caviar. After that time, the importer could not meet his or her contractual obligations without violating the law and would therefore be excused from those obligations (as, of course, the customer would be excused from paying). Because it has special powers to change the law, the government cannot always take advantage of this excuse. It cannot escape its contractual commitments by changing the law for that very purpose. Nonetheless, because changes in the law are inevitable and desirable, the United States is excused if it cannot comply with a contract because of changes in the law that are "relatively free of Government self-interest."[68] That surely describes passage of the ESA. No one could seriously contend that the law of endangered species protection traces its origins to the desire of the United States to escape its water delivery commitments.

To the surprise of many observers, though, in 2001 the Court of Claims (a specialized court that hears claims seeking monetary awards against the United States) gave hope to water users everywhere that they might be entitled to compensation for restricted deliveries. In *Tulare Lake Basin Water Storage District v. United States*, the court ordered the United States to compensate irrigators in California's Central Valley after diversions were reduced to protect the threatened delta smelt.[69] The *Tulare* court decided that restricting water delivery was the equivalent of physically occupying property. That brought it within a rule announced by the Supreme Court in 1982. In a case called *Loretto v. Teleprompter Manhattan CATV Corporation*, the Court held that any "permanent physical intrusion" on property by the government, no matter how small, requires compensation. Writing for the court, Justice Thurgood Marshall pointed out that such intrusions "chop through the bundle [of property rights], taking a slice of every strand,"[70] and produce "a special kind of injury," direct occupation by a stranger.[71]

A categorical requirement for compensation for physical intrusions on land seems appropriate given the special importance of the right to exclude others from land, which protects the owner's privacy and autonomy as well as his or her economic interests. It should not, however, be extended to water shortages. Holders of water rights, unlike owners of land, do not own the physical manifestation of their property, the molecules of water that pass through their pipes or channels. They own only a right to use that water. Moreover, the expectation of any particular quantity of water is always tentative, subject to the possibility that nature itself may withhold water. Finally, water rights do not invoke privacy or autonomy interests. Losses from restrictions on water deliveries or diversions are strictly economic. They are more appropriately analyzed under the court's general test, which is one of fairness under all the circumstances.[72] Under that test, the fact that western water users have never had reasonable expectations of year-to-year stability suggests that foreseeable delivery reductions should not require compensation.

Even if one were to accept the reasoning of the *Tulare* decision, it would not apply to Klamath Basin water shortages. In the *Tulare* case, federal law had forced reductions in deliveries from a state-operated water project. Although the contracts included shortage clauses, those clauses ran only to the state; they said nothing about the potential for federal liability. As already explained, that is not the case in the Klamath Project, where deliveries are made under contracts explicitly providing that the United States is not liable for water shortages.

Nonetheless, emboldened by the *Tulare* decision, and committed to the idea of standing on their sacred constitutional rights, Klamath Basin irrigators filed suit in October 2001, seeking compensation "in an amount as yet unascertained, estimated at approximately $1 billion," for the water deliveries they were denied that summer. In 2005, the court of claims rejected their takings claim, ruling that they could seek damages only for breach of federal water delivery contracts.[73] Although it did not expressly resolve their contract claims, the court offered little comfort to irrigators on that score, either. It noted that the vast majority of the water contracts in the basin expressly absolve the United States of liability for shortages due to drought or other causes and quoted with approval the Ninth Circuit's holding in *O'Neill v. United*

States that such shortage clauses preclude liability. With respect to the small number of contracts that do not include broad shortage clauses, the court emphasized the right of the sovereign to override contract obligations through general legislation and noted that other courts have held that the ESA provides a valid excuse for failure to meet water contract obligations. Finally, rejecting the argument that the *Tulare* decision required a different result, the court said, "With all due respect, *Tulare* appears to be wrong on some counts, incomplete in others, and distinguishable at all events."[74]

Despite their failure to obtain relief through takings litigation, the Klamath Project irrigators still believe that justice as they envision it will prevail. They continue to retain a public interest firm that specializes in property rights litigation and to believe that the best way to preserve the status quo is to insist on full recognition and enforcement of strong property rights in water.[75] They are not, in other words, giving an inch.

The ESA in the Klamath Basin

The Klamath conflict erupted when federal officials concluded in the spring of 2001 that the ESA required minimum water levels in Upper Klamath Lake and minimum flows in the main-stem Klamath River. The crisis had been building, however, since the 1980s.

The Listings

The ESA first became a factor in water allocation in the Klamath Basin in 1988, when the Lost River sucker and shortnose sucker (see fig. 7) were listed as endangered. Although the addition of a species to the federal protected list is frequently a highly contentious and protracted process, the decision to list those fish passed almost unnoticed. By 1982, FWS had identified both sucker species as possibly qualifying for listing. Populations declined drastically shortly thereafter. Between 1984 and 1986, the shortnose sucker almost disappeared, and the spawning population of the Lost River sucker decreased by half. Dams, especially the Chiloquin Dam on the Sprague River, had blocked nearly all of the suckers' historic spawning habitat. Both species had experienced almost no spawning success in nearly twenty years.[76] Their situation became even more precarious in 1986, with a major die-off in Upper Klamath Lake.[77] Both Oregon and California had already listed the suckers under their state endangered species laws. Only thirteen comments were submitted in response to FWS's 1987 announcement that it intended to list the two species as endangered.[78] None of the commenters, including the City of

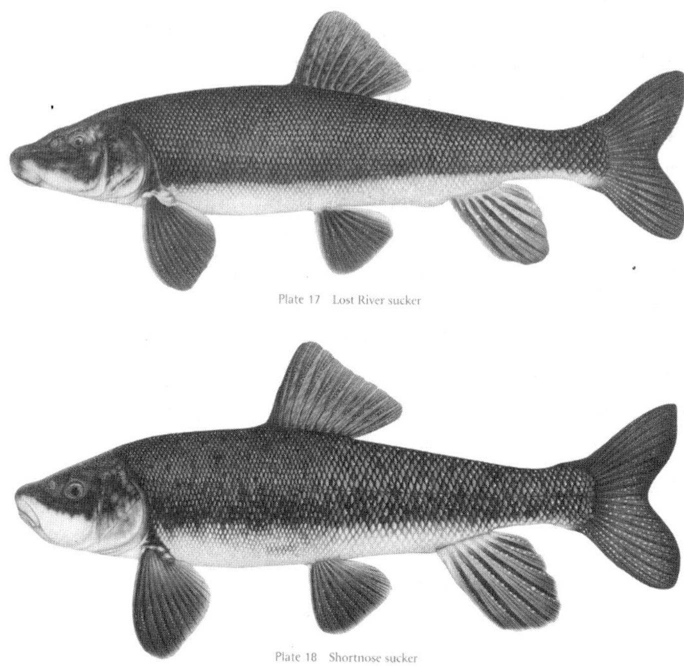

FIGURE 7
The endangered Lost River and shortnose suckers. (Illustration © Joseph R. Tomelleri, reprinted from: Peter B. Moyle, *Inland Fishes of California* [Berkeley, CA: University of California Press, 2002].)

Klamath Falls, the California Department of Fish and Game, and the Oregon Department of Fish and Wildlife, opposed the listing.

In part, that was surely because the species' situation appeared so dire that listing was inevitable. Beyond that, no one seems to have anticipated that the listing might have serious impacts on operation of the Klamath Project. When it proposed to list the suckers, the FWS identified a number of federal actions that might require consultation, including dam licensing by the Federal Energy Regulatory Commission; national forest management along the Sprague River and Upper Klamath Lake; and wetlands permit issuance by the Army Corps of Engineers. Irrigation was mentioned only obliquely, with a reference to "leases or other arrangements between the Klamath Tribe and local irrigation interests that would result in the diversion of water from the Williamson or Sprague Rivers."[79] The final listing rule added a mention of the Bureau of Reclamation, but again without any signal that existing project operations might have to change. It noted only that "management of canals and diversion structures" by the Bureau might affect the suckers.[80]

As was its practice at the time, FWS did not designate critical habitat at the time of the sucker listing. The explanation for that omission rang hollow, however. FWS concluded that critical habitat would be difficult to identify because the vast majority of the species' historic spawning grounds were already blocked by dams. FWS also asserted (again, as was typical at the time) that critical habitat would provide little in the way of conservation benefits for the species because "agency personnel are well aware of the distribution of both species."[81] As a result, the agency found that critical habitat designation was not "prudent or determinable."

In 1993, FWS finalized a recovery plan for the two sucker species. Recovery plans are supposed to provide road maps of the steps needed to bring the species to the point where it no longer requires protection. They set out a list of possible conservation measures, establish criteria for recovery, and estimate how long it will take and how much it will cost to get to that point. Sucker populations were so low, however, and the reasons for their decline so uncertain, that FWS acknowledged that it could not describe the steps necessary to achieve recovery. The best it could do was to call for the establishment of a secure population of at least five hundred fish for each sucker stock within twenty years.[82]

Water use in the basin became more complicated in 1997 with the listing of coho salmon (see fig. 8) in southern Oregon and northern California as threatened. Unlike that of the suckers, listing the coho did not fly under the radar. By that time, several other Pacific salmon runs had been listed; environmental, agricultural, timber, fishing, and hydropower interests were all sensitized to the possible implications of listing for the long-standing practices that had degraded the watershed. In the proposed listing, NMFS identified agricultural diversions, alteration of stream flows, blockage of spawning habitat, elevated water temperatures, forestry practices, hatchery operations, and overharvest in nontribal fisheries as significant threats to coho. It was no secret, therefore, that operation of the Klamath Project could be affected by coho listing. Nonetheless, the public response was muted in comparison with today's ESA controversies. Sixty-three people testified at six public hearings in the region, and a total of 174 written comments were submitted on the question of whether coho ought to be listed in any part of their West Coast range, which extends from central California to the Canadian border.[83]

In 1999, NMFS designated all accessible river reaches within the range of the southern Oregon–northern California coho ESU as critical habitat. For the Klamath Basin, that included the Klamath main stem from its mouth to just below the Oregon border, where Iron Gate Dam blocks salmon passage farther upstream, as well as the Trinity, Scott, and Shasta rivers upstream to their first blocking dams. Adjacent riparian zones are also included. As has

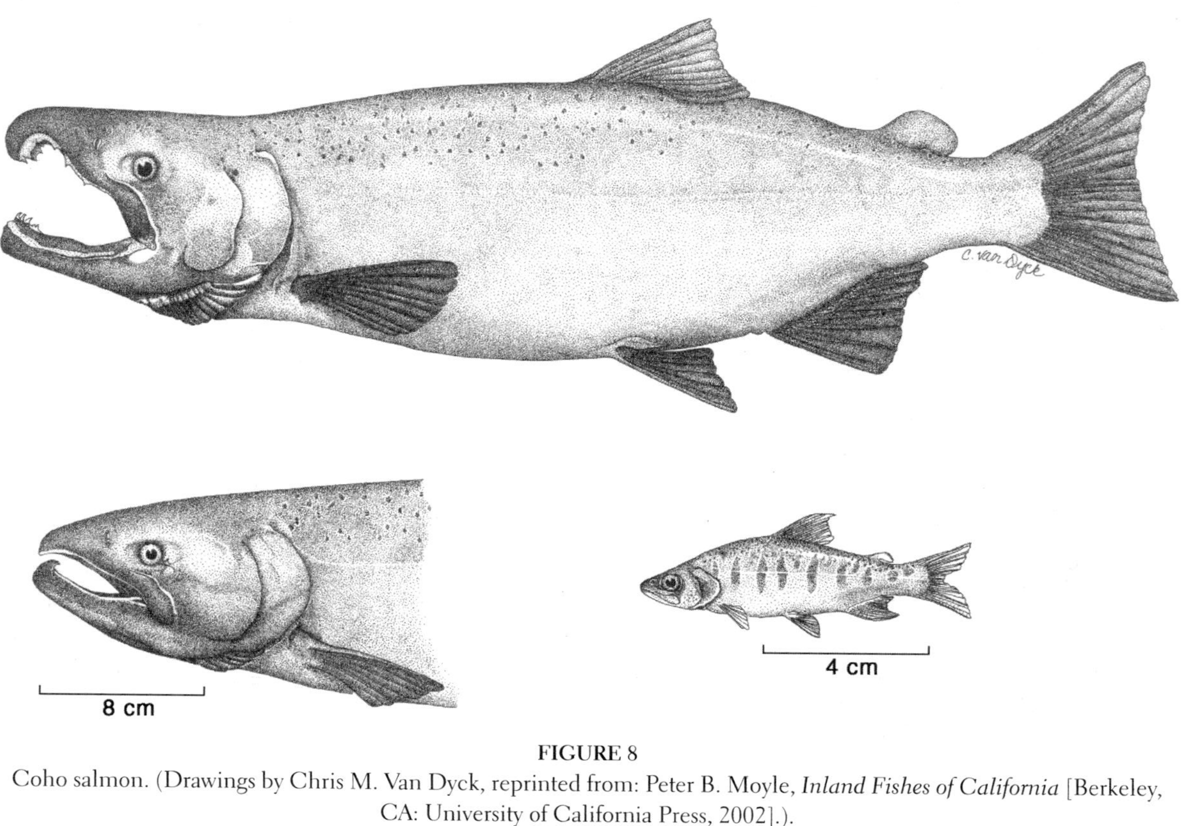

FIGURE 8

Coho salmon. (Drawings by Chris M. Van Dyck, reprinted from: Peter B. Moyle, *Inland Fishes of California* [Berkeley, CA: University of California Press, 2002].).

frequently been the case, this critical habitat designation was a focal point for controversy. More than five thousand comments were submitted, many from riparian landowners opposing the designation on the assumption that it would bring heavy regulatory impacts. At the request of the Lower Basin tribes, their lands were specifically excluded from the critical habitat designation. NMFS expressed the belief that other mechanisms would ensure that the tribes made their proportionate contribution to coho conservation.[86]

Designation of the main-stem Klamath as critical habitat for the coho does not automatically protect its flows. Establishing adverse modification of critical habitat, like establishing jeopardy, is not simply a mechanical process. The critical habitat designation identifies water quality, quantity, temperature, and velocity, all of which can be affected by diversions, as essential features of the critical habitat. It does not, however, identify specific required values for those features.[87] In order to find either adverse modification or jeopardy, NMFS has to do a more specific analysis and determine that proposed federal actions will produce conditions harmful to the species.

The Impacts of Listings

The ESA's prohibition on "taking" listed species has played almost no role in the Klamath water conflicts. It is quite difficult to use section 9 to protect aquatic species, both as a legal matter and as a political one. Take has always been easiest to show, and therefore to sanction, when an action intentionally and unequivocally leads to the death, injury, or capture of an animal. There is not a lot of sympathy for someone who captures endangered turtles, for example, with the hope of selling them to collectors at a high price, or (in most parts of the country) for someone who shoots an endangered wolf. But the problems for fish in a system like the Klamath come from actions that are more difficult to condemn. They result from the combination of many diversions, large and small, a number of hydropower dams, and agricultural and timber harvest practices basin wide. None of those actions are intended to harm fish, and each of them contributes to some socially valuable activity. Each by itself might well be harmless, and even demonstrating that the combination is harmful can be difficult. Tracing the marginal effect of any one of them is virtually impossible.

That complicates any attempt to prove a violation of the ESA's take prohibition by any of the smaller actors in the system. The U.S. Supreme Court suggested in *Babbitt v. Sweet Home Chapter of Communities for a Great Oregon*[88] that the take provision can be violated only by an action whose proximate and foreseeable result is actual injury to an identifiable member of the listed species. In the case of diversions under the western appropriative water rights doctrine, that means that the government might face the daunting challenge of having to identify the point at which demands on the system became too heavy for the fish to endure.

Even if that showing could be made, the politics of seeking sanctions against individual diverters or others who contribute to the fishes' problems are daunting. It might well seem unfair if regulators, or for that matter conservation groups, targeted only some diverters. On the other hand, pursuing all diverters at once would produce an administrative nightmare and encourage united opposition. It is not surprising that to this point neither FWS nor NMFS has made any attempt to enforce section 9 in the Klamath Basin.[89] Even the environmental groups active in the basin, some not normally shy about litigation, have not attempted to use section 9. In this respect, the Klamath Basin is typical. There have been few attempts anywhere to enforce the ESA's prohibition on take against water users or, for that matter, against users of terrestrial resources.[90] As we mentioned earlier, the hollow victory gained by ESA proponents in *Sweet Home* inevitably meant that the most exposed diverter, the Klamath Project, would become the focus of ESA enforcement in the basin.

Unlike section 9's prohibition on taking, section 7's consultation provision has played a large role in the Klamath water conflicts. Operation of a federal irrigation project, even under the perpetual contracts that govern much of the Klamath Project's deliveries, is subject to section 7 consultation requirements. The Ninth Circuit has held that operation of the Klamath Project, specifically, remains subject to the ESA's consultation requirements despite the existence of water contracts long predating the ESA.[91]

Consultation on project operations began shortly after the sucker species were listed. Conflict followed almost immediately. The very first BiOp, issued in 1991, concluded that operation of the project as proposed by the Bureau of Reclamation was likely to jeopardize both sucker species. In 1992, the driest year on record since construction of the Klamath Project,[92] FWS again concluded that the Bureau's proposed long-term operation plan would jeopardize the continued existence of the suckers. To protect the fish, FWS directed that more water be retained in Clear Lake and Gerber Reservoir. When the Bureau indicated that it would follow FWS's direction, project water users sued. They had to go all the way to the U.S. Supreme Court to establish their right to bring the suit,[93] but ultimately they prevailed on the merits. The federal district court for the District of Oregon ruled that FWS's requirements were arbitrary and capricious because the record did not show that minimum elevations in Clear Lake and Gerber Reservoir would help avoid jeopardy, either in those lakes or in the larger project area.[94] Although there are sucker fish in Clear Lake and Gerber Reservoir, the dominant population of both species lives in Upper Klamath Lake. Moreover, sucker populations in Clear Lake and Gerber Reservoir, unlike those in Upper Klamath Lake, have been stable in recent years.[95]

The 1992 BiOp also set minimum lake levels for Upper Klamath Lake, which were not challenged. In 1994, another critically dry year, water levels at Upper Klamath Lake fell below the minimum prescribed in the 1992 BiOp, despite some curtailment of irrigation deliveries.[96] The listing of the suckers, in other words, had not fundamentally changed the status quo. The Bureau of Reclamation was continuing to give agricultural water demands priority over the environment. It was, however, at least paying some attention to the fish.

Perhaps thinking that annual fine-tuning would allow it to make the most of any available irrigation water, the Bureau soon abandoned its long-term plan in favor of yearly operation plans. Those plans were immediately challenged from both sides. The 1997 plan called for limiting September flows out of Upper Klamath Lake through Link River Dam to 1,000 cubic feet per second (cfs). PacifiCorp, the operator of Link River Dam, indicated that it would not follow that plan, because doing so would violate the minimum flow requirements of its FERC license, established to protect fish in the lower reaches of the Klamath. Reclamation and PacifiCorp thereafter modified the contract for operation of Link River Dam so that it called for implementation of the 1997 operating plan, contingent upon FERC concurrence. Irrigators filed suit, asserting third-party beneficiary rights to enforce the contract. The Ninth Circuit rejected their claim and held that the ESA governed operation of the dam notwithstanding the earlier contract or the irrigators' water rights.[97]

The situation became even more difficult with the 1997 coho listing. Water supplies for irrigators were now squeezed from both ends of the basin. FWS was convinced that survival of the sucker species required that the Upper Basin Lakes, which double as the project's reservoirs, remain full, while NMFS insisted that the coho needed minimum downstream flows. Maintaining both would leave little water for irrigation withdrawals.

A series of above-average water years between 1995 and 2000 temporarily relieved some of the pressure. The Bureau of Reclamation's water juggling act fell apart, though, in 2000. Disagreements among the technical advisors about minimum flows needed to support the coho complicated preparation of the annual operating plan. The Bureau did not adopt a final plan until late April. It did not complete a draft biological assessment until November, long after the plan had gone into effect, and the final biological assessment was not ready until late January 2001, when the plan had essentially expired. Long before that, the Pacific Coast Federation of Fishermen's Associations had filed suit, claiming a violation of ESA section 7.

The outcome of the suit was a forgone conclusion. The Bureau knew that consultation was required before putting its plan into effect, but it had failed even to begin the consultation process until the plan was virtually complete. As it was bound to do, the court ruled in *Pacific Coast Federation of Fishermen's Associations v. U.S. Bureau of Reclamation* that the Bureau had violated section 7 by implementing its operating plan for the 2000 water year without ensuring that the plan would not jeopardize listed species or adversely affect their critical habitat.

On April 3, 2001, faced with no formal operating plan and an agency that appeared at best indifferent to its ESA responsibilities, the district court enjoined irrigation deliveries from the Klamath Project.[98] The injunction would apply whenever flows at Iron Gate Dam fell below the minimum recommended for coho in the Hardy Report, prepared for the Bureau by an outside expert. It would apply until formal consultation was completed, and resulted either in a "no jeopardy" opinion by NMFS or adoption by the Bureau of reasonable and prudent alternatives to prevent jeopardy.

With the water situation already near the breaking point, the Klamath Basin had endured a critically dry winter in 2000–2001. By the time the injunction was issued in early April, the gravity of the situation was clear. The Bureau of Reclamation was forecasting record low inflows to Upper Klamath Lake. Nonetheless, the Bureau's draft operating plan called for operating the project as in the dry years of the 1990s. In April, FWS and NMFS released final BiOps on project operations for the 2001 irrigation year, concluding that the proposed operation of the project would jeopardize the continued existence of both the suckers and the coho. As required by the ESA, both agencies offered reasonable and prudent alternatives they believed would avoid jeopardy. FWS called for Upper Klamath Lake to be maintained at the preproject minimum elevation level of 4,140 feet, with allowances for brief dips just below that level. NMFS called for minimum flows below Iron Gate Dam ranging from a high of 2,100 cfs in early June to a low of 1,000 cfs from July through September. Those flows exceeded the minimums established by FERC in the license for Iron Gate Dam but were less than those recommended in the draft Hardy Report.

On April 6, 2001, the Bureau of Reclamation issued its final 2001 operations plan, in which it committed to providing the lake levels and flow levels demanded by the wildlife agencies. Presumably the Bureau was motivated at least in part by its desire to get the injunction imposed in the fishermen's suit lifted, so that some water could flow. Because the year was critically dry, however, meeting the demands of the wildlife agencies left little water available for irrigation. The 2001 operations plan provided for delivery of the full allotment of irrigation water, some 70,000 acre-feet, from Clear Lake and Gerber Lake. It provided for deliveries to the wildlife refuges only as needed by the sucker species, not to support leased land farming. In a drastic departure from past practice, the 2001 plan allotted no water at all from Upper Klamath Lake for irrigation. That meant much of the acreage within the project would be left dry.

Irrigators immediately went to court to block implementation of the plan. Among other things, they argued that the best available science did not support the claim that listed fish needed higher lake levels and stronger instream flows. The court concluded that the plaintiffs were unlikely to prevail, because they had shown no more than a disagreement with the agencies' scientific conclusions. Furthermore, although the court conceded that implementation of the plan undoubtedly would cause the irrigators some economic harm, that harm did not clearly outweigh the harm to the fish, fishermen, and tribes that irrigation deliveries above those provided by the plan would cause. Finally, the court noted that if the 2001 plan or the BiOps supporting it were set aside, the ESA and the injunction in the earlier litigation would require that irrigation deliveries be cut even further. The court denied the requested injunction and urged the parties to resolve their disagreements about the basin's water needs outside the courts.[99]

Because the Bureau had now fulfilled its consultation requirements, the injunction in the fishermen's suit was lifted on May 3.[100] That did not mean, however, that the water flowed freely. The summer turned out to be as dry as predicted. The headgates were kept closed to maintain Upper Klamath Lake at its pre-project minimum level of 4,140 feet above sea level. A summer of confrontations, accusations, and recriminations followed, as described in chapter 1. As discussed in more detail in the following chapters, however, the crisis of 2001 has not altered the status quo in the Klamath Basin as much or as quickly as might have been expected.

CHAPTER 6

Water Wars Become Science Wars

> The obvious purpose of the requirement that each agency "use the best scientific and commercial data available" is to ensure that the ESA not be implemented haphazardly, on the basis of speculation or surmise. While this no doubt serves to advance the ESA's overall goal of species preservation, we think it readily apparent that another objective (if not indeed the primary one) is to avoid needless economic dislocation produced by agency officials zealously but unintelligently pursuing their environmental objectives.
>
> *Bennett v. Spear* (1997)

Like an earthquake, the 2001 closing of the headgates of the Klamath Project set off a series of aftershocks. Although those shocks continue to reverberate in the basin and nationally, they have not felled any of the basin's basic institutional structures.

In the short term, the irrigators' plight drew widespread national and regional sympathy and moral support, especially in the rural West. Politicians rushed to provide dollars to the Upper Basin. In 2001 and 2002, the federal government turned on the disaster relief spigot, as it has done so often in the past when farmers faced economic crises. But fundamental change has proven elusive. In Congress, for example, the Klamath quickly became a symbol of the need to "reform" (code for "roll back") the Endangered Species Act. Although that movement had the support of several influential legislators, it fell short of success. The Democratic capture of both houses of Congress in the 2006 elections makes near-term revival of attempts to gut the ESA unlikely.

Reform efforts from the other direction have also stalled. The crisis of 2001 emboldened Indian tribes and Lower Basin fishermen to press for reductions in Upper Basin water use. So far, though, the Bush administration, the usual bias in favor of the status quo, and the fragmented structure of government in the basin have all worked against lasting change. As a Congressional Research Service study reported, "There is no one entity that represents the Basin and has authority to resolve the issue. Rather, the Basin has more than 25 inter-agency and regional working groups."[1] Each agency is constrained by its own mission and budget. Each can address only part of the problem, and each tends to favor short- as opposed to long-term solutions.

The money that poured in to the Upper Basin following the crisis helped buy a measure of peace. So did the series of wet years that followed 2001, which, together with a new (and legally questionable) interpretation of its ESA responsibilities, helped the Bureau of Reclamation make full irrigation deliveries from 2002 through 2006. The Klamath Basin faded from the national spotlight, replaced by more urgent concerns in the wake of the September 11 terrorist attacks, the invasion of Iraq, and increasing awareness of the threats posed by climate change.

The peace that currently prevails in the basin, though, is fragile and surely temporary. The underlying problems have not been addressed, despite the good intentions and sincere efforts of many stakeholders. There has been a great deal of "problem-solving" activity, involving to varying degrees all interested parties and government agencies. But all of the efforts have been ad hoc, and the measures pursued have been partial, internally inconsistent, and unrealistic. No one has articulated an overall vision for the basin, much less a road map to achieve that vision.

The lack of a repeat crisis has allowed the status quo to persist, favoring irrigators. But it has also dissipated much of the rage that unified irrigators in 2001, perhaps reducing their chances of winning a lasting political victory. Difficult years for salmon have increased the leverage and visibility of the commercial fishing industry in the Lower Basin, enmeshing the Upper Basin irrigators and the Bureau of Reclamation in the volatile politics of salmon conservation. Market forces continue to stress farmers in the Upper Basin, making them ever more vulnerable to new economic shocks, some of which have already materialized. Meanwhile, the fate of the main-stem Klamath River dams hangs in the balance of relicensing proceedings on PacifiCorp's hydropower projects.

We return in the next chapter to a more detailed treatment of the post-2001 attempts to find a solution to the Klamath Basin's water conflicts. First, though, we need to explode a myth that complicates the search for solutions.

The myth is that science can determine policy decisions, making it unnecessary to resort to those other messy decision-making processes.

The Costs of Science Centrism

The Klamath stakeholders, like their counterparts in most American environmental conflicts, seem to share a general faith that science will produce a single, "correct," solution (although, of course, they disagree as vigorously about the nature of that solution as believers do about the one true faith). The kind of blind faith in the primacy of science that permeates so many environmental debates is rooted in the eternal but futile search for perfect rationality. As the great environmental philosopher John Passmore observed, "The Enlighteners accepted the Socratic doctrine that vice is always a form of ignorance, that if man once learns what is best for him to do, he will necessarily act in that way."[2] Of course, the horror and brutality of the twentieth century, which continues in many parts of the world, have destroyed the hopeful vision of endless progress through science, reason, and technology. But somehow the core Enlightenment idea that the "right" science can lead society to the "right" decisions lives on.

While we are believers in the power of science to illuminate the world around us, we are also acutely aware of the limits of science's ability to resolve human conflicts. In this chapter, we detail how all sides turned to science in the Klamath conflicts, show that appeals to science have failed to bridge the deep divides in the basin, and explain why science alone can never resolve this sort of conflict.

The Lure of Science

It should come as no surprise that the first response of the Bush administration to the 2001 Klamath Basin water crisis was to turn to science, because science carries great power in environmental conflicts. Science is both a substantive tool for understanding the causes of environmental decline and a rhetorical tool for building political support to address that decline. In recent years, both advocates for and skeptics of government intervention in high-profile environmental controversies have insisted that science must form the primary basis for decisions, yet they have sharply diverged in their evaluation of what outcome science demands. The Klamath controversy typifies these battles for the scientific high ground, which simultaneously demand both too much and too little of science.

That science must play a role in natural resource management decisions goes almost without saying. It is obvious that protecting endangered species requires knowledge of their needs, that rebuilding depleted fisheries requires a sense of their population dynamics, and that deciding whether and to what extent to log national forests requires information about how that decision will affect the physical and biotic environment. Not surprisingly, the law has responded to the need for scientific input. Any number of legislative and regulatory mandates require that environmental and natural resource management agencies seek the advice of scientists, consider the best available scientific information, or obtain outside scientific review of their decisions.

But there is more to the emphasis on science than concern about substantively getting decisions "right." Science supplies the fundamental underpinnings of environmentalism. The modern environmental movement is heir to the Enlightenment's substitution of science, broadly defined, for religion as the fundamental norm for organizing society. There are, of course, important ethical, religious, and spiritual strands to modern environmentalism, but the environmental movement has been heavily science driven. The icons of the environmental movement from its earliest days to the present have been scientist-advocates. Rachel Carson, Barry Commoner, René Dubos, Aldo Leopold, Paul Sears, and Edward O. Wilson, to name just a few, fit this mold. Their scientific credentials have helped to persuade the public of the importance of environmental goals and to identify steps needed to achieve those goals.

Environmental law is even more indebted to science. Environmental law breaks radically with the western legal tradition. It seeks to protect not living humans but natural systems and future human generations, two constituencies left out of the traditional legal (and political) calculus. Furthermore, environmental law challenges the primary objective of law, which has been to protect settled expectations. The environmental law project is forward looking with a vengeance and has little respect for the past. Indeed, it sees the legacy of the past as the source of current problems and demands replacement of traditional views with a new paradigm of human-nature relations.[3] Science is supposed to provide both the justification for change and a fair mechanism for distributing its costs.

Science is a politically appealing justification for any policy choice that must be made in the face of fierce disagreement within the political community. Science promises objective, rational decisions. It is supposed to be free of emotion, a characteristic that may seem especially important to the champions of the environment. Without the cover of science, they might face the prospect of defending public implementation of what could be described as a mere taste, and perhaps a quirky one at that, for environmental protection.

Science also promises decisions free of the corrupting influences of special interests. Probably because they are seen as above the ordinary political fray, scientists enjoy a high level of public trust.[4] Decisions that can be presented as scientific instantly gain a special level of credibility. Republican consultant Frank Luntz described the political benefits of framing policy decisions in scientific terms in a memorandum that became infamous when it was posted on the Internet by environmental interests:

> The most important principle in any discussion of global warming is your commitment to sound science. Americans unanimously believe all environmental rules and regulations should be based on sound science and common sense. Similarly, our confidence in the ability of science and technology to solve our nation's ills is second to none. Both perceptions will work in your favor if properly cultivated.[5]

Completing the trifecta, coating regulatory decisions with a scientific gloss can insulate decision makers from the political consequences of their judgments. The American public is notoriously scientifically unsophisticated. Few Americans are able to evaluate claims that particular policy decisions are objectively required by available scientific data. Even public interest groups may have a difficult time overcoming that hurdle, because highly specialized knowledge and a sizable investment of time are often necessary to unpack scientized decisions. As a result, agencies can use the cloak of scientific objectivity to hide, and therefore to evade political responsibility for, their value choices.[6]

The Limits of "Scientific" Policy Making

Insisting that agencies "follow the science" could ensure accurate decisions, constrain agency discretion, and defuse controversy if two conditions were fulfilled. First, the available scientific data would have to be reliably complete, precise, and relevant to the decision (or capable of being made so within the time frame allowed for decision making). Second, it would have to be certain that the agency would strike the same balance as the larger society between competing goals. Unfortunately, in the real world it is rare for either of those conditions to be satisfied.

The scientific information available to support resource management decisions is typically incomplete, ambiguous, and contested. An array of critical interpretive judgments, not fully determined by the data, are needed to translate that kind of science into policy. The more limited the data, the larger the universe of potential interpretations. The human tendency to interpret ambiguous evidence in a way that reinforces preexisting beliefs can exacerbate controversy by entrenching sharply contrasting interpretations.

Even if the data were perfect, however, decisions would not be reducible to an algorithm. Environmental conflicts are not like math problems. The first step in resolving such conflicts is defining the problem, an inevitably subjective process. In the 1970s, a pair of urban planning professors coined the term *wicked problems* to describe planning problems that require articulation of a vision of the desirable future community.[7] Different members of the community define wicked problems quite differently, depending on their own goals, values, and beliefs. Their definition of the problem, in turn, determines the very different solutions they see as acceptable, or even conceivable. The diverging views cannot be objectively identified as "right" or "wrong." They are simply different. To make matters worse, steps that might be taken toward a solution are frequently not easily reversible. They create "facts on the ground," such as roads or infrastructure, as well as human expectations. Trial and error is therefore a high-risk, high-cost approach to wicked problems.

Allocating the Klamath Basin's water resources is a wicked problem. There is no single "best" mix of farming, protection of native ecosystems, and production of fish for harvest. The value of competing water uses depends on one's perspective. So does the universe of potential "solutions." Some will see it as acceptable to take farmland out of production in order to free up water for other purposes. Others will not. Some will think the basin could do without salmon or suckers if that would make continued irrigation possible. Others will recoil in horror from such a suggestion. None of these views is objectively right or wrong; they simply reflect different values. Science can help us understand the consequences of various choices, but it cannot ultimately tell us which choices to make.

Uncertainty and value conflicts interact. Under conditions of uncertainty, people with strongly held values tend to interpret the available evidence as confirming their views,[8] and to reject even seemingly compelling evidence inconsistent with those views.[9] As a result, different people can draw very different conclusions from the exact same evidence. The deeper the value divide and the less complete the evidence, the more likely it is to reinforce, rather than reduce, conflict.[10]

Focusing on the Real Questions

Given those limitations, environmental policy decisions can certainly *draw on* science (and frequently must do so if they are to make any sense), but they are almost never *determined by* scientific evidence. Overemphasizing the centrality of science to decisions can actually exacerbate controversy and distract attention from the fundamental causes of conflict. Most natural resource conflicts boil down to disagreements about values and priorities. In a rare case, science might reveal a way to accommodate all competing values. Short of that, though, science will not resolve the underlying conflicts.

Contested resource decisions are essentially never objectively determined by the available scientific evidence. Subjective judgments of one sort or another always play a role. The real issues are how those judgments will be made, by whom, and how the role of "improper" or irrelevant biases and values can be minimized. Of course, what bias is regarded as improper is always in the eye of the beholder. Environmentalists calling for more or better science do so because they think current science mandates have not done enough to achieve substantive conservation goals. Critics in the regulated community, by contrast, believe current science mandates have not done enough to protect against unnecessary and unproductive regulation. Both sides claim to want more science and less judgment, but a more accurate assessment is that both want the inevitable judgments to be more closely aligned with their own policy preferences.

The flashpoint for disagreement is often the appropriate burden of proof. Environmentalists want regulatory agencies to be more cautious about approving activities that may affect listed species, applying the precautionary principle to impose protective regulations even if the supporting evidence is less than certain. The regulated community, on the other hand, wants the agencies to be more cautious about imposing regulatory restrictions on their actions and, therefore, using the rhetoric of "sound science," calls for application of the demanding standards of certainty imposed on claims of proof in the research science community.[11] Advocates on both sides are not shy about emphasizing the "scientific" underpinnings of their own views and accusing their opponents of misusing or even "abusing" science.

Science and Spin in the Klamath Basin

The nature of the problems and the governing law ensures that arguments about the scientific grounding of policy decisions flourish in the endangered species context. Conservation is costly, not just in terms of its economic consequences but also in terms of its impact on lifestyles and chosen identities in rural communities. Conservation policy lies at the crux of a value divide in American society that is difficult to bridge through rational discussion. There are people who believe strongly that other species have a right to exist or that people have an obligation to protect nature. There are others who believe just as strongly that private property and the right to make one's own moral choices, including choices about the use of nature's bounty, are the very foundation of American liberty. Most Americans probably share both sets of beliefs at some level and struggle to balance them. Most are uncomfortable with or feel little is to be gained by arguing openly about the relative priorities to be assigned to conservation and economic self-determination, though, and so are happy to argue instead about what science "requires."

The ESA exacerbates the tendency to focus on the scientific aspects of policy choices. It repeatedly calls on federal agencies to use the best available scientific information in decisions and to involve outside scientists in those decisions.[12] Agency practice seems to confirm the primacy of science. A formal policy requires that all information used in listing decisions, preparation of biological opinions, and development of recovery plans be evaluated by biologists "to ensure that any information used . . . to implement the Act is reliable, credible, and represents the best scientific and commercial data available."[13]

As we explained earlier, both the nature protection movement in general and environmental law in particular have always seen science as a core foundation. Environmental activists have long believed that science is the best support for their cause and that combining science with law provides considerable leverage. Recently, though, the opponents of environmental regulation have learned to exploit the uncertainties behind "scientific" policy decisions. Emphasizing science no longer works reliably in favor of environmental interests. By 2001, the "sound science" movement had been whittling away at environmental progress for a decade in the context of pollution control regulations. The Klamath Basin, though, was the first place that the conservation community came up against scientific uncertainty in a high-profile context that squarely threatened to undermine the law's authority and legitimacy.

Framing the Dispute

As we explained in chapter 5, the ESA forbids federal actions that would jeopardize the continued existence of a listed species, which by regulation have been defined to mean actions that would appreciably reduce the likelihood of a species' survival and recovery. In 2001, the Fish and Wildlife Service and the National Marine Fisheries Service independently decided that the Bureau of Reclamation's plans for operating the Klamath Project would violate that standard. Each claimed to have strong scientific support for its conclusion.

By the time the critically dry winter of 2000–2001 hit the Klamath Basin, the coho salmon that persisted below Iron Gate Dam had been listed as threatened and two sucker species in the Upper Basin were near extinction. Nonetheless, the Bureau of Reclamation proposed to operate the Klamath Project as it had done in earlier dry years, cutting back only slightly on irrigation deliveries. The wildlife agencies objected, invoking their scientific expertise in support of their view that the Bureau needed to both send more water downstream for the coho and keep more in Upper Klamath Lake for the suckers.

In a BiOp detailing the effects of proposed project operations on the suckers, FWS concluded that the Bureau's proposed operations would significantly reduce habitat for larval and juvenile phases, block access to spawning areas, make toxic algal blooms more likely, and exacerbate water quality problems in Upper Klamath Lake and other key locations. The BiOp did not confess to any significant doubt about its conclusion that higher minimum lake levels were needed to protect the suckers from extinction. In discussing its interpretation of the available data connecting lake levels to sucker status, FWS acknowledged that it had made some conservative assumptions in order to give the species the benefit of the doubt.[14] A few pages later, though, the agency stated flatly that the higher lake levels it called for were necessary to facilitate spawning and reduce fish kills.[15]

NMFS was more forthcoming about the thin state of the evidence. Its BiOp acknowledged "the substantial degree of uncertainty" regarding the status of the coho.[16] But, adopting a series of conservative assumptions, NMFS concluded that, because it would result in the worst habitat conditions in forty years, the Bureau's proposal posed "an unacceptable risk" to the coho.[17] NMFS did not explicitly reference the legal requirement that it give listed species the benefit of the doubt, but its conclusions were clearly significantly motivated by the desire to protect against a mistake that could wipe out the species.

Environmentalists, who had long argued that the wildlife agencies should follow the scientific evidence, welcomed the BiOps, which they were confident simply reflected the scientific realities. One went so far as to describe the science behind the opinions as "bulletproof."[18] Irrigators, who had already prevailed once in a lawsuit challenging requirements for water retention in the Upper Basin imposed by FWS, disagreed. They unsuccessfully sought to enjoin implementation of the Bureau's revised operations plan, arguing that the best available science did not support the wildlife agencies' claims that more water was needed to protect suckers and salmon.[19]

National Research Council Review

When they lost in court, the Klamath Project irrigators sought political relief in the form of general ESA reform or a targeted ESA exemption. To their chagrin, the Bush administration refused to convene the God Squad and did not endorse any of the general ESA reform measures. Instead, the administration sought review of the science supporting the BiOps by an independent expert panel. At the request of the departments of the Interior and Commerce, the National Research Council, the research and public outreach arm of the National Academy of Sciences, convened a multidisciplinary review committee. The committee's preliminary report, released early in 2002, returned the Klamath controversy to the media spotlight.

The National Academy of Sciences is a nonprofit nongovernmental organization founded in 1863 for the purpose of providing scientific advice to the nation. It has since spun off the National Academy of Engineering and the Institute of Medicine; together the three are now referred to as the National Academies. The members of each entity are the top scientists in their fields, elected by their peers. Originally, the members themselves provided advice when requested by the government, but the requests quickly outstripped the capacity of the limited membership to respond. In 1916, the academy established the National Research Council (NRC) to facilitate the temporary recruitment of specialists from the scientific community to help with the increased demand for scientific advice occasioned by World War I.

Today, the NRC conducts hundreds of studies each year, most at the request of Congress or executive branch agencies. The requesting agency works with NRC staff to frame a statement of task defining and bounding each study. Once the questions are framed, the NRC appoints a committee of experts to conduct the study. Most committee members are academics, but they may also come from government or industry. They are recruited with the intent of representing not only all relevant disciplines but also a range of perspectives. Committee members must not have any financial interest in the outcome of the study. They are not paid for their service. All must be credible experts in their field, but the vast majority are not members of the National Academies.[20] The process of selecting committee members involves a certain amount of networking; potential members are often suggested by others who have served on NRC committees and governing boards.

NRC committees are given a time frame, typically about eighteen months to two years, to study the issue and produce a published, peer-reviewed report. They usually meet several times, in the field or in National Academies facilities in Washington, D.C., and Irvine, California, in open session to gather information and in closed session to deliberate. Committee members must be willing and able to participate in meetings and do their share of the work of writing a potentially lengthy report on top of their full-time jobs. Reports typically represent the consensus of the entire committee, although every committee member has the right to issue a separate explanation of his or her views.

Before they are made public, NRC reports must go through rigorous internal and external peer review. The process is cumbersome and expensive, with a typical study costing about $250,000 or more. Requesting agencies foot the bill for the studies but have no editorial control over committee reports. Because NRC committees are widely viewed as both expert and independent, the high costs are viewed by client agencies as worthwhile. NRC reports typically carry considerable weight in the worlds of politics and public opinion.

In practice, the process of selecting committee members and the expectations of the NRC staff who work with each committee tend to push committee reports toward relatively middle-of-the-road positions. Often, reports identify the parameters of a problem but refuse to render concrete policy advice. Such committee reports are generally understated and address controversial issues in general terms. While they can be critical of agency policies and actions, they tend to shy away from direct criticism of agency scientific conclusions. Recently, committees have been more willing to opine that the scientific evidence points in at least general policy directions. For example, in 2002, the NRC recommended that the United States Army Corps be authorized to begin an aggressive ecosystem restoration experiment on the Missouri River.[21] The more specific the policy advice provided, of course, the more the NRC becomes vulnerable to criticism. The Missouri River report did not sit well with Senator Kit Bond of Missouri or downstream navigation interests who feared the loss of navigation releases. Typical NRC reports may earn considerable scientific respect but do not automatically change the political landscape.

The committee established to review the Klamath BiOps departed from the NRC norm both with respect to its process and, even more so, in the substance of its preliminary report. The committee was constituted in the fall of 2001, holding its first meeting on November 6. It was asked to deliver a preliminary report on an unusually fast track. The first draft was sent for peer review on December 14, and the report was released to the public on February 6, 2002.[22] William Lewis, an eminent limnologist at the University of Colorado and veteran of many NRC committees dealing with the use of science to manage large ecosystems, was appointed chair. Eleven other members, from disciplines as diverse as economics, engineering, ecology, and law, rounded out the committee. Although nearly all were research scientists, many also had considerable experience at the interface of science and policy—for example, as expert witnesses in litigation over science-laden choices. They had seen the rough-and-tumble world of environmental policy making. Nonetheless, they were clearly surprised by the reaction to their preliminary report.

The committee was asked to review and evaluate the science underlying the 2001 BiOps. Its preliminary report minced no words. The committee found "strong scientific support" for FWS's BiOp "except for the requirement for specified minimum lake levels in Upper Klamath Lake."[23] Although it was kindly phrased, the report essentially cut the legs out from under the BiOp. The minimum lake levels were the key provision of the BiOp and the source of the conflict with irrigators. According to the NRC committee, the available data did not provide scientific support for the assumption that higher lake levels would help the sucker species. The committee's assessment of NMFS's coho BiOp was equally harsh. There was, according to the committee, no "clear scientific or technical support for increased minimum flows in the Klamath River main stem,"[24] despite their intuitive appeal. Given the existing state of knowledge, the committee concluded that there was no substantial scientific basis for increasing lake levels or main-stem river flows above those of the previous ten years.

The preliminary report delivered an unexpectedly decisive victory to irrigators and the Bureau. The response was swift and, from those quarters, enthusiastic. Newspaper headlines were highly critical of the wildlife agencies and, by extension, of the ESA. The Bureau of Reclamation quickly issued a new ten-year plan for Klamath Project operations, relying heavily on the preliminary NRC report to justify maintaining the status quo. It hardly mattered, even to the wildlife agencies and environmentalists, that the committee had endorsed other aspects of the BiOps, including requirements for additional screening at key diversion points, improved access to sucker spawning habitat, and better interagency coordination. And no one seemed to notice that the preliminary report was just as critical of the Bureau's proposal to decrease lake levels and river flows as it was of the wildlife agencies' contrary recommendations.

Two years later the committee released its final report. That report was detailed and nuanced, a more typical NRC committee product. It urged a stronger focus on recovery of the Klamath Basin's suckers and salmon. Recovery, it argued, could not be accomplished without looking well beyond the Klamath Project, a point we return to later. With respect to project operations, the committee stuck up for the embattled wildlife agencies, expressly disagreeing with the criticism that the agencies had used "pseudoscientific reasoning" or "junk science" in their earlier BiOps. Still, the core conclusion remained the same: There was no substantial scientific evidence to support FWS's call for higher lake levels or NMFS's for higher river flows. The committee summed up its view of the 2001 BiOps as follows:

> The agencies can be expected, when information is scarce, to extend their recommendations beyond rigorously tested hypotheses and into professional judgment as a means of minimizing risk to the species. In allowing professional judgment to override site-specific evidence in some cases during 2001, however, the agencies accepted a high risk of error in proposing actions that the available evidence indicated to be of doubtful utility.[25]

Because it came out when events in the basin were less in the news, and undoubtedly also because its conclusions were more carefully hedged, the final NRC report got much less media coverage than the preliminary report. It has played a role in subsequent basin events but not as important a role as the preliminary report.

The Review's Effects

The preliminary NRC report triggered an interagency science war by changing the landscape for evaluation of the science behind the relevant policy choices. In 2001, the Bureau of Reclamation had adopted the wildlife agencies' operating recommendations even though it disagreed with them. Any other choice would have left the Bureau vulnerable to an ESA challenge. The preliminary NRC report, however, emboldened the Bureau to believe that it did not have to concede the greater expertise of FWS and NMFS.

Shortly after the preliminary report became public, the Bureau issued the long-term Klamath Project operating plan it had been promising since 1992. In a proposed plan for 2002 to 2012, the Bureau continued to assert that all water needs in the basin could be satisfied. It proposed to maintain irrigation deliveries while protecting fish and wildlife with a "water bank," voluntarily acquired through leases and other strategies, in dry years. The proposed plan was clearly influenced by the preliminary NRC report. While the Bureau backed off its earlier proposal to decrease river flows and lower lake levels, it insisted on maintaining the operational status quo.

In addressing the two key variables, Upper Klamath Lake levels and Klamath River flows below Iron Gate Dam, the Bureau hewed closely to the path laid out by the NRC committee. The committee's preliminary report had said that there was no convincing scientific justification for changing operational practices established over the prior decade. So the Bureau proposed to stick to those practices. Its plan called for maintaining Upper Klamath Lake at levels at or above average elevations for the period 1990 to 1999. Lake levels would be higher than the pre-project baseline in late spring but would be allowed to fall as much as 2 feet below pre-project levels in the fall, [26] and nearly 3 feet below pre-project levels in critically dry years.[27] Klamath River flows at Iron Gate Dam would also be closely tied to 1990 to 1999 averages. In critically dry years, river flows would be allowed to fall to 501 cfs in late July,[28] half the level called for in the Hardy Report.[29] The Bureau relied heavily on the NRC preliminary report to justify its low flow requirements, emphasizing that the NRC committee had found no scientific justification for deviating either up or down from 1990 to 1999 flows.[30]

ESA consultation on the ten-year plan was not finalized before the 2002 irrigation year began, so the Bureau requested limited consultation on project operations for April and May. Entrainment of suckers in those months is usually only a minor concern, and the Bureau promised to keep Upper Klamath Lake levels higher than pre-project levels for a similarly dry year, so FWS readily issued a "no jeopardy" opinion for the interim plan.[31] NMFS reluctantly agreed that the interim operation would not adversely affect coho, although the period from March to early June is the most critical time of the year for young salmonids.[32] The terse concurrence letter makes it clear that NMFS felt it had no choice.[33] NMFS emphasized, however, that its concurrence applied only to operations for April and May 2002 and that it was seeking additional consideration of spring flows by the NRC committee.

Subsequently, both FWS and NMFS issued jeopardy opinions on the ten-year operations plan. In the text of its new BiOp, FWS held its ground against the NRC committee. As it had in the 2001 BiOp, FWS asserted that low water levels in Upper Klamath Lake, even within the operational averages of the prior decade, would jeopardize the suckers. FWS pointed to the same effects it had relied on in 2001: Low water would interfere with spawning by reducing access to spawning habitat at the lake margins and would increase the likelihood of adult fish kills by reducing water quality and limiting access to high-water-quality refuges.[34]

Not surprisingly, FWS felt the need to defend its view of the science against the conclusions in the NRC preliminary report. The agency painstakingly explained how water depth could affect water quality in terms of dissolved oxygen, pH, nutrient availability, and algal blooms and set out evidence supporting those connections. It also detailed the precise relationship between changes in lake depth and availability of habitats suitable for spawning and use by larvae, juvenile, and adult fish. Finally, FWS was able to point to favorable reviews of its 2001 BiOp by faculty at Oregon State University and the University of California. The agency had solicited those reviews in the summer of 2001, before the NRC study was commissioned, in response to the controversy generated by the water cutoff. The Oregon State faculty were experts on sucker biology who had authored many of the studies considered in the BiOp and had reviewed a draft of the 2001 BiOp before it was finalized. They endorsed FWS's conclusion that minimum water levels in Upper

Klamath Lake needed to be increased above those allowed in the 1992 BiOp.[35] Four anonymous University of California faculty also provided individual reviews. While they acknowledged the paucity of firm data, overall these reviewers concluded that the recommendation of higher lake levels was sound and supported by the available evidence.[36]

Although the text of its new BiOp openly challenged the NRC report's conclusions, FWS appeared to lose its nerve in formulating the "Reasonable and Prudent Alternatives" it called on the Bureau to implement. Instead of renewing its 2001 call for minimum lake levels above those proposed by the Bureau, FWS imposed three less controversial requirements. First, it required the Bureau to change its method of forecasting water availability. Measurements of the winter snowpack, taken each April, predict a range of possible inflows. The Bureau had traditionally adopted as its official forecast an estimate at the lower end of that range called the "70 percent exceedance level," because actual inflows are expected to exceed predicted inflows in seven of ten years. The 70 percent exceedance level provides a conservative approach to irrigation planning, making it more likely that inflows will be underestimated than overestimated. But it is not a conservative approach to conservation. The spring inflow estimates determine whether a year is categorized as dry or critically dry. In those years, the project is allowed to operate to lower lake and minimum flow levels. Systematically underestimating the annual water availability as the Bureau had been doing, therefore, increases stress on the listed fish. In the 2002 BiOp, FWS called on the Bureau to make water year decisions on the basis of a 50 percent inflow exceedance level in order to ensure that Upper Klamath Lake would not be "managed at artificially low levels."[37]

Second, FWS directed the Bureau to reduce entrainment of juvenile suckers at Link River Dam.[38] The only thing remarkable about this requirement was that it still needed to be addressed. Entrainment had been recognized as a problem since the fish were listed; the first BiOp, issued in 1992, had directed the Bureau to screen the A Canal. That had still not been done, showing just how skewed the power dynamics were in the basin before the environmental groups went to court and the water conflicts hit the national spotlight. Until that point, there had been essentially no consequences to the Bureau's utter disregard of its ESA obligations. By 2001, no one seriously contested either that entrainment was a problem for the fish or that screening could make it less of one. The Bureau had finally agreed to screen the A Canal. FWS demanded that it also take steps to reduce entrainment at Link River Dam.

Third, the 2002 sucker BiOp called for the Bureau to do additional studies of the impact of water quality on the sucker species. The details were left for the future. In general terms, FWS directed the Bureau to develop a model for predicting low dissolved oxygen conditions in order to facilitate improved management of summer lake levels, to report on the use of water quality refugia (areas where water quality is better than the average) during the summer, to assess how population monitoring might be improved, and to develop a sucker die-off monitoring plan.

NMFS also issued a jeopardy opinion for the coho. Like FWS, NMFS took issue both with the Bureau's claim that it would operate the project within 1990 to 1999 parameters and with the NRC report's conclusion that operation within those parameters would sufficiently protect the fish. First, NMFS latched on to the report's statement that depletion of river flows below the 1990s reference levels could threaten the coho. As NMFS analyzed the ten-year plan, the proposed operations would likely result in flows lower than those during the reference period.[39] Second, NMFS took on the NRC committee's conclusions, asserting its own greater expertise with the species and system and explicitly appealing to the need for a precautionary approach. While acknowledging the need for more empirical work, NMFS reiterated its concerns about the effect on coho of habitat reductions it estimated at 20 percent to 35 percent during the winter and early spring period most critical to the fry.[40] In response to the NRC committee's assertion that no evidence supported the "conjecture" that high spring flows might increase smolt survival, NMFS pointed out that the strongest returning population in recent years, the adult 2001 year-class, had experienced exceptionally strong spring flows during its 1999 out-migration.[41]

NMFS also quoted the ESA consultation handbook, which directs the wildlife agencies to "provide the benefit of the doubt to the species concerned with respect to . . . gaps in the information base."[42] Noting that it could take several coho life cycles to gather scientifically rigorous evidence linking main-stem Klamath River flow rates to coho population trends, NMFS determined that in the interim it was required to take "a cautious approach" to evaluating the effects of the Klamath Project.[43] Interpreting the available evidence in light of that need for caution, NMFS concluded that the Bureau's proposed operations would be expected to increase the risk of coho extinction by decreasing reproductive success and the survival of juveniles.[44]

Like FWS, however, NMFS backed off from its 2001 "reasonable and prudent alternative" (RPA). It still called for higher flows than the Bureau wanted to provide, but it lowered its target for spring peak flows and allowed the required flows to be phased in gradually, so that they would not need to be achieved until 2010. That time would allow the Bureau to create a water bank through voluntary transactions, essentially buying the water needed for fish rather than simply withholding it from irrigators. Subsequently, NMFS biologist Michael Kelly charged that the phase-in was adopted at the urging of the Bureau, without any independent NMFS biological analysis.[45] NMFS's 2002 BiOp also called for a research program to evaluate the assumptions behind the Hardy Report, which had led to the minimum flow requirements that were criticized by the NRC committee. Finally, again at the urging of the Bureau, NMFS concluded that because the Klamath Project is not the only water diverter upstream of Iron Gate Dam, it should not bear the full brunt of restoring flows. Based on the distribution of irrigable acreage in the Upper Basin between project and nonproject farms, NMFS agreed that the Bureau need contribute only 57 percent of the flows needed by the coho. In an effort to make the BiOp satisfy the law, NMFS directed the Bureau to initiate a process for identifying sources to provide the other 43 percent of needed flows.[46]

Reclamation agreed to operate the project for 2002 in accordance with the RPAs specified in the BiOps but made clear its disagreement with those opinions. Key points of contention included the scientific underpinning of the opinions, the extent to which the proposed actions were under the control of the Bureau, and the extent to which the Bureau should be responsible for remedying the sum of all threats to the species.[47]

Science and Judgment

The Bureau of Reclamation welcomed the NRC committee's preliminary report, and the wildlife agencies were forced to respond to it. Fisheries biologists working in the Klamath Basin were outraged by the report, which they felt unfairly denigrated their work and intensified the public criticism they were already experiencing. In the Upper Basin especially, they felt beleaguered by a local community that saw conservation as being at odds with its economic interests. The preliminary report threw gasoline on a smoldering fire, ratcheting up hostility that had already caused federal biologists to remove government license plates from their vehicles.[48] As one FWS biologist said, "Some people refer to it as combat biology."[49] The last thing these scientists needed was a bunch of outsiders lobbing bombs at them. Larry Dunsmoor, a biologist for the Klamath tribes, summed up their reaction: "It was very offensive to many folks here. . . . It has been a very painful thing to see everything we have worked for over the past decade [described] as useless."[50] They particularly bridled at the way the NRC report was held up as "the best available science," and their own work, although the NRC had not used the term, was suddenly regarded as "junk science."

Perhaps the most outspoken scientific critic of the NRC preliminary report was Doug Markle, a fisheries biologist at Oregon State University. Markle is a sucker expert, an author of many studies relied on by FWS in the 2001 BiOp, and a critical reviewer of that BiOp in both draft and final form. In a paper published in *Fisheries*, the journal of the American Fisheries Society, Markle and his student Michael Cooperman pointed out that disagreements about the interpretation of evidence "are normal in science."[51] They charged that the committee's interpretation was rushed, simplistic, and unhelpful to public understanding. Klamath Tribe biologists issued a commentary making similar points.[52] NRC committee chair Lewis responded in kind to Markle's criticisms. The critics' main purpose, he wrote, was "to discredit the committee rather than to deal in a useful way with some of the important issues that the committee's report has highlighted."[53] With one breath, Lewis acknowledged that professional judgment is an essential aspect of (at least) applied science.[54] With the next, though, he concluded that a "strictly scientific approach" to evaluating information (clearly in his view the committee's approach but not the approach of its critics) is essential to environmental problem solving even if it disturbs people by challenging their assumptions.[55]

In the meantime, the State of Oregon had asked its Independent Multidisciplinary Science Team, a panel created to advise the state on its salmon conservation program, to review the 2001 Klamath Basin BiOps. The team issued its report in April 2003. Its conclusions were strikingly different from the NRC committee's. With respect to the suckers, the Oregon panel concluded that lake levels play a role in fish kills. It acknowledged that "no strong scientific data" linked fish kills with lake levels between 1990 and 2000 but pointed out that "typically, from such a short time series it is difficult to determine scientifically whether a relationship does or does not exist."[56] The team agreed with FWS "that lake level management is one of several appropriate management tools to reduce conditions that may lead to fish kills" but also noted that "lake level management alone will not prevent sucker die-offs."[57] With respect to the coho, the team noted that data were "scarce and incomplete" but concluded that NMFS's minimum flow requirements were "conceptually sound."[58]

In part, Markle and Cooperman were reacting to the media coverage rather than the report itself, which had not used the words "junk science." But directing their anger at the report and its authors was understandable. The preliminary report had, perhaps unwittingly, revealed how thin the scientific information supporting policy decisions can be. And it had done so with phrasing that played into the rhetoric of the sound science movement, lending the committee's considerable scientific credibility (again perhaps unwittingly) to the view that a "scientific" approach to policy leaves the status quo in place until there is very strong evidence that change is needed. Responsibility for the spin that followed the preliminary report, however, cannot be entirely laid at the committee's door. Both the committee and the scientists working in the basin were trapped by an incorrect but enduring public vision of science as a process that separates true from false. The committee had said that the most controversial requirements of the two BiOps were not supported by scientific evidence. The committee had not said that the lack of scientific support made them either wrong or unjustified, but it was an easy leap to those conclusions for the press and the affected communities.

The Klamath experience illustrates how the fundamental disputes in resource conflicts, although often described on all sides as fights between "good" and "bad" science, are really about the judgments needed to translate scientific data into regulatory decisions. As NMFS biologist Jim Lecky pointed out, BiOps are policy, not research science: "If a biological opinion was a science document, on a par with those that appear in peer-reviewed journals, it would conclude that we don't have enough information to make a decision."[59] Not deciding, however, is not an option for resource managers and regulators. Choosing what action, if any, to take in the face of uncertain data requires several types of judgments: *scientific judgments*, extrapolations from limited data to form beliefs about the functioning of a species or system; *management judgments*, decisions about the most viable and effective way to address a problem; and *policy judgments*, judgments about societal goals, their relative importance, and the acceptability of different types of error. All three played crucial roles in the sequence of regulatory events that produced the 2001 BiOps, and all were unnecessarily obscured in the subsequent battle over the science supporting the BiOps.

Scientific Judgments

Judgment is an inherent aspect of the scientific process of learning. At the frontiers of knowledge, science is a messy process characterized by competing explanations. Research scientists must constantly exercise judgment in deciding what to test, what explanations to accept, and which data to give more weight to when some are consistent with one explanation and others point in a different direction.

Scientific judgments are closely intertwined with judgments about the desirability of avoiding different types of error, but the latter are not in fact "scientific." Research scientists in many fields do not claim that they have "proven" their point unless the data meet a specific level of statistical significance, providing 95 percent confidence that an observed effect is not attributable to chance alone. There is nothing magic about that confidence level. It has become customary because it serves the goals of research science; it keeps scientists from prematurely accepting a hypothesis as proven and moving on, likely down an unproductive research path. However, as Tom McGarity has so aptly written, "Statistical significance is an issue of pure policy."[60]

Furthermore, conventions about statistical significance have limited force even within the research community. They prohibit only claims of proof, and only if those claims rest on a single study. They do not prevent scientists from believing a connection is real on the basis of far less conclusive evidence or from acting on that belief—for example, in choosing their next research project. Nor do they prevent an accumulation of studies, each of which falls short of statistical significance, from being taken as a whole to prove a connection. Even if only a single study is available and it falls short of conventional statistical significance, a persuasive explanation of the relationship between an alleged cause and effect may be sufficient to win acceptance in the scientific community.

An additional scientific judgment step, beyond those inherent in the research process, is often required when research science is applied to resource management. Much of the ecological research that forms the fundamental basis for resource management efforts is conducted by academics and funded by general research programs. Not surprisingly, academic researchers focus on locations and systems that are convenient to study and fit their research goals. Those are not necessarily the same systems that require management. Management controversies may bring targeted research funding, but quite often, especially early in the management cycle, agency personnel must extrapolate results from small-scale manipulation to large-scale management, or from one location, system, or species to a very different one.

The Klamath BiOps required numerous scientific judgments. Those most directly connected to the controversy were about the effect of water levels in Upper Klamath Lake on the endangered suckers and of flow levels in the main-stem Klamath River on the threatened coho salmon. As is so often the case in natural resource management, those judgments had to be made on the basis of very limited information.

Scientific interest in the suckers and salmon was not high until they were listed under the ESA. The earliest data correlating environmental conditions with the status of the suckers, therefore, dated only from 1990. The limited available data were spotty and had not been collected systematically. Thus, when it produced its biological opinion in 2001, FWS knew it had little to go on. Applying its established interpretation of the ESA, that the benefit of the doubt in section 7 consultation must go to the listed species, FWS called for lake levels to remain higher than the Bureau proposed and even higher than they had been kept in recent dry years.

The NRC committee criticized the agency's scientific judgments, reasoning that the available data contradicted FWS's claim that low water levels in Upper Klamath Lake might contribute to mass die-offs of adults or impede juvenile recruitment, so that even a cautious interpretation of those data could not support FWS' call for higher water levels. The committee's view was surely a tenable one, but not incontestable. It is not always easy to tell whether available data confirm or refute a particular hypothesis. The data, limited as they were, showed that adult fish kills had occurred in years of high, low, and average summer lake levels.[61] That data straightforwardly support the committee's interpretation that lake levels are not the crucial factor in mass mortality events but also leave open the possibility that, as argued by the Oregon State biologists, fish kills result from a combination of water levels and weather conditions. Within the ordinary bounds of scientific practice, scientists could have drawn (and did draw) differing conclusions from the data.

The picture is similar with respect to the impacts of low spring lake levels on recruitment. Because lake levels are closely related to the availability of spawning habitat, the NRC committee agreed that it was "a reasonable hypothesis" that lake levels might suppress spawning.[62] Little data were available to test that hypothesis. There were six years for which April lake levels could be compared with larval abundance, and there were relative abundance data for year-classes from mass mortality events that could be used to compare water levels with spawning success. The committee concluded that the available data suggested only a weak or indirect relationship between lake levels and larval recruitment. Again, this was a plausible interpretation but not the only possible one. The population age distribution extrapolated from mass mortality events did not show a correlation with mean water level during spawning, bolstering the committee's view. The larval abundance data could be read either way. Five of six points on the graph of spring water levels versus larval abundance suggested a reasonably strong correlation between the two. The degree of credence given the outlying sixth point was crucial to the interpretation. It might have been discounted without offending the norms of scientific practice; as the committee noted, measurements of larval abundance had a high degree of sampling variance, so that it was difficult to have confidence in the accuracy of any particular point.[63] The counterintuitive nature of the committee's conclusion—that spawning success is not related to the availability of spawning habitat—could have led reasonable scientists to interpret the equivocal evidence the other way.

In sum, as both the regulatory agencies and the NRC committee acknowledged, the limited data available could not be said to either conclusively prove or conclusively disprove the supposition that higher spring lake levels improved recruiting success. Scientific judgments interpreting such limited and equivocal data reflect the educated intuition of the scientists making them, but those judgments are also nearly inextricably bound up with other views about what actions are possible and about the appropriate degree of risk of ecological versus economic harm.

Management Judgments

In the Klamath Basin, FWS and NMFS had to make management judgments about where to focus their regulatory efforts. Both chose to focus heavily on the Klamath Project, relying on the section 7 consultation process to drive changes in project operations. Other possibilities, including section 9 enforcement proceedings against private irrigators who divert water above Upper Klamath Lake and section 7 consultation for other federal actions, such as management of national forest lands in the Lower Basin, were essentially ignored. That choice drew considerable criticism in the final NRC report,[64] because the committee believed that regulation of the Klamath Project alone would be both inequitable and ineffective.[65]

We remain persuaded, as we argued in print before the final NRC report was published, that any lasting solution to the Klamath conflict must extend beyond the boundaries of the Klamath Project. That does not mean, however, that the regulatory agencies made improper, or even incorrect, management judgments. The rule of law requires that regulators enforce applicable statutes, but those statutes often leave considerable implementation discretion. In deciding how to exercise that discretion, agencies necessarily take into account both the availability of levers to push—that is, where they can successfully intervene—and the extent to which those levers can move the system—that is, the potential effects of intervention. In the Klamath situation, regulators were entitled to consider that section 7 consultation proceedings, as angry as they might make people, would almost certainly be less controversial than section 9 enforcement. When the section 7 process produced a judgment that the headgates at Upper Klamath Lake had to be closed, that judgment was endorsed not only by the regulatory agencies, but also by the Bureau of Reclamation, an agency project irrigators had every reason to believe would give full consideration to their interests. Even so, the closing produced a firestorm of outrage that reverberates even today on the Web and in the local community. A direct attack on irrigators above the project through section 9 probably would have produced an even more extreme reaction, likely including charges of black helicopters and conspiracies. It is understandable that the wildlife agencies have avoided such a provocative action.

The regulatory agencies also had reasonable grounds to believe that targeting the Klamath Project would provide the greatest conservation return on enforcement efforts. The project, unlike private irrigators, has a direct line to federal budget decisions. Its operation is the highest-profile ongoing federal action in the basin and the one with the strongest local political support. Reducing federal water deliveries was calculated to bring both attention and a substantial infusion of federal conservation dollars to the basin. Indeed, the water crisis of 2001 has brought federal and state money for both conservation and economic relief, as discussed in the next chapter. Even with the benefit of hindsight, it cannot be said that regulators made a clear error in focusing their efforts on the Klamath Project.

Policy Judgments

The sequence of regulatory events that produced the controversial BiOps of 2001 included a number of policy judgments. Such policy judgments logically precede, and provide the context for, the scientific judgments. Congress has provided vague indications of how many of these judgments should be made but has generally left a broad space for agency discretion. Both regulatory agencies and their critics frequently leave their policy judgments unexplained, unacknowledged, and perhaps even unrecognized. Policy judgments essential to regulatory choices, therefore, often remain quite opaque to the general public.

The first set of policy judgments in the Klamath sequence were those required to list the suckers and salmon under the ESA. First, FWS and NMFS had to decide which fish to group together as "species." The statute provides only that the term *species* include subspecies and, for vertebrates, "distinct population segments," which is not further defined. Identifying groups for protection has been particularly challenging for Pacific salmon. The genetic basis of much of the observed life history and morphological variation in salmon is poorly understood. Within recognized salmon species, runs are often largely, but not completely, reproductively isolated from one another by the time and location of spawning.

In 1991, believing that runs should be protected if they represented a unique evolutionary unit, NMFS developed a policy for identifying distinct population segments of salmon.[66] The policy provides for protection of groups that are "substantially reproductively isolated" from others, so that they promise to evolve as a separate lineage and "represent an important component in the evolutionary legacy of the species." In 1995, NMFS identified the coho salmon stocks in the Rogue, Klamath, Trinity, and Eel river basins, together with those in several smaller basins in the same area, as a single distinct population segment.[67] The agency found a relatively large genetic distance between the northern and southern fish in this evolutionarily significant unit and noted that fish from this group were more likely to spend the ocean portion of their life cycle off the California coast than their cousins from more northerly rivers.

Neither of these distinguishing traits amounted to a bright line. The ESU itself showed considerable genetic diversity, and its ocean distribution overlapped with other ESUs.[68] Faced with groups of fish that were not perfectly distinct from each other, genetically or in their ocean behavior, NMFS had to make judgments about where to draw lines. It might have excluded Rogue River salmon from the group or included those in the Elk River to the south. Because nature did not provide bright lines, any choice the agency made could be criticized as arbitrary.

Once the wildlife agencies had identified listable "species," they had to make policy judgments about the degree of acceptable risk to those species. The statute defines a species as *endangered* if it is "in danger of extinction throughout all or a significant portion of its range,"[69] and *threatened* if it is "likely to become endangered in the foreseeable future."[70] That language makes clear that endangered species must be in worse condition than threatened ones, but it can hardly be considered a definitive explanation of the degree of risk needed to support listing in either category. The listing agencies have not made any effort to describe in general terms what degree of risk over what period of time they think makes a species endangered or threatened. Their individual listing decisions frequently provide little information about the degree of risk facing the species, no doubt in part because robust estimates of the probability of extinction are unavailable. In listing the coho salmon, NMFS noted that the population had dramatically declined from historic levels; that coho were absent from many streams in the region that had once harbored them; and that a high proportion of the naturally spawning fish in the region were first-generation hatchery fish.[71] In listing the suckers, FWS noted that the populations had declined by as much as 50 percent in the last several years and that no significant recruitment of young fish had been observed for eighteen years.[72]

Once the species were listed, NMFS and FWS had to determine what level of risk would fall below the jeopardy threshold and precisely what it means to "insure" that jeopardy is "not likely."[73] The agencies' joint regulations suggest caution in this determination: "Action[s] expected to . . . reduce appreciably the likelihood of both the survival and recovery of a listed species in the wild" are considered to jeopardize the continued existence of the species.[74] As with their listing determinations, the regulatory agencies did not clearly address the extent to which they believed the Bureau's proposed operation of the project would reduce the likelihood of either survival or recovery of the listed species.

The Intertwining of Scientific and Other Judgments

Even with the best of intentions it is difficult to separate the three kinds of judgment. When the services opined that the Bureau's proposed operation of the project would cause jeopardy, they were necessarily making both scientific and policy judgments. Undoubtedly, those judgments were influenced by unstated management judgments about what levers could be turned in the system and about the reaction their decisions would provoke. The NRC review committee may also have had a hard time separating types of judgments. The committee's charge was to review the science underlying the 2001 BiOps. The committee read that charge (unnecessarily, in our view) as requiring that, in deciding whether scientific evidence adequately supported the regulatory requirements, it apply norms of research science that require high levels of certainty to support a claim of "proof."[75] In addition, the committee's evaluation of the science may have been affected by its policy preferences. The committee chair wrote that "it is obvious" that the regulatory agencies will make professional judgments in a way that privileges the species they are charged with protecting, but that "where the economic stakes are high," special attention should be given to the role of speculation in those decisions.[76]

It seems that the committee chair, at least, believed that overregulation would generally be the norm under the ESA, so that regulators would need to be reined in when their zeal threatened to impose high economic costs on society. The empirical evidence available, however, is directly to the contrary. Political pressures already impede overaggressive ESA implementation quite effectively.[77] That the committee as a whole may have shared the chair's view is supported by its divergent treatment of the lake level and diversion point screening requirements in the 2001 FWS BiOp. The call for higher lake levels was criticized because it lacked substantial scientific support. But the committee endorsed FWS's call to screen the main diversion point from Upper Klamath Lake to the project's irrigation works, even though it acknowledged that the "benefits of this measure to the population are unknown."[78] Presumably the committee believed this less controversial step, which did not threaten to deprive farmers of their livelihood, required less supporting evidence. If the committee was indeed inclined to demand clearer scientific support for the BiOps because of their perceived economic consequences, that policy judgment may have affected its scientific judgments.

Science Hits the Courts

Like almost every other step in the Klamath Basin in recent years, the 2002 BiOps led to litigation. Like the political reaction to the 2001 BiOps, the litigation focused on the scientific justification for specific river flows and lake levels. As explained in chapter 5, Upper Basin irrigators had first taken their concerns about the science behind ESA limitations on Klamath Project diversions to the courts after the 1992 BiOp. After the Supreme Court endorsed their right to sue, the irrigators succeeded in getting the courts to strike down minimum elevations imposed by FWS on Clear Lake and Gerber Reservoir.[79] Their challenge to the 2001 BiOps, however, fell victim to the typical deference shown by courts to agency scientific judgments.[80]

The very different operating plan adopted after the NRC committee's preliminary report brought the downstream fishing interests, who had precipitated the 2001 crisis by forcing ESA consultation, back to court. Represented by Earthjustice, a premier environmental public interest law firm, the fishermen first sought to block implementation of the interim 2002 operating plan. They contended, among other things, that the plan lacked an adequate scientific foundation, pointing out that the river flows it proposed were considerably below those recommended in the draft Hardy Report and called for by the NMFS 2001 BiOp.[81] In May 2002, the trial court refused to order increased flows. In defense of the Bureau's actions, the United States had cited the interim NRC report questioning the scientific link between higher flows and salmon survival. In the face of that report and NMFS's newly articulated concurrence with the low spring flows, the judge concluded that the plaintiffs had not sufficiently proven that those flows would harm the coho.[82] In 2001, the judge had agreed with NMFS that the Hardy Report represented the best available science.[83] Now she endorsed the Bureau's determination that the NRC report had supplanted the Hardy Report in that role.[84]

When the Bureau adopted its ten-year operating plan with NMFS's concurrence, the fishermen renewed their challenge. The Yurok and Hoopa tribes intervened to support the suit. The district court rejected NMFS's attempt to limit the Bureau's responsibility to 57 percent of the flows needed to support salmon in the long run, ruling that the Bureau must ensure that operation of the Klamath Project would not cause jeopardy even if other actions contributed to the threat. The district court upheld the phased approach of the BiOp, under which the full flows that NMFS considered necessary for the salmon did not have to be provided until 2010. The Ninth Circuit subsequently overturned the phasing, however, because the BiOp lacked any analysis of the effect of eight years of low flows, encompassing the complete life cycle of five generations of coho.[85] The court rejected the Bureau's argument that the phased approach was a way to harmonize the conflicting flow conclusions of the Hardy and NRC reports. Reasoning that NMFS had made a judgment that the long-term flows it called for were necessary, the court refused to allow those flows to be reduced by half for eight years without some explanation.

On remand, NMFS offered more explanation of its decision to allow the Bureau eight years to achieve the full flow requirements, but still did not prevail. The district court held that NMFS needed to fundamentally rethink the BiOp, not just better rationalize it. The court ordered NMFS and the Bureau to reinitiate consultation, taking into account new information that had emerged since 2002. Pending production of a valid BiOp, the court prohibited any irrigation diversions by the Klamath Project inconsistent with the long-term flow requirements of the 2002 NMFS BiOp, "the only portion of the Biological Opinion that remains valid."[86]

The Landscape Talks Back

Nature always has the last word in scientific disputes. In the fall of 2002, shortly after the new ten-year operating plan had been put into effect, nature decided to speak up. The message was striking but not exactly clear.

The year following the crisis had begun with substantial optimism. The winter rains arrived as they had not the prior year. As water rose in the national wildlife refuges, the birds returned, showing no lingering ill effects from the lack of water in 2001.[87] Interior Secretary Gale Norton, Agriculture Secretary Ann Veneman, and Oregon senator Gordon Smith opened the A Canal headgates with great fanfare on March 29, proclaiming that water supplies seemed to be sufficient to meet the needs of both farmers and fish.[88]

Within weeks, however, that optimism had given way to another dry year. By the end of April, although irrigation deliveries had not yet reached their peak, reduced flows below Iron Gate Dam stranded juvenile salmon in puddles; young coho were rescued by biologists from two low water areas.[89] By July, Reclamation had revised its water forecast down from "below average" to "dry." The Bureau began further ramping down releases to the river in accordance with the changed forecast and asked irrigators to make efforts to conserve water.[90] Nonetheless, Klamath Basin farmers were provided with water while flows below Iron Gate Dam were reduced just as the (unlisted) fall chinook salmon began returning to the lower Klamath River.[91]

A massive salmon die-off ensued. At least 34,000 fish died in the lower forty miles of the Klamath River in September 2002 (see fig. 9).[92] It was the first known major fish kill of adult salmonids on the Klamath.[93] The immediate cause of the deaths was an epidemic of two common parasitic diseases,

FIGURE 9
Dead salmon line the banks of the lower Klamath River near its mouth at Klamath, California, on September 28, 2002. (AP Photo/The Herald and News, Ron Winn. Reprinted with permission.)

triggered by crowding of the fish into the low, warm waters at the mouth of the river. Frustrated fishermen, Indians, and environmentalists, convinced that the juxtaposition of the die-off with implementation of a new Klamath Project operating plan providing lower river flows was no coincidence, delivered dead fish to the steps of the Department of the Interior's headquarters in Washington.[94]

Scientific battle lines were immediately drawn as to the causes of the disease outbreak. The Bureau of Reclamation and the Bush administration initially argued that, given the distance between the project and the fish kill, it was "premature" to attribute the kill to project operation.[95] Environmentalists and the State of California, though, blamed the die-off on the Bureau's decision to supply irrigation water, which resulted in river flows 25 percent below those of the crisis summer of 2001. At first the Bureau refused to release additional water, on the contested ground that the water in the upper reaches of the system was so warm it would do more harm than good. The Bureau did, however, eventually provide a two-week "pulse" release from Iron Gate Dam, increasing the flow from 800 to 1,300 cfs.[96] It is unclear whether that pulse helped the fish.[97]

California's Department of Fish and Game issued a preliminary report on the fish kill in January 2003 and finalized that report in July 2004. It concluded that a combination of low September flows, warm water temperatures, an above-average run of returning chinook, and perhaps restricted fish passage from unfavorable channel conditions had precipitated the disease outbreak. Of that list, Fish and Game attributed the most importance to flow, noting that the other conditions had all been worse in 2001, when no die-off occurred,[98] and that flow is the only controllable risk factor.[99] FWS came out with its own report in November 2003. It generally agreed with the state agency's assessment that a combination of low river flows and a large salmon run had caused the epizootic, adding that the unusually early return of the run might also have contributed.[100] Based in part on those reports, the Yurok Tribe contended that the Bureau of Reclamation was responsible for the fish kill and had violated its trust duties to the tribe. As described in chapter 4, however, the tribe was unable to get relief from the courts.

Fallout from the events of 2001 and 2002 continues to this day in the ocean salmon fisheries. The Klamath fall chinook generally return to their natal streams four years after their birth, or three and a half years after their trip to sea as juveniles. In 2005, the returning Klamath run of fish born in the dry fall of 2001 was so small that it forced drastic cuts in ocean harvests even though the run on the Sacramento was expected to reach record numbers.[101] The 2006 returns, born of the fish that survived the 2002 fish kill to spawn, were equally small, prompting the nearly complete closing of northern

California's ocean salmon fishery, even though NMFS temporarily reduced its target for Klamath stock escapement.[102] The fishing restrictions, in turn, resulted in a declaration of economic disaster by the Department of Commerce.[103] The Secretary of Commerce personally asked the chair of the House Appropriations Committee to provide $60 million in emergency assistance for hard-hit fishing communities. By the spring of 2007, although it appeared that the salmon season might be close to normal, the Pacific Fishery Management Council was proposing to amend its salmon regulations to allow more catch of Klamath chinook in years when conservation goals were forecast not to be met.[104] The council deemed protection of the fishing economy more important than protection of the fish.

The economic plight of the salmon fishermen today is in many ways worse than that of the Klamath irrigators in 2001. Most fishermen depend on fishing for their livelihood, and they support many small businesses in coastal communities. A good 2006 crab season in California offset some losses, but there are fears that the industry may not survive another year without access to salmon. After the Democrats took control of Congress in November 2006, the federal relief spigot was temporarily turned off for fear that they could not control the requests from farmers for disaster aid.[105] Instead of a check, the salmon fishermen got a consolation prize: The federal government was directed to develop a recovery plan for the Klamath salmon by April 2007.[106]

NMFS issued its plan in July 2007.[107] It is a framework rather than a detailed roadmap to recovery. After explaining what is known of the current status of the salmon, it details the conservation efforts taken over the past twenty years, as well as ongoing regulatory actions. It then sets out a laundry list of potentially helpful restoration actions various parties could take, if they so chose. The plan emphasizes restoration of tributaries because they typically provide the best spawning habitat but notes that "mainstem habitat may nevertheless play a critical role in . . . coho salmon survival in rivers such as the Klamath where tributary conditions are particularly inhospitable."[108] Other actions identified as desirable include the purchase of tributary water rights for dedication to instream flows and preparing a total maximum daily load (TMDL) under the Clean Water Act to address high nutrient levels, low dissolved oxygen, and elevated water temperatures in the Lower Klamath mainstem. Although TMDLs have been produced for many tributaries, California does not expect to develop one for the mainstem Klamath until 2009. The plan does not identify mechanisms for carrying out most of the various actions it recommends but does estimate the total cost of recovery at over the $1.875 billion projected by the California Department of Fish and Game.[109]

Another new problem has appeared in the Klamath Basin since 2001. The water in Upper Klamath Lake and in the string of reservoirs behind the hydropower dams that extend to just below the California border has always been murky. High levels of nutrients, both naturally occurring and added by farm runoff, make the warm, shallow Upper Basin waters an excellent soup for algal growth. Algae harvested from Upper Klamath Lake are marketed commercially as a dietary supplement. One ad on an herbal remedy Web site describes blue-green algae "harvested from the pristine Upper Klamath Lake in the Oregon Cascades" as a "nutrient dense superfood that contains a full spectrum of easily digestible minerals, vitamins, protein, and chlorophyll."[110] But in recent years algal blooms in the reservoirs have become a health concern. Beginning in 2005, every summer has brought warnings from the EPA and California water agencies against swimming or boating in Iron Gate and COPCO reservoirs because of high levels of the blue-green alga *Microcystis aeruginosa*, which produces a toxin capable of causing liver failure. Mats of *Microcystis* have been found floating on the Klamath River more than 125 miles below the dams, prompting EPA to advise people to avoid any direct contact with Klamath River water during algal blooms. The Lower Basin tribes and the environmental group Klamath Riverkeeper have filed separate suits related to the algal blooms. The tribes have sued PacifiCorp, claiming that its dams amount to a nuisance. Klamath Riverkeeper has sued both PacifiCorp and California's Department of Fish and Game, which operates a salmon hatchery just below Iron Gate Dam, claiming that releases of fish parts, fish waste, and fish food from the hatchery are contributing to algal blooms on the lower river.

Did the Crisis Trigger Learning?

If there is one thing all the various interests in the Klamath Basin agree on, it is that too little is known about the needs of the fish, both upstream and down. The crisis of 2001, and especially the reviews of the science that followed that crisis, drew painful attention to the shortage of information. It also drew national and state attention to the basin and generated some new funding. Six years down the line, it is fair to ask how much has been learned, or at least how much progress has been made toward learning.

If one simply counts programs and dollars, the picture looks encouraging. Efforts were already under way in the Upper Basin to coordinate scientific work focused on restoration among the various agencies and stakeholders before the train wreck. Those efforts continue, through FWS's Klamath Falls Ecosystem Restoration Office, the Upper Klamath Basin Working Group, the Bureau's Conservation Implementation Program, and any number of stakeholder groups and workshops. A Science Team convened by the

Working Group oversees the granting program and provides recommendations for additional research. In the Lower Basin, pre-2001 efforts focused on the fishery resources also continue, largely under the umbrella of the Klamath River Basin Fisheries Task Force and the Ecosystem Restoration Branch of the FWS's Yreka Field Office. Basin wide, there are digital libraries, a Klamath Basin Coordination Group, and regular conferences.

On a deeper level, there is some reason for optimism. There appears to be a higher level of trust among disparate interests in the basin, which translates into greater willingness to share data and work together on the scientific questions. A large number of studies have been done in the basin since 2001, mostly with funding from the Bureau, by various federal, state, and tribal agencies. The information from those studies is now being synthesized in the renewed consultation process, which is being carried out far more cooperatively than in 2001. Then, the Bureau came up with its proposal for operations more or less in a vacuum and delivered it separately to NMFS and FWS for review. This time, all three agencies are working closely together, hoping to find a plan that will protect the fish while supplying irrigation water. The connection between the Upper and Lower basins is also more explicitly recognized than it was before the crisis. FWS and NMFS have developed new models that cover both lake and river and are trying hard to figure out how best to divide the water that does not go to irrigators between the two. The federal agencies, at least, are now acutely aware of the limits of science and openly talking about the need for policy judgments.

Nonetheless, in some key respects there seems to have been little progress. The system is a difficult one to study, and the listings are still recent. Since 2001, studies of the suckers seem to confirm the NRC committee's view that water quality, the most important parameter for adult survival, is not closely tied to lake elevations. That may lead to more flexibility in the next BiOp. The effect of lake levels on habitat and what is limiting sucker recruitment are proving more difficult to understand. Downstream, the flow needs of the coho remain controversial. Early in 2006, at the request of the Bureau of Reclamation, the National Research Council convened a new Committee on Hydrology, Ecology and Fishes of the Klamath River Basin. That committee was asked to review the final Hardy study (which had not been available when the first NRC committee issued its report), as well as a Bureau of Reclamation study of historical flows that forms the baseline for the Bureau's operations plans; evaluate the implications of those studies for coho and other anadromous fish; and identify gaps in knowledge. The committee's report, issued late in 2007, was highly critical of the Bureau's natural flow study. It also found flaws in the Hardy study, but concluded that its flow recommendations would probably be better for salmonids than the current flow regime.

Meanwhile, in the midst of another dry year, a lot of hopeful thinking is going on in the basin. There is hope that ongoing wetlands restoration work will improve spawning and rearing habitat for the suckers; that new storage capacity can be developed, perhaps in the Long Lake Valley southwest of Upper Klamath Lake; and that the needs of upstream fish, downstream fish, and irrigators can all be met. And while agency personnel congratulate themselves (with justification) on their newfound level of cooperation, environmental groups still feel like outsiders watching as the ecosystem deteriorates further.

CHAPTER 7

Searching for Solutions

> We water guys never confront the hard issues. . . . We find a temporary fix and hope we're retired before we have an answer for it. Then if our kids are attorneys, they can make a living sorting it out.
>
> Tom Levy, general manager of the Coachella Irrigation District

This chapter focuses on how the law has influenced four major institutional responses to the water crisis of 2001—the political process, litigation, the marketplace, and ad hoc stakeholder-driven consensus negotiations. We recognize that these four approaches overlap, but we find it useful to begin by considering them separately to highlight their fundamental differences and the strengths and weaknesses of each. Because litigation and stakeholder processes are closely tied to the role of science to mediate environmental disputes, this discussion overlaps to some extent with that in the previous chapter, but the focus is different. In this chapter, we explore the unfamiliar "black box" of "in your face" political and legal contests into which resource conflicts involuntarily thrust scientists.

The lessons we derive are not especially hopeful for progress toward a sustainable balance in the basin. All parties have been forced to act negatively, primarily using politics and litigation to cancel or block gains by other interests. Each approach can confer major short- and longer-term advantages on one interest, but none offers a complete solution. The one positive note is that the relicensing of Iron Gate Dam has at least created a forum for the negotiation of a broader solution, although it has yet to produce one.

The Major Players, Positions, and Strategies

Six major sets of interests compete for long-term power in the Klamath: irrigators, the Bureau of Reclamation, the wildlife agencies, Indian tribes, fishermen, and environmental organizations. Oversimplifying, their interests can roughly be characterized as maintenance of the status quo, minimal change, and varying degrees of ecosystem revival. The irrigators, tribes, and downstream fishermen have been the primary affirmative actors. Environmental groups have a less defined role; primarily, they have sought to influence state and federal agencies through the political and judicial processes. The federal agencies, although they seemingly hold the reins of power, were initially reactive before being forced to take a more proactive role.

The irrigators' primary objective is to maintain the status quo, which gives them access to the bulk of the basin's water at low cost. They would be happy to see the ESA go away. Failing that, they want it implemented with minimal impact on irrigation deliveries. They have sought that objective in part through politics and in part through litigation.

In contrast, the Indians, downstream fishermen, and environmentalists want to change the way water is allocated. They have differing priorities, but all seek generally to revive a degraded ecosystem and redesign the human footprint on it with a reduced agricultural base. With scant political influence in the executive branch under the Bush administration, they have had little choice but to rely on litigation. Downstream fisheries interests had the most to gain from litigation and made frequent use of it to expand the problem-shed to the entire Klamath basin. They have also used the legislative process to gain short-term financial relief.

The federal agencies have contrasting goals. On one side, the Bureau of Reclamation is closely aligned with the irrigators, with a primary goal of maintaining the water status quo. As a federal agency, the Bureau cannot be openly hostile to, or completely ignore, the ESA, but it seeks ways to comply with the act that favor its irrigation constituency. The wildlife agencies, FWS and NMFS, have a complex relationship with the Bureau and the environmental interests. Their mission is conservation, and many of the career employees identify strongly with environmentalists. But each of the wildlife agencies is housed in a larger department with a more complex mission, and each must deal with the realities of limited political and practical power. They have tended to seek consensus or compromise positions and as a result have found themselves at various times aligned with and pitted against each of the other interests.

In theory, both the Bureau of Reclamation and the wildlife agencies are simply neutral dischargers of their duties and promoters of the public interest, but that naive model of agency behavior went out of fashion years ago. The Bureau is a good example of "public choice" at work. *Public choice* is a theory of agency behavior derived from neowelfare economics. It posits that government agencies are motivated in much the same ways that individuals are, pursuing their own selfish interests. Instead of seeking to maximize personal wealth and satisfaction, they seek to maximize resources and power. In the chilling words of its Nobel prize–winning developer, James Buchanan, public choice theory is "politics without romance."[1] That describes today's Bureau of Reclamation well. The wildlife agencies are difficult to capture in a sound bite, but they are less amenable to a public choice explanation; the law seems to make them the key power in the basin, but the reality is quite different.

As a young agency, the Bureau married technical expertise with idealistic vision. It brought skilled engineers to the romantic work of settling the arid West with vibrant irrigation communities. That vision faded with the reclamation era, leaving an agency focused, in the view of many of its critics, almost entirely on consolidating its power and maximizing its budget. Until about 1970, the Bureau was a powerful vassal state that owed nominal fealty to its overlord, the Secretary of the Interior, but enjoyed a large degree of independence because it had the support of powerful legislators and regional constituencies. Today, it remains powerful in some areas, but its glory days are long past, diminished by the rise of environmental law on one hand and the stagnation of irrigated agriculture in the West on the other. Its future lies in beginning to restore some of the damage done to river basins by its projects and in serving mundane municipal needs, not in new irrigation works.

In the end, although the public choice model describes the Bureau accurately, it fails to capture the root problem of government in the Klamath Basin, which is a regime weakened by division. The basin illustrates what Professor William Buzbee calls the tragedy of the regulatory commons.[2] The tragedy of fragmented authority is that because no one individual or agency can ever be held fully responsible for failure, no one has much incentive to take the risks that are a necessary part of problem solving. In that situation, the most powerful force tends to be the status quo.

Fragmentation is certainly a problem in the Klamath Basin. There is plenty of regulation, but it is so fragmented between states and among federal agencies that it is no match for the scope of the problem. No agency can control all the relevant parameters. The development of a sustainable Klamath requires cooperation among all levels of government and a blurring of hierarchies. Traditional regulatory patterns and institutions encourage tunnel vision, confining each agency to its own geographic scope and mission. Not surprisingly, none has taken "ownership" of crafting and implementing an alternative vision for the basin.

The lack of strong public leadership, in turn, makes it difficult for anyone to challenge the status quo. The groups trying to do so remain relatively weak outsiders struggling to bring attention to their concerns. Bringing stakeholders together can theoretically overcome the institutional fragmentation problem, but so far stakeholder processes have remained at the margins in the Klamath Basin. Although several stakeholder institutions have been launched, none has the power or voice of those that have emerged in, for example, California's Sacramento–San Joaquin Delta or on the Truckee River in Nevada.

The law itself can also inhibit creative problem solving by constraining flexibility. From a conservationist perspective, that is both a blessing and a curse. On the one hand, only strict judicial interpretation of the ESA has allowed any inroads to be made on the traditional allocation of water to out-of-stream uses. Absent that sort of rigid boundary, in the Klamath Basin as elsewhere, environmental interests would have little chance of dislodging the status quo. On the other hand, too much rigidity can reinforce the tendency toward tunnel vision and leave little room for evaluation of alternative approaches that might fulfill conservation objectives in a fairer and more effective manner.

The most effective combination is likely to be a statutory hammer big enough to bring the status quo interests to the table, together with a forum for negotiation that encourages broad thinking and allows some trade-offs. In the Klamath Basin, the ESA has provided one half of that combination; so far the other has been missing. The hydropower relicensing process might provide it, although optimism on that score is fading as this book goes to press.

2001 and the Problem of Baselines

Establishing baselines is important to environmental policy choices in two distinct respects. First, conservation goals are generally set with reference to some baseline historic or "normative" condition. We take up the issue of goals in the final chapter.

Baselines are also important anywhere change is sought because they provide a benchmark against which to measure how rapidly transitions should occur and what costs can fairly be imposed on its victims. Before detailing the various responses to the 2001 crisis, therefore, we set the stage by considering the quantifiable economic effects of that crisis on the irrigation community. We recognize the shortcomings of this measure; we do not mean to suggest that only economic impacts matter, on either side of the environmental protection question. Nonetheless, it is the most objective measure available and inevitably plays a role in debates about future directions for the basin.

We also recognize that numbers of this sort (like the incomplete scientific data we discussed in the last chapter) are always open to different interpretations. The choice of comparison period can be crucial. Here we adopt the period immediately prior to the water crisis as the relevant comparison. That advantages the irrigators relative to others, because it masks a steady decline in farm income and treats as a given the damage done by agriculture to the ecosystem services economies over the past hundred years. We think it is a useful measure, nonetheless, because it fairly represents the practical status quo and the "shock" of ESA enforcement. We begin with a look at how cultivated acreage and crop sales in 2001 compared to acreage and sales in full-water years. We use those numbers to calculate the actual dollar losses suffered by irrigators and the irrigation community.

Before 2001

Between 1969 and 1998, real personal income from farming and agricultural services declined by more than 50 percent in Klamath County, Oregon, and Modoc County, California. Today, farm income constitutes only about 1 percent of personal income in Klamath County and 8 percent in Modoc County.[3] Still, 1998–2000 is a useful baseline period because irrigated acreage remained relatively constant even as the area's economy shifted to a more diverse model. During those years, an average of 201,753 acres were cultivated in the Upper Basin. Barley, irrigated pasture, and alfalfa accounted for 130,742 acres, a number that jumps to 146,231 when other hay crops are added. Wheat and oats are also grown on the Tule Lake National Wildlife Refuge lands, and 19,934 acres are planted in potatoes, onions, and the specialty crops of horseradish and peppermint. The total gross crop value was $97,879,000. Potatoes, which represented only 5 percent of the acreage in Klamath County, accounted for 21 percent of the overall value of crop production.

After 2001

After the 2001 shutoff, crop acreage in the Tule Lake Irrigation District in California remained almost the same, at 61,429 versus the baseline 61,803 acres. The Oregon portion of the Upper Basin took a much larger hit. Total crop acreage in Klamath County dropped from 124,997 to 82,900 acres. Within the project boundaries, crops were grown on only 47 percent of the pre-2001 baseline acreage.[4] Crops were actually harvested on slightly over 56,000 acres in

Oregon's portion of the project. A small percentage of the reduction in crop acreage was attributable to factors other than the water crisis; some 2,500 acres of sugar beets were taken out of production due to the closing of two northern California sugar refineries for reasons unrelated to water availability. Initially, farmers held off on planting row crops such as onions and potatoes, but eventually those crops were grown on about half the usual acreage. Many growers of those high-value crops had long-term and futures contracts, which gave them incentives to seek alternative sources of water. A fair number were able to get water from new wells, purchases from other landowners, and irrigation district transfers. In the end, the yield per acre for onions and potatoes dropped less than 5 percent. Alfalfa and hay acreages were reduced by about 20 percent, but in the end those farmers also did quite well.

Fallowed acreage and resulting lost income do not tell the whole economic story because so much disaster relief flowed into the basin following the 2001 crisis. Estimates of the damages and the disaster payments vary considerably. The Klamath Water Users Association claimed that the value of crops grown in the area was $110.8 million and that losses ranged between $160.7 and $222 million.[5] The first independent post-2001 study noted that dynamic adaptation strategies such as new wells and water transfers complicated measurement of the actual economic impacts. In addition, crop prices were affected by extrinsic factors. Using a more conservative regional multiplier than the water users, the study estimated that crop production values dropped by $24 million in Klamath County and $23 million in the Tule Lake Irrigation District. Adjusting for land within the project but outside Klamath County, the crop loss figure from fallowed acreage comes to $54 million.[6] An additional $10 million can be tacked on to account for rises and declines in crop prices.[7] However, the most relevant figure is net farm revenue, because that is the most accurate reflection of what individual farmers actually lost and the hardships they suffered. Accounting for additional expenses such as well drilling and adjusting for those farmers who were unable to find alternative employment, the study puts the net loss figure at between $27 million and $46 million. The important point, however, is that shutoff loses were shared between the irrigators and federal tax payers. As is often the case, disaster payments immediately followed the crisis.

Using Federal and State Legislative Processes

Crises beget political responses, and the events of the summer of 2001 cried out for political relief. Klamath irrigators immediately resorted to existing programs designed to protect farmers from both natural disasters and the international commodity markets. Those programs left the losses unevenly distributed. Growers who owned their land were able to shift substantial portions of their losses to federal taxpayers, but farmworkers and growers who relied on leased land were unable to do that. The irrigators also used their political influence, which belies their modest numbers, to get targeted economic relief from the states of California and Oregon as well as the federal government. Finally, they tried hard to mute the future power of the Endangered Species Act, seeking to ensure that it would be implemented only in a manner compatible with irrigation water deliveries.

None of this is surprising or inherently illegitimate. In many ways, politics is a better crisis mediator than lawsuits or the harsh discipline of the market. Politics can provide money without imposing a benefit-cost test and can soften or remove inappropriate or unpopular legal restrictions far more quickly and less expensively than litigation or the endless talk shows that consensus processes tend to become.

Flavors of Politics

Not all politics, of course, is alike or of equal merit. The word conjures up both the idealized self-governance legacy of ancient Greece and the nightmare of the use of state power to dominate and marginalize the weak.[8] People have been struggling to define the elements of "good" politics since Aristotle separated politics from ethics. In the western tradition, political theory has focused on a search for what makes state action legitimate and how to constrain the exercise of state power to protect those most vulnerable to abuses. With apologies to more high-minded political philosophers and political scientists, we put these sophisticated theories aside, adopting instead three relatively simple working definitions of politics.

Each of the three definitions of politics we consider gives a clue to the incentives it creates. The first is the standard definition from American constitutional tradition: Politics is the representative process and whatever outcome it produces, within the boundaries set by the Constitution. Enactment of new laws (and repeal of old ones) by the Congress and adoption of new policies and interpretations of existing laws by the executive branch are the legitimate and expected outcome of the electoral process. Responsiveness to that process promotes accountability and facilitates public participation in policy choices. "To the victors go the spoils," as the old adage says. We call this model "plain vanilla politics." Of course, the real world does not always work in the idealized fashion this model assumes, which is why we consider other models as well.

The second definition is the deliberate use of government processes to redistribute public (and private) resources. The eminent political scientist Harold Lasswell put the distribution of resources at the center of politics when he defined political science as "the study of influence and the influential."[9] Building on this tradition, Helen Ingram, the leading political scientist of western water politics, has characterized the politics of water in the twentieth century as distributive. As she sees it, other values, including social equity, efficiency, and the environment, have often been crowded out as Congress rushed to construct water projects, large and small.[10] Elected officials are often most comfortable in the role of Santa Claus, bringing gifts to their constituents, because distributional politics historically have been seen as a win-win situation, questions of efficiency aside. We call this "cash-flow politics."

Third, politics can mean the raw use of legislative or executive power to cancel or block the results of "true" representative democracy. We call this "dirty politics," because it strikes most observers as undesirable even when it is perfectly legal. The line between plain vanilla politics and dirty politics can be difficult to draw, since the administrative agencies charged with carrying out the law often have a range of legitimate interpretations available to them. Dirty politics often has more to do with motive than with the substance of the decision. In plain vanilla politics, legislators and agency personnel try to effect what they perceive to be the will of the voters. In dirty politics they pursue their own vision, or that of their rich and powerful friends, because they can. In the worst examples, they use the system to reinforce and consolidate their power for power's sake. While it can be hard to identify, dirty politics is an important part of the political landscape and a key reason for building rigidity and oversight mechanisms into institutions as part of the "rule of law."

All three types of politics have played a role in the Klamath Basin. Old-fashioned distributive politics has been the dominant political response, despite some dramatic examples and allegations of very dirty politics. Farmers, Indians and downstream fishermen have all extended their hands for federal and state handouts, as have the wildlife refuges.

Plain Vanilla Politics

The crisis summer occurred just after the Republican party had consolidated its power by adding control of the White House to majorities in both houses of Congress. The irrigators tried unsuccessfully to use Republican hegemony to eliminate the ESA from the Klamath Basin or, better yet, from the country. Initially, the irrigators were largely ignored by the new Bush II administration. As we mentioned in chapter 6, their calls to convene the God Squad, with the power to exempt Klamath Project operations from the ESA, were ignored.

Still, the administration made no secret of its support for farmers and responded enthusiastically to Oregon's Republican senator Gordon Smith's request that it intervene in favor of the irrigators. In the early fall of 2001, President George W. Bush flew to Portland and met with Senator Smith, who faced what seemed a potentially difficult reelection in a blue state.[11]

Senator Smith sponsored several bills to roll back the ESA, or at least to shift the fiscal burden of ESA compliance to the government. The Senate narrowly rejected (52–48) a rider he proposed that would have removed the FWS's power to protect fish habitat under the ESA. From 2000 to 2006, the Republican majority put forward several efforts to weaken the ESA, but each was blocked. Finally, the 2006 midterm elections drastically altered the political landscape. Congressman Richard Pombo (R-CA), chair of the House Resources Committee and the leading critic of the ESA, was defeated, and the Democrats captured both houses of Congress. The campaign to weaken the ESA persists, however, within the Department of the Interior as of mid-2007.[12]

Cash-Flow Politics

Unable to bring down the ESA, at least so far, the Klamath Project irrigators have settled for substantial government checks and other forms of direct relief. Disaster payments complemented the existing farm subsidy programs available to the basin.

Farmers are the beneficiaries of a long evolution of thinking about the role of government in natural disasters and the inability of the United States, and other developed countries, to develop a rational agricultural policy. In this section we digress a bit to trace the history of the expectation that government should bear the brunt of the burden of coping with natural disasters. That history is especially relevant to areas known to be drought or disaster prone like the Klamath Basin; residents of those areas might be expected to adapt to foreseeable conditions rather than continuing to assume that the government will repeatedly open its coffers like an especially generous slot machine. The reality remains, however, that Americans are far more likely to try to outwit nature than to adapt to nature's realities. Government disaster payments reinforce that tendency by continually bailing out those who are unable to hold nature back.

In law, natural disasters are labeled "Acts of God" to signal that no person is legally liable for the damages they cause. The term is, of course, a fiction that less and less accurately describes what happens when a disaster occurs. Natural disasters are born in large part from the human belief that nature can be outwitted through good engineering and politics. Initially, it was enough to outwit nature by pouring concrete. To minimize the damages from floods and droughts, America dammed rivers to minimize flood damage and built storage reservoirs to buffer arid areas against drought.[13]

When engineering failed to do the job, the initial assumption was that victims would have to cope on their own. By the eighteenth century, charities were raising money for the victims of hurricanes and other disasters. The roots of federal assistance date from the early years of the Republic; as early as 1803, Congress appropriated money to help rebuild Portsmouth, New Hampshire, after an extensive fire. Not until the New Deal, however, was it taken for granted that the federal government bore primary responsibility for disaster aid. Into the twentieth century, disaster relief was seen primarily as a local and private responsibility. For example, after the 1906 San Francisco earthquake, $9 million were contributed by private relief organizations and other cities. The federal government's role was limited to mobilizing the army to prevent looting and to distribute private charity.[14]

That changed after the great 1927 Mississippi River flood showed how tenuous the U.S. Army Corps of Engineer's control of the river was.[15] At their height the floodwaters covered some 16 million acres along the Lower Mississippi. Roughly 700,000 people were displaced, nearly half of them African Americans. Congress responded with a large Lower Mississippi public works program. Shortly thereafter, the New Deal response to the Dust Bowl firmly established the expectation that victims of natural disasters were entitled to federal relief. A brief review of that history shows not only how our present disaster policy has developed but also what might have been.

In 1935, a high-level committee was formed to propose remedies for the ecological and social disaster called the Dust Bowl.[16] Its chair was Morris L. Cooke, one of a small group of New Dealers who tried to reorient agricultural policy in a way that would now be defined as sustainable.[17] The committee, following a classification system originally developed by John Wesley Powell, identified lack of rainfall as the fundamental reason "the agricultural economy of the Great Plains will become increasingly unstable and unsafe. . . ."[18] The committee's primary recommendation was a Great Plains land-use policy based on the inherent limitations of the region for intensive agriculture and human settlement, or what would now be called genuine environmentally sustainable development. It stated directly that humans would have to adapt to the unforgiving climate of the Great Plains, not the other way around. "The basic cause of the present Great Plains situation is an attempt to impose upon the region a system of agriculture to which the Plains are not adapted, to bring into semi- and arid regions methods which, on the whole, are suitable only for a humid region."[19]

The committee's report addressed the issue of carrying capacity with a level of frankness that would be hard to find in today's government reports:

"Whether or not the region can adequately support the population now residing within its limits is a question which cannot be at present answered. In the long run a transfer from cropping to grazing would undeniably reduce population in some areas."[20] This bold diagnosis of the need to reduce the intensity of settlement was too far ahead of its time. President Franklin Roosevelt, who considered himself a forester, was ready to see planting trees as the answer to almost all pressing problems of land degradation. In the end, rather than address the root problem, the government was satisfied with incremental measures such as shelter belts and new farming methods such as fallowing, greater crop diversity, contouring, and stubble retention. While widely praised at the time, those measures created the current dysfunctional rural welfare economy, sustained only by subsidies. That early Great Plains report and the response to it demonstrate how tempting it is to ignore the hard questions, optimistically believing that technology can overcome any constraints imposed by climate and landscape.

Money began to flow in large amounts after World War II. In 1950, Congress passed the first federal disaster aid program. Originally federal aid went to local governments, but in 1969 it was extended to individuals in response to Hurricane Camille's devastation of the Gulf Coast.[21] By then, expectations were set for the federal treasury to open when a flood, hurricane, earthquake, or drought occurred.

The proper design of public disaster policy is a complicated issue. The idea of relief for victims is appealing and in many cases, such as following the September 11 terrorist attacks or hurricanes Katrina and Rita, irresistible. But not all disasters are equal, and not all victims are equally deserving. Nature may be the proximate cause of "natural disasters," but human choices typically determine the amount of damage.[22] Many types of natural disaster are recurring and foreseeable. Yet people continue to organize their economic lives in ways that are vulnerable to predictable events. At a minimum, more advance adaptation needs to be built into our disaster mitigation policies, especially for those who choose to live in inherently risky areas.

Drought is a good example. It is predictable, occurs in stages, and is not life threatening (at least in the United States), and steps can be taken to mitigate its impacts before it occurs. The leading student of drought, Donald Wilhite of the University of Nebraska, notes that severe droughts continue to be treated as aberrational, even though over the past one hundred years they have hit between 10 percent and 30 percent of the West. United States drought policy remains centered on responses after drought occurs, primarily in the form of victim compensation and ad hoc economic reallocations. The nub of the problem is what economists call "moral hazard"—the idea that people are more likely to engage in risky behavior if they think someone else will cover the costs when things go wrong. Farmers in arid areas, and people who buy homes in flood plains, don't see themselves in that description, but they might behave differently if they knew they would not be bailed out.

John Wesley Powell urged a very different approach to drought: avoiding agricultural development in arid areas unless no other reasonable options are available. Once settlement has occurred, prudence would still counsel taking steps to limit vulnerability in advance of disasters, rather than simply responding after they occur. This is a hard and intensely unpopular lesson to absorb, though, requiring as it does changes in both behavior and long-settled expectations. Only Australia, occupying the driest inhabited continent and prone to frequent, severe, and prolonged droughts, has come close to it. In 1989, Australia officially recognized that climate variability was the norm.[23] In 1992, it adopted a National Drought Policy premised on the need to shrink agriculture in the interior regions most prone to drought. The policy emphasized the need to keep agriculture at levels consistent with environmental and (less subsidized) economic sustainability. To that end, drought assistance was shifted from post-drought damage payments to pre-drought preparedness and risk management.

The United States is still at the other end of the spectrum. American drought policy has three prongs: disaster relief, temporary adaptation, and longer-term planning. Disaster relief has been the primary response in the Klamath Basin. Two spigots were turned on in aid of the stricken irrigators: One provided a flow of federal dollars, the other a flow of groundwater.

According to a 2001 report, there are twenty-eight general programs for which U.S. farmers affected by drought might be eligible.[24] That is apparently not enough for Congress, though, which often adds ad hoc allocations in response to high-profile droughts. In 2001, Congress appropriated $20 million for direct payments to the 1,110 Klamath Project irrigators.[25] About $4 million of that was spent on paying farmers to plant cover crops and to temporarily idle about 17,000 acres of land.[26] The bulk of the rest went toward conservation activities. The 2006 budget proposed $22 million in funding for the Klamath Project for the water bank, fish passage improvements, and other conservation programs. Slightly more was proposed for 2007.

Even absent disaster, many farmers in the United States are eligible for government payments. Like their counterparts elsewhere, Klamath Basin farmers are subject to a schizophrenic agricultural policy under which the United States provides generous subsidies to the ever-shrinking pool of American farmers, while at the same time promoting international free trade, which hits smaller farmers hard in places with limited infrastructure. Starting in 1933, the federal government has spent billions to support farmers through a variety of subsidy programs. Subsidies have continued even as the United States has opened its markets to food products from all over the world, and as the number of full-time farmers has progressively fallen. For many people farming remains a way of life, but one that can be supported only by off-farm income and subsidies. Nationwide, some 93 percent of farm households have off-farm sources of income, as do most farmers in the Klamath Basin. A few statistics tell the story of modern agriculture in the United States. In 1930, 21.5 percent of the workforce was in agriculture, and farms grew an average of five crops. Since the 1930s, the number of farms has decreased by 63 percent, and farm size has risen by 67 percent; by 2000 most farmers grew only one crop.[27] The bottom line is that the taste for subsidies has remained strong among farmers, despite their free market rhetoric. Today, as in the 1930s, federal crop subsidies also help cushion the vagaries of climate, without regard to the economic position of the recipient.

Despite pressure from the World Trade Organization and developing nations, the United States seems unable to give up agricultural subsidies. It has, however, added the pursuit of environmental objectives among the activities for which farmers can be paid. In 1996, Congress passed a farm bill, grandly styled the Federal Agricultural Improvement Reform Act (FAIR), that was intended as a major step toward weaning farmers from subsidies and encouraging them to engage in affirmative risk management. In that spirit, the legislation consolidated the federal crop insurance programs into a new Risk Management Agency within the Department of Agriculture. Despite its name, though, the new agency essentially continues traditional administration of the federal crop insurance and related programs. Klamath farmers also benefited from a major shift in agricultural policy that opened a new source of grants. Although it has continued the crop subsidy program, Congress has progressively added resource conservation programs. Those programs pay farmers to withdraw highly erodible or environmentally sensitive land from production for a period of time and to plant species that help restore the soil. In 2006, nearly $2 billion was spent on this program; $259 million of that amount went to conserving isolated wetlands.

Klamath Basin farmers have benefited from both general and special payment programs. Federal crop insurance is available for a wide range of commodities in the basin, including potatoes. A separate disaster relief program covers noninsured crops. In theory, the crop insurance program is subject to the Department of Agriculture's risk management program. Irrigated lands are eligible only if adequate water delivery facilities and supplies are available at the time of enrollment or the farmer has a "reasonable expectation" of receiving adequate water. These Department of Agriculture programs backstop the Bureau of Reclamation, which has done an excellent job as the traditional risk manager for irrigators, providing carryover storage in most basins to smooth out climate variability.

Even with the help of two Cabinet departments, risk protection is incomplete for water users. Farmers are not insured against nondrought risks, including the risk of ESA enforcement. To provide federal insurance for the loss of water to the needs of endangered species "would place the federal government in the somewhat awkward position of being both water allocator and the insurer against reallocations."[28] Of course, it is not always easy to tell whether water shortages should be attributed to nature or to bureaucrats. Although farmers are fond of referring to "regulatory droughts," meaning that water use has been curtailed not because nature failed to provide adequately but because environmentalists demanded more than their appropriate share, regulatory restrictions are needed only when there is not enough water for all.

In the Klamath Basin, that ambiguity was resolved in favor of the farmers. The Farm Security Administration, which administers the crop insurance program, determined that the 2001 water crisis resulted from a drought, and thus the crop losses were compensable. The result was $4.3 million in payments for uninsured crops and $1.1 million for insured crops.[29] Those amounts are much smaller than the actual damages suffered by the irrigators because, as is typical in the West, few farmers have enrolled in the crop insurance programs. There is little incentive to do so when the Bureau, like a Labrador retriever, is always ready to help and, unlike a Labrador retriever, has ready access to cash. The cold logic of neowelfare economics, which supports the Department of Agriculture's efforts to make farmers become responsible risk managers, is easily overcome in the wake of a disaster with appealing victims. Congress, it seems, can't resist offering supplemental emergency appropriations after disasters materialize.

The federal spigot was opened wide for the Klamath Basin after 2001. The 2002 Farm Bill directed $50 million specifically to the Klamath Basin as part of the nationwide Environmental Quality Incentives Program of the Natural Resources Conservation Service (NRCS). By the end of 2003, 2,700 landowners in the Klamath Basin had received payments for a variety of land and irrigation-system improvements on 66,869 acres.[30] Flood irrigation was eliminated on 16,006 acres. Some 18,500 acres were dedicated to environmental protection, including 2,241 acres of enhanced and new wetlands and 2,692 of riparian forest buffers. The NRCS was able to expand the number of improved acres to 84,497 by the end of 2006 and to improve irrigation of 37,209 acres.[31] Federal aid does not inevitably flow from a disaster, however. Not all victims are politically equal. As we mentioned in chapter 6, salmon fishermen did not fare nearly as well as farmers when the Klamath water crisis moved downstream.

Dirty Politics?

Whether federal subsidies to Klamath irrigators (and other farmers) are good policy can certainly be questioned on economic and social equity grounds, but the irrigators cannot be blamed for taking advantage of the goodie bags the government made available. The more dubious use of politics is to bend existing laws to the benefit of the irrigators. There have been allegations of that kind of dirty politics in the Klamath Basin, but, if it has occurred, it has been subtle and below the radar. Existing administrative and legal processes have not been directly supplanted. Rather, the George W. Bush administration has pushed the limits of its discretion under the ESA and the Reclamation Act to maintain the pre-2001 water delivery regime to the extent possible and has made no secret of its preference for farmers (and the Republicans who represent them in Congress) over environmentalists and downstream fishing interests (and their Democratic representatives) in California. The Bush II administration learned an important lesson from the Reagan administration: "Reshaping" congressional mandates is often more effective than openly refusing to follow them. One approach is to reinterpret statutes in a way that seems faithful to the letter of the law but eviscerates its spirit.

The use of power politics to override normal administrative processes and undermine environmental law in the Klamath Basin has been alleged but not yet proven. In 2002, as we explained in the previous chapter, the Department of the Interior reversed its 2001 decision to withhold irrigation water. After a summer of full irrigation deliveries, the fall brought a massive die-off of chinook salmon in the lower Klamath River. Later reports by state and federal wildlife agencies agreed that low river flows related to Klamath Project operations contributed to the fish kill. Subsequently, the *Wall Street Journal* reported that Karl Rove, President Bush's powerful political advisor, had said at a meeting of top Department of the Interior managers in January 2002 that the administration would side with the irrigators.[32] The story's implication was clear: that Interior had followed political direction, rather than looking dispassionately at the available science and governing law, when planning project operations for 2002.

Outraged editorials followed in the *New York Times* and the *Sacramento Bee*.[33] Senator John Kerry of Massachusetts, in the midst of his run for president, demanded that Interior conduct an investigation. The department's inspector general did look at the allegations but concluded that Rove's comment had not driven water delivery decisions. In the summer of 2007, the *Washington Post* revived the allegations of dirty politics in the Klamath in a series on the pervasive influence of Vice President Dick Cheney on the Bush administration's policies. Jo Becker and Barton Gellman reported that Cheney had called Sue Ellen Wooldridge, then deputy chief of staff to Interior Secretary Gale Norton, early in 2001, before the headgates were shut off, looking for ways to moderate the impact of the ESA on Klamath Project irrigators.[34] Later, according to the *Post* account, it was Cheney who decided that the administration would be better served by seeking NRC review of the science than by invoking the God Squad, which would put it on record as endorsing extinction; who called the National Academies to urge that they take on the review; and who made sure that the 2002 operation plan called for higher irrigation deliveries.

Cheney would not be the first high executive to practice hands-on natural resources management. In 1937 President Franklin Roosevelt made a trip to the Olympic Peninsula to support creation of a national park there. The Forest Service was strongly opposed to conversion of what was then Olympic National Monument into a park, because that would mean transfer of forest lands to the enemy National Park Service. After cross-examining the regional forester and refuting "every statement [he] made about timber requirements and supply," FDR ordered him removed from the Portland office, an order that Secretary of Agriculture Henry Wallace never carried out.[35]

Despite the latest sensationalistic charges, there is still little evidence of direct White House interference in the Klamath Basin. The National Academies have denied that Cheney played any role in the decision to empanel a Klamath review committee, and we think that particular charge is unlikely to be true. Although the Klamath Basin may have seemed small and politically unimportant to the East Coast establishment, the events of 2001 raised precisely the sorts of issues—of the appropriate use of science in policy—that are the NRC's bread and butter.[36] Once the decision was made to empanel a committee, we are confident that the vice president's views played no role in that committee's report.

The reality of his influence on the agencies' response to the report is probably more complicated than the *Post* story suggests. Even the story's authors acknowledge that there is no direct evidence of Cheney being involved at that level; as they put it, "Characteristically, Cheney left no tracks."[37] Regional officials at both the Bureau of Reclamation and the Fish and Wildlife Service believe they made decisions on the basis of the best available scientific information and without interference from higher-ups. However, at least one line scientist strongly dissents. NMFS biologist Michael Kelly alleges that political officials overrode agency scientists' views. High-level political influence need not be heavy handed to make a difference. Officials at both the Bureau and the wildlife agencies must have realized that Washington was interested in the outcome of the Klamath decisions. No doubt the wildlife agencies were also a bit intimidated by the criticism they received in the NRC report, especially coming as it did on the heels of a court ruling that FWS had been overaggressive in demanding that water be left in the Upper Basin. On the basis of the current evidence, it appears to us that Rove's and Cheney's actions simply provide a graphic illustration of the impact elections can have on the administration of federal law. Contrary to Ralph Nader's claims in the course of the 2000 election, it does matter which of the two major parties holds executive power, and indeed it matters which individuals hold key policy positions.

Groundwater: The Other Available Water

Like disaster payments, "free groundwater" helped farmers in the Klamath Basin weather the crisis of 2001. Throughout the West, groundwater often serves as a major drought reserve. Water law has long ignored the hydrologic cycle, treating groundwater as distinct from surface water. California has never subjected groundwater to regulation and has consistently rejected the argument that it even has the statutory power to do so. Oregon does treat groundwater as subject to the state's appropriation system, but Klamath irrigators were able to get groundwater when they needed it on both sides of the state line.

Law and science combine to make groundwater legally accessible. It is much more difficult to manage groundwater than surface water. Most states, not surprisingly, wait as long as possible to step in, leaving it to the courts to mediate conflicts between users. For surface water, science generally paints a pretty accurate picture of the impacts of diversions on the system, and the appropriative rights system (at least in theory) orders the priorities of different users. A junior surface irrigator who takes water before another with senior water rights is clearly "stealing" the senior's property. That means that a system of surface priorities can be consistently and fairly administered when necessary. The closing of the Klamath Project headgates in the summer of 2001 illustrates the ease of administering surface water rights in a drought.

Groundwater shortfalls are more complicated on both counts. From the science side, although much is known about aquifer behavior, their hydrology and precise underground dimensions are typically not as well understood as those of surface waters. "Out of sight, out of mind" still accurately describes treatment of this valuable resource, even as courts recognize that scientific understanding has moved beyond the "dark arts" theory of capture.[38] From the legal point of view, aquifers are seldom pumped dry. Instead, they are "mined," meaning that more water is extracted than replenished, at least for a time. Whether mining is occurring may be hard to determine, since replenishment times are not always well understood. Even if it is clear that an aquifer is being mined, that is not necessarily a bad thing over the short run. Mining an aquifer in several dry years and allowing it to replenish itself in wet ones is a rational strategy for smoothing out short-term variability in precipitation. In effect, groundwater can be used as an enormous carryover storage reservoir. The problem is not mining per se, it is the inability to confine it to levels that are sustainable over the long run. Finally, it is difficult to know who to blame if groundwater is being overused. All pumpers contribute to the lowering of water tables, and all suffer from it. Absent a registration and priority system like that which governs surface water rights, it is not clear that any one pumper is wrongfully harming any other.

Because of these complications, managing groundwater takes an aggressive regulatory scheme or a high degree of cooperation among users, complemented by replacement water. In general, the threat of an agricultural crisis or an end to urban growth is needed to trigger limits on groundwater access. Truly arid New Mexico was the first state to apply the rule of prior appropriation to groundwater, seeking to protect its artesian agricultural basins along the Texas border, but even it has only managed to slow groundwater mining. Steve Reynolds, legendary state engineer and the model for Norman Buckman in John Nichols's novel, *The Milagro Beanfield War*, developed a unified system for managing surface and groundwater that effectively subordinated most groundwater rights to surface rights. His system laid the foundation for the state's current approach, which keeps Albuquerque growing and the Rio Grande alive by allowing new groundwater use in the Rio Grande Valley only to the extent that prior surface rights are retired.

In contrast to New Mexico, Arizona mined its groundwater with abandon to support the growth of Phoenix and Tucson along with cotton and pecans. The state's leaders correctly bet that the federal government would eventually fund an aqueduct to bring water from the Colorado River, rather than leaving the growing metropolises high and dry. The late Senator Carl Hayden capped his career by convincing Congress to do just that, but the Central Arizona Project did not come without a price. Arizona was required to adopt an aggressive conservation regime to bring its aggressively mined aquifers back to safe yield. That regime, which combines cropland retirement and aggressive urban conservation, remains a work in progress. The point, though, is that the New Mexico and Arizona experiences demonstrate that the most effective way to conserve groundwater is to prohibit new pumping or require that it be offset by retired surface rights.

The Role of Groundwater in the Klamath Conflict

Neither California nor Oregon has followed this path. The legal regimes are different in the two states, but in both cases capture has become the de facto rule in the Klamath.

Western states initially adopted the common law rule of capture, which allows landowners to pump groundwater with essentially no limitations, even though they rejected that rule for surface water. It soon became apparent that some restraints must be imposed on groundwater capture. As conflicts intensified, states adopted two different approaches to moderate the common law rule. Some, including California, left it up to the courts to develop rights-sharing doctrines. Others, including Oregon, extended the prior appropriation system to groundwater. In both cases, the early rules were developed before much was known about the movement of water within the ground or between ground and surface. The early law, therefore, ignored the hydrologic relationships between ground pumping and surface flows.

At the beginning of the twentieth century, California courts created a baroque sharing regime similar to the law of riparian rights for surface waters. The California rule gives all those who hold rights in land overlying an aquifer correlative rights to the water. Any surplus can be appropriated to serve non-overlying land. The rule is elegant, but figuring out who holds what rights requires long and costly litigation. That has generally been cost effective only in the southern part of the state, and even there only with the creation of special rules for intermunicipal adjudications and special districts to practice conjunctive management, making sure that aquifers recharge. Because the transaction costs are so high, the California rule is seldom actually applied and remains poorly understood even by the bench. When the parties to an adjudication in Santa Barbara agreed to use the rule to settle their rights, they had to hire a water law expert (author Tarlock) to write a letter reassuring the judge that the settlement was consistent with California law. As a practical matter, the rule on the ground in California remains very simple: "People who have access to groundwater can just pump it."[39]

Oregon has followed the prior appropriation model for groundwater regulation since 1927 and has had a unified system for governing surface and groundwater rights since 1955. In theory, access to groundwater should be more difficult in Oregon because new pumping should have to be shown to be consistent with prior uses. In reality, though, Oregon, like other states following this model, has found it difficult to limit pumping. The reason is the difference in hydrogeology between surface and groundwater. If a surface diverter interferes with another's senior rights, the damage is usually immediately observable—the senior user gets less water. The remedy is equally obvious—the junior diverter must curtail use. New pumping of groundwater doesn't usually leave senior pumpers dry, however. Instead, it lowers the water table, making it more expensive for everyone to get water out. In theory, one could limit new pumping by defining groundwater rights in terms of a specific water pressure or water table elevation, but that would be difficult to administer. Instead, the most common approach among states that ostensibly manage groundwater use is to wait until an overdraft is so severe it cannot be ignored and then close the basin to new entrants and impose uniform conservation standards on established wells.

In response to the 2001 Klamath water crisis, California immediately encouraged pumping in the Tule Lake area. In May $5 million of emergency aid was allocated to the Tule Lake area. The Department of Water Resources used the money to drill ten deep wells, which irrigated about 20,000 acres. That was great for the Tule Lake farmers, but as often happens with groundwater pumping, it simply pushed the problem to other users. Wells create a cone of depression as water moves toward an area of low pressure, which means that aggressive pumpers win the race for water and surrounding landowners lose it. Since the Klamath basin slopes southward into California and six of the ten new wells were placed right on the state line, California's new water came at Oregon's cost. The big loser was the small town of Malin, Oregon, which saw the water level in its best domestic well drop 40 feet. The town had to switch to a backup well, which produced hard water with a sulfurous odor.

Oregon also rushed to help its farmers exploit groundwater. Surface and groundwater relationships were not well studied in the Klamath because of the historic near-exclusive reliance on surface supplies. The state used that uncertainty to permit new wells in 2001 and in 2005 to deny a petition submitted by the environmental group WaterWatch Oregon demanding the withdrawal of all unappropriated waters in the Klamath Basin from appropriation.

The Bureau of Reclamation helped finance the new water rush, spending $7.6 million in 2004–5 to pay for new wells as a way to augment the basin's supplies. While pumping was increasing, the United States Geological Survey was studying groundwater use. It reported in May 2005 that water tables in the area had dropped between 2 and 20 feet.[40]

Law and Litigation

Resort to the law, whether in the form of litigation or lobbying for legislative change, is not cheap. Why do parties to resource conflicts invest so much in lawyers' fees, as opposed to putting that money into on-the-ground farm or ecosystem improvements? The answer is that the potential payoff is large, and the law and science of those conflicts encourage litigation and other efforts at legal regime change. Two aspects of natural resource problems combine to foster litigation. As we demonstrated in chapter 6, the science behind resource management decisions is almost always contestable. That sort of uncertainty, combined with legal mandates to use the best available science, lets all parties hope to gain from litigation. Second, as we showed in chapters 4 and 5, the extent of the legal entitlements to water in the Klamath Basin is highly uncertain and contested. The irrigators can argue that any regulatory restrictions violate their vested property rights, the tribes can argue that in fact their rights have priority, and the environmental groups can argue that the rights of the fish trump all. If everyone is firmly convinced of the moral and legal rightness of their position, and by extension the wrongness of their adversaries' positions, negotiation is not likely to produce a resolution that satisfies everyone. Some arguments, in other words, must be resolved by a higher authority.

Law has played a central role in the Klamath dispute. The Reclamation Act shaped the water status quo, and the ESA perturbed it. Every interest group in the Klamath Basin sees hope in the law, and all have tried to use it to their advantage. In this section, we ask what those efforts have done for the sustainability of the basin. To lay the groundwork for that discussion, we begin by outlining the basic role of the legal system in natural resources conflicts like this one and the incentives for all sides to head to the courthouse.

In the United States, law serves three great functions, each of which has been invoked in the Klamath Basin. First, law protects legitimate entitlements from interference. In jurisprudential terms, it does corrective justice. Protecting entitlements is noncontroversial to the extent that the entitlements are universally recognized. No one complains about the government prosecuting bank robbers, or about courts awarding damages for the victims of a drunk driver. But the existence of entitlements in the Klamath Basin is hotly contested. The irrigators believe they have property rights in water and that the federal government therefore owes them compensation for withholding "their" water in 2001. By the same token, though, the Lower Basin tribes and fishermen believe they have an entitlement to a healthy Klamath River salmon run and that the Bureau of Reclamation interfered with that right when it cut instream flows in 2002 in favor of irrigation deliveries.

Second, law protects minorities from the tyranny of the majority. The Upper and Lower basin tribes obviously have the best claim in the Klamath Basin to this kind of protection. But others can also portray themselves as victims with some justification. Lower Basin fishermen have made good use of their victim status at the hands of irrigators. Even the irrigators themselves claim to be victims. They see themselves as a small remnant of a unique experiment caught in a vice of changing societal values and market forces. That is a hard role for faux minorities to play. The Bureau of Reclamation will continue to guarantee them water until Congress tells it otherwise in unmistakable terms. Still, there is no question that the irrigators are economically vulnerable, and the government is unlikely to rescue them from the globalized market. Their plight reminds us that they must be treated fairly in any long-term basin-wide program.

The law has begun, haltingly, to redress some of the power imbalance in the basin. Enforcement of the ESA, combined with the doctrine of federal Indian reserved rights, for example, has given the Indians power the political process denied them. Whether that power will translate into a better life for tribal members or a healthier Klamath ecosystem is another question.

Finally, law vindicates the public interest as reflected in legislation, helping to protect the results of "good" politics from the constant threat of "dirty" politics. In the Klamath Basin, what the public interest requires and where the line should be drawn between legitimate interpretation and illegitimate undermining of the law are hotly contested.

To nonlawyers, it may seem strange that so much reliance has been placed on the courts to solve the problems of the Klamath Basin. Courts cannot fund new reservoirs to augment supply, remove dams that block fish runs, or develop an alternative vision for the landscape. Although courts are powerful actors, they are institutionally required to be reactive. They must wait to be presented with a dispute. When their authority has been properly invoked, they can resolve factual disputes, interpret statutes (or oversee agency interpretations), and decide whether federal agency decisions are adequately explained and supported by the evidence. Much ink has been spilled on the questions of what it means for courts to be "activist" and how free courts should be to disturb the status quo. The important point is that even the most activist court cannot resolve complex environmental conflicts like that in the Klamath Basin independent of the political branches. At most, courts can stimulate the political branches to more directly or aggressively address a problem. They cannot themselves devise or implement comprehensive solutions.

That the Klamath Basin is still such a troubled and contested landscape after two decades of nearly constant litigation is ample evidence of the limited power of lawsuits to provide enduring fixes. Still, the courts serve a function that the political branches cannot duplicate. In the Klamath Basin, litigation has been driven by two factors: the failings of the political system and the need for a broader approach to the ecological and social community than any one law offers.

Americans tend to have a deeply ingrained faith in judges, who are seen as less political and less corrupt than politicians. At the height of President Franklin Roosevelt's attempt to pack the Supreme Court with sympathetic justices to achieve his political goals, Justice Louis Brandeis was asked how the Court maintained its high standing in the public eye relative to Congress and the executive branch. His reply was short and to the point: "We do our own work."[41] Brandeis was following the model of early English judges, led by the great Lord Edward Coke, who created the model of the heroic judge standing as a bulwark against tyranny, in the late sixteenth and early seventeenth centuries. Ever since *Marbury v. Madison* established the Supreme Court's power to decide the constitutionality of acts of Congress,[42] that vision of the judiciary has flourished in the United States.

Still, it took the political upheaval of the 1960s to bring the federal courts to the point where they could play a significant role in water allocation decisions in the Klamath Basin. Courts today are far more active in policing the actions of federal administrative agencies than they once were. In the progressive era and then during the New Deal, when the administrative state began to take on its present form, its architects had little interest in facilitating either legislative or judicial restraints on administrative action. Administrative agencies were expected to bring to their tasks both technical expertise and a level of independence from the political process that would allow them to pursue the public interest more effectively than the other branches. The courts acquiesced, granting agency decisions an extraordinary level of deference. Through the 1960s, they routinely upheld agency action without any review of its factual predicate and with only the most cursory examination of the rationale behind it.[43]

This restraint reflected both the New Deal deference to expertise and a rosy view of politics that supposed that all interests were adequately represented and the process would produce reasonable compromises among them.[44] That view collapsed in the 1960s.[45] Environmentalists, together with consumer activists and others, rejected the assertion that their interests were adequately considered in administrative decisions. The work of political scientist Marver Bernstein provided theoretical grounding for those concerns and laid the foundations for modern "rule-of-law" environmental litigation.

In a 1955 book with the pedantic title *Regulating Business by Independent Commission*, Bernstein challenged the conventional view, arguing that agencies could be "captured" by the regulated community to the point that they would ignore, or at least not give enough weight to, other perspectives. According to the capture hypothesis, instead of providing meaningful input into deliberation about the public interest, industry representatives co-opt governmental regulatory power in order to satisfy their private desires. Regulated entities are well organized and generally well funded, and they often have strong interests at stake, which they do not share with the polity as a whole. These entities have much to gain by ensuring that they have control over government decisionmakers and that the decisionmakers whom they do control remain in office.[46] Put in modern terms, the capture idea is a variant of public choice theory, discussed earlier. Agency employees may share the perspective and values of the industry they regulate, based on common training, past work experience in industry, or the hope of a lucrative future industry job. Agencies may be more subject to capture than the legislature, simply because the number of staff who matter for any one decision is far smaller than the number of legislators needed to enact a law.[47]

A version of capture theory played a major role in the development of environmental law. Environmentalists looked at federal agencies like the Department of Transportation and the Forest Service and saw perpetual engines of environmental destruction single-mindedly pursuing their missions of paving over the nation and turning all its trees into lumber with no heed for the adverse consequences. They thought that environmental values deserved more consideration and that courts were the institution most likely to agree. Framing their argument as a call for agencies to obey the rule of law, environmental groups mounted a guerilla litigation campaign, seizing on a few statutes that seemed to call for consideration of environmental values.

That nascent campaign hit pay dirt with a 1965 federal appellate decision that allowed a citizen organization to challenge a federal hydropower license issued for a pumped-storage plant on Storm King Mountain in New York state. Plaintiffs argued that the plant would destroy the beauty of the lower Hudson Valley and adversely impact the Hudson River's striped bass population. The court not only listened to the complaint, it also remanded the license decision and delivered a lecture to the Federal Power Commission (FPC), saying that the commission had an affirmative duty to take a comprehensive look at the justifications for and environmental impacts of power plant proposals.

Judges, especially in the influential District of Columbia Circuit, soon announced a more general "hard look" doctrine calling for stricter judicial policing of administrative agencies. Separation of powers requires that judges not substitute their opinions on the merits for decisions within the agencies' discretion. But courts can insist that agencies justify their decisions with coherent analysis. This test still immunizes decisions from judicial control within a wide zone of administrative discretion, but it can help prevent agencies from making decisions for the wrong reasons, for no reason, or contrary to a strong scientific consensus. The hard look "revolution" has been steadily limited as Presidents Reagan, Bush I, and Bush II appointed more conservative members of the federal judiciary. Still, the idea that judges should use their power to police the administrative state remains very much alive, bolstered by environmental-era statutes in which Congress, listening to charges of agency capture, limited agency discretion.

The need for judicial oversight remains alive as well, particularly in the implementation of controversial laws like the ESA. Even under conservation-minded administrations, FWS and NMFS tend not to protect endangered species without litigation when conservation clashes with strong economic interests. In the Bush II administration, this tendency has been magnified by general hostility to the law. In the administration's first four years, fewer than thirty species were listed, barely more than 10 percent of the number listed in the same period by the Clinton administration. Not a single species reached the protected list without the prod of litigation.[48]

Environmentalists have also been driven to the courts by the lack of an available forum for broader problem solving. Aggressive implementation of the ESA, which can only be obtained through the courts, is the strongest lever environmental interests have to bring status quo interests to the negotiating table. Although the ESA is at the heart of the Klamath story, by itself it is not adequate for resolving the basin's water problems. It is almost entirely a tool for preventing new harms to listed species. It cannot force the restoration of ecosystems degraded by decades of unrestrained resource extraction. In that respect, as Professor Reed Benson has noted, the ESA is much like western water law. Both "work best preserving the status quo—that is in preventing changes that would adversely affect the interests they protect."[49]

If it can be made to seem rigid enough, however, the ESA has the potential to trigger broader negotiations toward systemic change of the resource-use patterns, social structures, legal rules, and institutions responsible for ecosystem degradation. Or at least that's the hope. There is some evidence that it is possible. In the 1990s, fears that the listing of the California gnatcatcher would shut down Southern California housing construction helped persuade the state to enact an innovative ecosystem protection law, the Natural Community Conservation Planning Act.[50] Concerns that protection of the threatened delta smelt might shut down the pumps that move vast quantities of water from northern to Southern California for farms and cities pushed not only the state but also water users into endorsing the state-federal Bay-Delta accord that created CalFed, discussed in more detail in Chapter 8.[51] In Texas, the prospect of losing control of a major aquifer persuaded the state to regulate groundwater pumping for the first time.[52]

Pushing ESA enforcement to the point of a train wreck in the hopes of triggering structural change is a high-risk strategy, however. By the 1990s, the ESA was already a favorite target of the Republican-controlled congress. During the Clinton administration, the Department of the Interior spent much of its energy defending the ESA against efforts to repeal or drastically roll it back by devising a series of administrative reforms, including safe harbor permits and "no surprises" protection for habitat conservation plans, intended to soften the law's impacts on traditional resource exploitation.[53] The ESA can be seen as the legal equivalent of a preemptive nuclear strike. It is powerful enough that it might deliver a decisive knock-out blow; but if it leaves the opposition standing, it may trigger devastating retaliation. That is a particularly high risk in the context of western water conflicts, where the opposition is armed with an equally "macho" legal weapon, the doctrine of prior appropriation.

Left to its own devices, the government might choose never to use such a risky weapon. But the choice is not entirely the government's to make. The ESA nuclear arsenal is available, through the law's citizen suit provision and doctrines that allow judicial review of agency actions, to any person with standing to sue. The ability of outside parties to invoke the courts means that underenforcement carries its own risks for those it might be expected to benefit. The 2002 coho BiOp, as described in chapter 6, bent too far in favor of irrigators, requiring them to provide just over half the flows needed to support the fish and giving them eight years to do that. Not surprisingly, the courts held the plan unlawful and, in 2006, ordered the Bureau of Reclamation to release water, at the expense of the project, to support the coho.[54] In retrospect, perhaps the Bureau (and its client irrigators) would have done better had they pushed a bit less hard. The tango of ESA negotiations and litigation, in other words, is a delicate one for all involved.

The Hope and Peril of Markets and Beyond

The tunnel vision of the various legal regimes that govern natural resource management and the limited ability of courts to redress the deeply ingrained systemic flaws in those regimes have led to a search for other paths to durable solutions. Two candidates have emerged: collaborative processes and the discipline of the market. Both increase the power of private actors. That can be seen as a sharp departure from the past several decades of resource management, which have been dominated by a regulatory model. Or it can be seen as a logical extension of the environmental era's suspicion of agencies—if constraining agency discretion and allowing citizens to enforce the law is not enough, perhaps the agencies ought to have less control of the initial decisions. A third way to view increasing private power in public decisions is as an effort, often well intentioned, to turn the clock back a full century, to the days before government regulation was expanded to rein in imperfect markets.

Collaborative Processes

In recent years there has been a great deal of enthusiasm for place-based, ad hoc, collaborative processes to address resource management conflicts. These processes are thought to offer more flexibility and less hostility than command and control regulation enforced by "rule of law" litigation. They are also experiments in more direct democracy. As resource conflicts have become sharper, traditional legal processes for resolving them have encountered increasingly stiff political resistance. The risks of changing the traditional approach can seem low and the potential gains high. Commodity-user groups have always been involved in resource management, sometimes formally and sometimes informally. The new collaborative processes formalize their participation, making it more transparent, and extend similar access opportunities to previously excluded groups, including environmentalists, Indians, and at-risk communities. In addition, by involving agencies with different missions and from different levels of government, such processes can help overcome the problems of fragmented authority and cross-boundary effects. The West has been a particularly fertile ground for collaboration; environmentalists and ranchers and other landowners have been able to find common ground in opposing a variety of development threats. At their best, these novel processes can create opportunities for agencies and interest groups that might otherwise be at cross purposes to see how their missions (and legal obligations) can be combined to produce a bioregional solution.

Law professors Jody Freeman and Daniel Farber have coined the phrase *modular regulation* to describe governance regimes that mix intergovernmental coordination with stakeholder participation. They hail modular regulation as the next logical step in the evolution of the regulatory state. The hope is that collaborative processes will produce creative substantive outcomes, which will more readily gain acceptance because stakeholders have participated in their achievement. According to Freeman and Farber, "Modularity requires that institutional form follow function wherever possible, meaning that the goal of the modular enterprise is first to diagnose problems and second to devise solutions and match institutions capable of implementing them."[55] Creating, nurturing, and overseeing these sorts of cross-cutting novel institutions are daunting tasks. The enthusiasm for such institutions is in some ways a measure of how bleak the current political landscape is and how poorly suited more traditional institutions seem to environmental conflicts.

While they have some promising features, these untested experiments seem to us to pose a high risk that process will swamp progress, producing neither harmony among stakeholders nor long-term ecosystem protection.[56] Complex stakeholder processes can be likened to trying to fit together the pieces of a jigsaw puzzle representing a Jackson Pollock painting, with no real expectation that a clear picture will ever emerge. We prefer an approach that begins by defining the goals of the process. The first product should be a map that, within the constraints of fixed settlement patterns, designates the landscape characteristics of a functioning ecosystem and identifies workable indices of function, difficult as that challenge is. The next step is to find fair and effective mechanisms to implement and sustain the desired ecosystem. In chapter 8, we explore in detail why this has not yet happened in the Klamath and what might bring it closer to fruition.

The Discipline of the Market

The Klamath Basin is in transition between the so-called old and new Wests. One difference between the two lies in the foundations of their economies. The old West's economy rested on resource extraction. The new West's economy rests on services that facilitate resource enjoyment. But there is another important distinction connected to how the region's path is determined. In the old West the federal government, through its role as the major landholder, self-consciously chose what it saw as the best future for the region and pursued that vision. Today, those choices are more likely to be mediated through the accretion of individual decisions, that is, the market.

Markets decide how technologies, clothing styles, and music rise and fade as tastes change. The same holds true for land use. Just as "Indians" were supposed to vanish in the face of a superior white civilization in the nineteenth century, market enthusiasts today argue that marginal agricultural communities should wither away (a gentler process than the forcible removal of the Indians) if they cannot make the transition to a "modern" service economy. In many areas of the rural West, the market is hard at work creating precisely that sort of transition. Parts of the northern Great Plains are emptying out, reverting to a modern form of frontier, with low population densities located long distances from market-service areas. In the San Joaquin Valley, one of the nation's prime agricultural areas, the transition is even more dramatic in the opposite direction. Urbanization is spilling over from the Bay

Area and Los Angeles, rapidly shifting thousands of acres from farm to urban uses. Both types of transition are economically rational, forecast and blessed by economists. Farmers, environmentalists, and urban commuters all have the opportunity to bid for available land. The result should be that resources find what economists like to call their "highest and best use," the use for which people will pay the highest price.

That markets might determine the future of the western landscape is deeply disturbing, in a way that at first seems inconsistent or hypocritical, to many farmers, ranchers, and longtime westerners. These are politically conservative groups, as the red and blue maps of the 2004 presidential election so starkly revealed. They strongly support robust protection of what they see as their property rights against government interference. But they also want those rights protected against the discipline of the market. Those positions are not necessarily as inconsistent as they might seem. Markets, as environmentalists have long recognized, often do not fully capture intangible values, such as the sustainability of established communities, multigenerational connections to the land, or, for that matter, the health of ecosystems. The market can be just as dangerous a threat as the government to westerners for whom farming or ranching is a way of life, not just a job.

Western rural resistance to the discipline of the market has been most clearly revealed in disputes over federal grazing policy. For years, environmentalists and free-market economists have criticized the federal government's grazing permit program as inefficient and environmentally destructive.[57] Environmental damage aside, the cost-benefit numbers are astounding: In fiscal year 2004, the federal government collected $17.5 million in grazing fees but spent $132.5 million on grazing management.[58] Fees are set not by market forces but by a formula based in large part on permittee costs. The market for permits, such as it is, is limited to livestock producers. The Clinton administration tried to change that. Its efforts to raise grazing fees were shot down by Congress amid fierce western opposition, and its attempt to create a new category of "conservation use" permits was invalidated by the courts as inconsistent with the governing legislation at the behest of a livestock industry association.[59] Even so, private conservation groups found a way to use their market power, purchasing grazing permits from willing sellers, then surrendering the permits to the Bureau of Land Management (BLM, the major manager of federal rangelands) and removing livestock.[60] That worked for a time because BLM in the Clinton administration cooperated, but in 2002 William Myers, the solicitor of the Department of the Interior, issued a new legal opinion concluding that BLM was required to offer surrendered grazing permits to other ranchers.[61] We believe Myers's opinion misreads the governing law,[62] but for purposes of this discussion it is enough to note that the grazing permit example illustrates just how intense opposition is to opening resource-use decisions to the market.[63]

Klamath Project farmers are like the ranchers who oppose robust market treatment of grazing permits in the sense that they see themselves as a culture with a right to continued existence, rather than as an industry that should properly be subject to stiff competition. They are buffered to some extent from the harshness of the market by cheap water, a diversified crop base, and the ability to supplement their income with nonfarm sources. They are not entirely immune to market pressures, of course. Like other farmers in the West, they face the prospect of global competition and rising temptations to sell their land or water rights. Because they are more secure than farmers and ranchers in other parts of the West who are facing threats from energy development and second-home sprawl, though, members of the Klamath Basin irrigation community have fewer incentives to cooperate in reshaping their landscape.

The most economically marginal lands in the Upper Basin lie outside the project boundaries.[64] Those lands are likely candidates for market-based water transfers to more profitable croplands or to instream flows.[65] Water transfers need not be permanent. Temporary transfers, through leases or water banks, can moderate the impacts of drought. In the appropriative rights system there are always senior water rights holders who can make their water available to others for the right price. The prolonged drought of the late 1980s and early 1990s stimulated interest in temporary transfers and water banks. Legally, temporary transfers are risky because of the "use it or lose it" rule that applies to appropriative rights. Water banking seeks to counter that rule by allowing irregular transfers to a "bank" without impairing the underlying right.

Water banking was pioneered in Idaho on the Snake River and adopted by California during the drought of the late 1980s and early 90s. In early 1991, California was facing its fifth consecutive year of drought. Major reservoir storage was just over half the average amount. Water banking played a major role in shifting water from agricultural to urban uses during the last years of the drought. An evaluation of the program concludes that it met the objective of providing emergency supplies, but that established procedures for the protection of third-party interests were bypassed.[66]

Experience in other locations shows that large-scale shifts of water away from agricultural use can trigger either positive or negative transitions. Where agricultural economies are marginal at the outset, surviving only because they have been protected from external water demands, shifting water away can leave the community in a static, semi-depressed condition. Other areas, though, can adjust to the transition through economic shifts that compensate for the loss of irrigated acreage. Typically, these more resilient communities enjoy higher-value agriculture and closer access to metropolitan centers, allowing them to capture many of the benefits of a transition economy. The experience of two areas in eastern Colorado, where water has been transferred from farms to nearby urban areas, illustrates these contrasting responses. The Arkansas Valley east of Pueblo is the darker example. The unslakable thirst of the growing communities on the Front Range of the Rocky Mountains has resulted in the retirement of over 60,000 acres of agricultural land in the Arkansas River Valley. Nearly 90 percent of the water once used to irrigate those lands has been sent out of the basin.[67] The valley has been left with a bleak economic future. The rapidly industrializing Platte Valley in northern Colorado is a more positive example of successful adaptation to change. Some farmers there have shifted to specialized agriculture. Others have used the economic value of their water rights as a retirement fund. New, less water-dependent industries are arriving as part of the continued eastward expansion of the Denver metropolitan area.

After the collapse of its timber economy, the Klamath Basin seemed to be headed in the direction of the Arkansas Valley even without loss of water. Today though, even without ready access to a major metropolitan area, it seems to be going in the other direction. Like the South Platte in Eastern Colorado, the Upper Klamath Basin is benefiting from its relatively unspoiled landscape and the abundance of outdoor recreational activities in the area. The Klamath Falls area has experienced modest growth; the population of the metropolitan area (if it can be called that) now stands at over 25,000. It is rapidly taking on the look of the new "cappuccino West." The Running Y ranch and spa, opened in 1996, is a beautiful, full-service golf and spa resort, as well as a second-home and retirement community. More generally, retirees are the crop of the future.[68] Baby boomers have not managed to eliminate old age, but they have redefined retirement and no longer seek only warm places. People are already talking about Klamath Falls as "the next Bend," expecting it to repeat the success of that central Oregon mountain community, which has built an economic surge on the appeal of a lifestyle centered around outdoor recreation. Nearby to the west is another possible model, the Medford-Ashland area, where theater and music draw both summer tourists and retiree residents. In 2007, Relocate America named the Klamath Basin among the one hundred best places to live in the United States.

Market solutions have been tried in the Klamath, but so far they have been used only to support the status quo. After the summer of 2001, the Bureau of Reclamation created a "faux" water bank in the Klamath. It is not a pool of water that is available to accept deposits and accommodate withdrawals but rather a series of ad hoc payments to irrigators for drilling wells or temporarily fallowing their land, a drought management strategy currently much in vogue. A preliminary assessment demonstrates the limitations of this faux banking. A 2005 GAO report concluded that although Reclamation had met its water bank targets, the actual reduction of water use was "highly uncertain due to the lack of effective flow measurement equipment and monitoring data for the Project." The net result was that the Bureau accelerated groundwater depletion without providing significant additional water for downstream coho salmon support.[69]

Can Hydropower Generate Compromise?

In the end, another federal agency with no constituency in the basin may be the most important player. Hydropower licensing provides a forum free of the macho posturing encouraged by the seemingly absolute law of prior appropriation and endangered species protection. PacifiCorp, which was recently acquired by multinational Scottish Power, operates the Klamath Hydroelectric Project, a series of five dams beginning with Link River and ending with Iron Gate just below the California border, as mentioned in chapter 3. Several of the dams were constructed before 1920, when with passage of the Federal Power Act (FPA) the United States asserted federal jurisdiction over private dams on navigable rivers. Iron Gate Dam, the largest and the most significant barrier to salmon passage, was licensed in 1956 and completed in 1960. Licenses issued by the Federal Energy Regulatory Commission, formerly known as the Federal Power Commission, run for fifty years and can be renewed for successive thirty- to fifty-year periods. The license for the Klamath Hydroelectric Project expired on March 1, 2006, but is extended annually under the same terms pending completion of the relicensing proceedings, which began in 2001. The ongoing relicensing proceedings show how sidestepping macho law may provide opportunities for compromise but also show how difficult it is to reach consensus agreements.

Since Iron Gate Dam was approved, three major changes affecting hydropower licensing have given environmentalists and downstream interests reason to hope that the relicensing proceedings might provide the impetus for a shift in the water status quo: First, the law now gives fish more leverage. Second, the idea of removing hydropower projects is no longer heresy. And third, FERC relicensing proceedings have become a forum for broad-ranging negotiations that can extend well beyond the project under consideration.

The general standard for hydropower licensing, which requires a finding that issuance of a license will be in the public interest, has always allowed consideration of the effects of hydropower projects on fish. In addition, as early as 1935 the FPA was amended to mandate that the FPC require licensees to construct, maintain, and operate fishways as prescribed by federal wildlife agencies.[70] Still, the FPC showed little interest in the environmental consequences of its licensing decisions until forced by the courts to take those consequences into account.

In the early 1960s, states and newly formed citizen groups began to argue that the FPC should not issue licenses where projects would have severe impacts on fish populations. The resulting administrative decisions and court cases were among the foundational precedents of what became environmental law. For example, failure of the commission to study the impacts of a pumped storage project on local striped bass populations was one of the reasons the Second Circuit remanded the license in the seminal 1965 case of *Scenic Hudson Preservation Council v. FPC*. In 1967, Justice William O. Douglas, the only environmentalist ever to sit on the Supreme Court, wrote an opinion holding that examination of a project's effects on fish and wildlife was required in hydropower licensing proceedings, setting the stage for the idea, now embedded in FERC law and practice, that the promotion of hydropower is not the commission's sole mission.[71]

Nonetheless, the commission continued to routinely ignore environmental concerns.[72] Finally, in 1986 Congress amended the FPA to explicitly require that FERC give "equal consideration" to fish and wildlife, recreation, and other environmental concerns in licensing as to power production and development.[73] Currently, therefore, effects on fish stocks, water quality, tribal water needs, refuge water needs, and the security of irrigation rights are all potentially relevant to relicensing decisions.

Because Congress recognized how reluctant FERC had been to take environmental interests into account, the 1986 amendments also added procedural mechanisms to focus attention on them. NMFS, FWS, and state fish and wildlife agencies are now asked to recommend conditions to limit and mitigate the impacts of hydropower projects on fish stocks. FERC must incorporate those recommendations into the license unless it finds them to be inconsistent with the purposes of the FPA.[74] The 1986 amendments also require that FERC consider the recommendations of affected Indian tribes.[75] In addition, of course, where a hydropower project may affect endangered or threatened species, ESA consultation is a required element of relicensing.

The second change is the growing acceptance of the once heretical idea that some dams have outlived their usefulness and should be removed. In 1997 FERC denied a relicense for a small dam in Maine and ordered its removal.[76] That precedent has emboldened downstream fishermen and Indians to seek removal of Iron Gate and smaller dams upstream on the Klamath River.

Third, FERC proceedings have become a forum for negotiating settlement between utilities and a wide variety of stakeholders with an interest in the relicensing. Traditionally, hydropower licensing followed a sequential procedure. The licensee developed its proposal, circulated it to the resource agencies for written comment, and then filed it with FERC. Once the application was filed, the public had the opportunity to comment, and environmental review began. Eventually, once the environmental analysis was complete, FERC would review the application, deciding whether to issue the license and subject to what conditions. Frequently, a lengthy round of requests for reconsideration and of lawsuits would follow. Relicensing was taking as long as twenty-five years for some projects. FERC, licensees, and stakeholders all agreed the process was more cumbersome than useful.

Beginning in 1997, FERC began encouraging license applicants to use a more collaborative procedure that would involve stakeholders from the beginning in face-to-face discussions and promote collaborative efforts to resolve disagreements about disputed issues in parallel with environmental review.[77] The collaborative model encourages the license applicant to negotiate with those who identify themselves as stakeholders, developing an agreement that is then presented to FERC for review and (the stakeholders hope) approval. Although FERC will include in the license only conditions with a fairly direct connection to the licensed project, the stakeholders are free to enter into additional contractual agreements covering whatever issues they are interested in and have authority over. Stakeholders generally include environmental groups; recreational interests; tribes; and a variety of federal, state, and local agencies. The settlement negotiation process, therefore, potentially provides a forum for taking a broad look at aquatic ecosystems and the socioeconomic systems tied to them. The process follows a contract negotiation model, though, meaning that its discussions are typically open only to direct participants, who often agree at the outset to keep the discussions confidential. In addition, a comprehensive settlement requires the agreement of all the stakeholders. That can be difficult and time consuming to achieve.

Because relicensing is a lengthy process, FERC requires that license holders begin it well before their existing license expires. PacifiCorp initiated the relicensing process for its Klamath project in December 2000. Initially, the company chose to use the traditional licensing process. When it met resistance to that plan, it agreed to "a structured collaborative process addressing the full range of resource and operational issues."[78] That agreement launched a process of protracted negotiations involving more than 140 stakeholder groups, though only about 25 are key participants. Although a deal was said to be close in early 2006, as of July 2007 no resolution had been reached.

As is typical of modern FERC hydropower proceedings, negotiations have progressed on a parallel track to environmental review and evaluation. In the spring of 2006, FWS and NMFS provided FERC with jointly developed fishway prescriptions under FPA section 18 requiring "volitional passage," meaning that fish could pass safely on their own both upstream and downstream, at all project dams.[79] PacifiCorp contended that satisfying those prescriptions would be prohibitively costly and ultimately futile because poor water quality upstream of the dams would limit fish survival. FPA amendments adopted as part of the comprehensive Energy Policy Act of 2005 allowed PacifiCorp to propose alternative fishway prescriptions and to have those alternatives accepted if they were no less protective and significantly less costly or better for energy production.[80] PacifiCorp's alternatives were starkly different than the agencies' prescriptions. The company proposed no passage at some facilities and nonvolitional "trap and truck" passage at others. It suggested that any efforts to improve passage for anadromous fish should be dependent on a joint determination by PacifiCorp and the agencies that self-sustaining populations could be established above the dams.

When the agencies refused to back down, PacifiCorp took advantage of another provision of the 2005 amendments to demand an expedited trial-type hearing before an administrative law judge on its claims that the agencies' prescriptions were both unnecessary and futile.[81] A number of other parties intervened. A five-day hearing was held in August 2006, accompanied by submission of thousands of pages of written testimony and exhibits, imposing time and money burdens the wildlife agencies and environmental interests had not anticipated. The result was good from their perspective, though. The judge ruled in favor of the agencies on almost all counts.[82] The agencies subsequently renewed their call for volitional fish passage, finding (with support from the hearing decision) that PacifiCorps' alternative proposals, while they would certainly be less costly, would not protect fish as effectively.

The agencies' insistence on installation of costly fish passage facilities has put dam removal squarely on the table. The Draft Environmental Impact Statement issued by FERC in September 2006 considers as one possible alternative the removal of two dams, Iron Gate and COPCO no. 1. Neither currently has fish passage facilities, and they produce relatively little electricity, so the economic case for removing them looks good, at least in comparison to compliance with the agencies' fishway demands.[83] The sale of PacifiCorp to multinational Scottish Power raised hopes that the new owners might find dam removal the more attractive option, especially if public pressure could be brought to bear. In early 2007, PacifiCorp sounded like it was at least open to discussion of dam removal, but its public stance subsequently cooled. It is hard to tell whether that is simply a negotiating position or the company is reluctant to give up any hydropower capacity, which has new value now that global warming has become a high-priority issue for state regulators.

As of mid-2007, relicensing seems to have stalled in the settlement negotiation process, becoming a hostage to the competing interests of the stakeholders. While the broad perspective available in FERC settlement negotiations offers considerable promise for making progress in ecosystem revival, it also carries very real costs. Where everything is on the table and everyone must agree, negotiations can easily fall apart. According to the *Los Angeles Times*, that is exactly what is happening. The paper reported in May 2007 that farmers were seeking a settlement agreement that would trade dam removal (which environmental interests want) for money to soften the blow of increased electricity costs and protection against future endangered species–based water restrictions, and that two of the more vocal environmental groups in the basin, WaterWatch and Oregon Wild, had basically withdrawn from (or been booted out of) the negotiations over their inability to get farming scaled back in the refuges.[84] As of this writing, it is not clear whether anything will come out of the negotiations or whether, if an agreement is reached that does not satisfy all basin interests, it would survive the inevitable litigation.

CHAPTER 8

When Is a Train Wreck a Good Thing?

I come no more to make you laugh.

William Shakespeare, Prologue, *Henry VIII*

The 2001 water crisis in the Klamath Basin was wholly foreseeable. The Bureau of Reclamation courted it by pushing the limits of water deliveries in a series of dry years. The irrigators went further, openly challenging the wildlife agencies with litigation when FWS first tried to require that water be left in the Upper Basin lakes. The Klamath tribes set the explosives in place by pushing for listing of the suckers. Finally, the downstream fishermen and their environmental allies lit the fuse when they demanded in 2000 that the ESA be enforced according to its letter.

Why wasn't the crisis avoided? In part because that would have required a series of changes to the institutions and expectations that guide water use in the Klamath Basin. As we detail in this chapter, those sorts of changes do not come easily. But more than that, no one had much incentive to look for a way around the crisis, and some participants had every reason to seek it, just as at the 1945 Potsdam Conference Churchill, Stalin, and Truman "perceived that they could enhance their power more certainly in a world of discord than of tranquility."[1] As we explained in chapter 1, environmentalists and environmental lawyers have deliberately used litigation to provoke political crises since the 1970s. Indeed, the 1970s wave of federal environmental laws were deliberately crafted to facilitate that strategy, including provisions allowing citizens to sue if the government failed to pursue robust enforcement.[2] In the Klamath Basin, the water allocation status quo was essentially static for nearly one hundred years, despite old and new legal doctrines intended to protect the interests of Indians and the environment. It's easy to see how crisis-triggering litigation could look like the only way to get those interests true recognition. At the very least, it would bring public attention to an area that had always been easy to ignore. There was even an attractive recent precedent: ESA protection of the northern spotted owl, driven at every stage by litigation, had shut down timber production on federal lands in the Pacific Northwest in the early 1990s. That brought the president out to the region and ultimately triggered a sea change in national forest management, accompanied by economic assistance to displaced timber workers.[3]

The irrigators too might have seen crisis as an opportunity. From their perspective, environmental regulation had been gradually nibbling away at their interests, producing noticeable, albeit not drastic, cuts in irrigation deliveries in the drought years preceding the crisis. The shutoff actually made it easy for them to make their case to the public: It's hard to get much sympathy for gradual reductions, but dry fields are an image everyone can understand. Given the traditional political power of farming interests in the United States and the apparent vulnerability of the ESA at the time, a drastic crisis might have permanently entrenched the status quo rather than dislodging it. When a Klamath-like crisis loomed on the middle Rio Grande near Albuquerque, that's exactly what happened: Congress passed a special rider forbidding the Bureau of Reclamation from reallocating water to protect the endangered Rio Grande silvery minnow.[4]

In the Klamath Basin, the 2001 train wreck has produced a series of disconnected ad hoc responses that have been helpful in small ways to various interests. It has not, however, fundamentally changed the law or the practice of water allocation, significantly reduced pressures on the ecosystem, or produced a new vision for the landscape. The Klamath Basin, like so many other parts of the arid West, remains poised for the next water crisis. In this chapter, we ask why the crisis has not provoked more drastic change and attempt to draw some modest positive lessons from a story that can only be characterized, on the whole, as a tragedy for all concerned.

The principal lesson is that the task of maintaining working rivers as rivers that also work ecologically is extremely difficult. Conservation of terrestrial resources on working landscapes is hard enough. But for reasons that we explain here, the challenges are even more daunting for water. Ecosystems cannot be fixed by treating only the symptoms of their deterioration. Yet environmental laws and governance institutions push strongly toward precisely that approach. As with health care, the United States offers high-quality (and high-cost) emergency conservation treatment but refuses to invest in basic preventive measures.

Like any history, this story does not have a true endpoint. Events continue to unfold in the Klamath Basin, but enough time has passed since the crisis to justify an evaluation of the lessons learned or not yet learned. As this volume goes to press in the middle of 2007, there are some modest signs of hope, but they are flickering and fragile at best. External pressures on irrigators continue to mount, as do stresses on the ecosystem. We believe some water will inevitably move from agricultural to environmental use in the Klamath Basin, but we suspect the transition will be slow and painful. Reed Benson, a participant in the Klamath water conflicts when he was with WaterWatch Oregon, analogizes resource conflicts to the grieving process. Like the loss of a loved one, he says, a change in resource allocation initially brings anger and refusal to confront the changed world, but eventually acceptance and adjustment follow. We hope he is right and that the Klamath Basin is approaching the acceptance stage. Before people can accept a changed world, though, they must have a positive vision of how they can fit into that world. At the end of this chapter, we try to sketch how that kind of vision might be developed for the Klamath Basin.

Water: The Different Resource

These days there is some room for optimism about the prospects of large-scale ecosystem management of terrestrial systems, especially those dominated by federally owned lands. The spotted owl crisis pushed the Forest Service to manage its lands in the Pacific Northwest on a region-wide basis and hastened a transition that was already in progress toward emphasis on recreational rather than extractive uses (although resistance continues, and the transition may yet be reversed by the Bush administration). In the northern Rocky Mountains, two leading natural resource scholars, Professors Joseph Sax and Robert Keiter, who were pessimistic about regional management in 1987, now have a more rosy outlook.[5]

Those experiments in ecosystem management on federally owned lands, however, enjoy three advantages over the Klamath situation. First, the coordination problems are less daunting. Getting ecosystem management to work at a basic level in the Pacific Northwest forests required only that individual units of the national forest system work together. In the Glacier National Park region studied by Professors Sax and Keiter, it is possible with coordination between national forests and the national park. In the Klamath and other western basins, basic ecosystem management requires the cooperation of the state water allocation agency, federal water project managers, state and federal water quality regulators, federal land managers, and perhaps state and local zoning and planning agencies. The second advantage of ecosystem management on federally owned lands is that history and the entrenched law of the past stand less in the way. Changing the trajectory of national forest management in the Pacific Northwest certainly upset timber communities. But no one could say they had a property right to cut a particular amount of timber every year. Water users, by contrast, strongly believe in their inalienable right to continue irrigating. Third, the landscapes involved—old-growth forests and the unspoiled Rockies—are more charismatic, enjoying a national constituency that probably does not exist for any aquatic system, certainly not for the little-known Klamath Basin.

The ongoing conflicts in the Klamath illustrate just how difficult it is to revive the West's degraded aquatic ecosystems.[6] The basin's problems stem from a long series of decisions, taken in good faith, about how the area's water should be used. To observe that it is hard to reallocate water is an understatement. Water conflicts are not simply about an abstract series of possible uses to which the resource could be put; they are about what water means to the inhabitants of an area.

William Lord describes water conflicts as the search for answers to two questions: What is? and What ought to be?[7] "What is" sounds like a simple question, but as we explained in chapter 5, there are enough uncertainties about water use and water rights that it can be quite difficult to answer. "What ought to be" is even more difficult, because it requires choices among competing landscape visions that implicate economic interests but also go much deeper. The necessary choices cannot be made without a vision of the future landscape, how fast to get there, and at whose expense.

In the Klamath Basin, the value conflicts those questions raise have been presented in the popular press only in the most simplistic terms, reduced to "fish versus farmers." In reality the conflicts are more subtle, and many of the participants less single-minded, than that picture. The conflicts that bubble to the surface reflect a deeper debate, not clearly articulated, about how western landscapes should be used and how their resources should be shared among the waves of humans who come to this unique region seeking their own vision of a better life.[8] Connecting all the area's battlefields, from the protection of salmon runs to the resolution of aboriginal Indian water rights, is the question of the ultimate future of the basin. Reducing that question to a simple dichotomy of fish versus farms obscures the fact that, rather than simple either-or choices, complex issues about the rate and geographic scale of transition must be dealt with.

The bottom line is that people in the West care deeply about water but in very different ways. They can be just as emotionally attached to the water filling an arrow-straight irrigation ditch as to water swiftly flowing from mountains to sea undisturbed by human hands.[9] In the Klamath Basin, these attachments manifest themselves in bitterness and distrust, but basically, the Klamath shows that people, even the same people, admire both working rivers and rivers that work.[10] When rivers must play both roles, as in the Klamath Basin, the resulting conflicts can be nearly impossible to untangle.

Reallocation: A Win-Lose Game

Although water reallocation is always difficult, it is particularly tough in places like the Klamath Basin, where the political power structure strongly favors the status quo and current water users have few options. The doctrine of prior appropriation and the Bureau of Reclamation's distribution of water have created a tight-knit irrigation community in the Upper Basin. It is difficult to introduce new values into such established water-use communities. The costs of changing the status quo are often high and concentrated on those established communities, which, not surprisingly, resist efforts to reallocate water in response to changed conditions or new societal goals. Because irrigators have historically held the reins of political power in rural communities and beyond, that resistance can be highly effective.

Students of water management have often observed that "water is different" in two important respects. Water rights, by comparison to land rights, face substantially greater risks of curtailment and loss. In addition, water rights have a stronger communal nature than is generally acknowledged for land rights. Appropriative rights are correlative, which means that users have interests in each other's use of water, although there is no formal sharing of rights. The correlative or community nature of water rights manifests itself negatively in the ability of other users to challenge a use as nonbeneficial or abandoned. Positively, user communities often cooperate to make sure that the risks of shortage fall equally on all community members.

The coalescence of a user community greatly reduces the risks of water shortfalls. The structure of water law, combined with the fragmentation of governmental oversight, allows user communities to shift the social costs of their water use to outsiders. No wonder they resist change, even in the face of crisis. For example, an assessment of the Upper Klamath Working Group's progress after the summer of 2001 found that agricultural interests had a great deal of trouble accepting the goal of restoring the Klamath ecosystem, wanted to focus on drought proofing the Upper Basin, and were not enthusiastic about including the Lower Basin in the process.[11] The 2001 shutoff of the headgates disturbed what they had come to see as the natural order of things. The impact was much more painful than the usual drought, and not just because the loss of water was so extreme. The loss of control was even more problematic.

Money: Not Always Welcome

Permanent water reallocation, to the extent that it has occurred in the West, has been driven either by a great disparity between the economic values of agricultural and alternative uses or by a dire threat to an ecosystem that has developed a powerful constituency. Neither of those conditions exist in the Klamath Basin, a remote and largely unknown ecosystem far away from the fiscal pull of urban areas.

As we explained in chapter 7, the majority of reallocations to date have been from agriculture to urban uses through the market rather than by regulatory fiat. There are few successful instances of reallocation of water from agriculture to environmental uses, the transition needed in the Klamath. The best example comes from the Newlands irrigation project east of Reno, Nevada. Over 50,000 acre-feet of water have been voluntarily shifted from agriculture to support the Stillwater National Wildlife Refuge. The refuge became a national issue after a major die-off of migratory waterfowl connected to agricultural diversions and polluted irrigation returns.

In the Klamath Basin, small-scale water transfers began in 1997 with the goal of restoring wetlands around Upper Klamath Lake. They have continued with mixed success. The good news is that modest reductions in irrigation can provide substantial benefits to the environment and the tribes. Counterbalanced against this is the resistance of irrigators to giving up their entitlements. Social cohesion within the irrigator community makes it hard for those individuals who would otherwise sell out. The Klamath Water Users Association, the voice of the Upper Basin's most committed farmers, reportedly scuttled congressional approval of funding for voluntary purchases of land or water rights in the region shortly after the 2001 crisis.[12] Some farmers who were prepared to sell complained that the association had usurped their ability to do so.[13]

No Drivers or Deep Pockets

It may seem counterintuitive, but change comes with more difficulty to small basins in remote locations than to larger basins in the path of urban growth. Size matters in the sense that larger, wealthier water users tend to have more options for adaptation. The small farmers that dominate the Klamath Basin have a smaller tolerance for risk than large corporate agricultural interests. Proximity to urban areas, and in particular connections to municipal water supplies, matters because it brings both political attention and money. One reason the federal government and the state of California have been willing to pour millions of dollars into attempts to revive the Sacramento–San Joaquin Delta is that the delta supplies drinking water to 23 million Californians.

One place where reallocation of water from agriculture is making progress is Nevada's Truckee-Carson Basin.[14] The Truckee-Carson has much in common with the Klamath. In the 1980s the ESA-listed cui-ui and Lahontan cutthroat trout, fish species of great cultural and economic importance to the Pyramid Lake Paiute Tribe, were declining because of agricultural diversions from the Truckee River into the Carson River Basin; the Stillwater National Wildlife Refuge at the end of the Carson River was not getting enough clean water to support the migratory waterfowl for which it was established; and an early federal reclamation project was clinging to its vested water rights. In 1990, Senator Harry Reid brokered the settlement of a long-running water dispute between California and Nevada over the waters of the Truckee River. His legislation required that the major interests in the basin, including the federal government, the states, the tribe, and the Reno-Sparks municipal water agency, negotiate a new operating agreement for the Truckee River.[15] The key irrigation district was left out of the negotiations on the assumption that the Bureau of Reclamation would adequately represent its interests.

The negotiations were anything but easy. After several false starts and nearly twenty years after the legislation, the negotiating parties reached agreement on a new Truckee River Operating Agreement (TROA) early in 2007, and it is working its way through the environmental review process. The agreement will benefit Reno-Sparks by providing it with more secure supplies in the event of drought and by reducing the risks of tribal opposition to acquisition of additional water rights in the future to support population growth. The tribe also benefits, through assurances of adequate flows to support the endangered fish. The major losers are the Newlands Project irrigators, who were shut out of the negotiating process and have already promised a lawsuit.

It remains to be seen whether the TROA agreement will stick. If it does, it will be because the combination of the ESA, tribal rights that had long gone unheeded, and the needs of a regionally important metropolitan area was enough to overcome the objections of irrigators. The Klamath Basin has the first two, but not the last. Without it, irrigators remain firmly entrenched as the water lords of the basin.

Regulatory Fragmentation

Political entrepreneurs are frequently urged to "take ownership" of a problem in order to find acceptable and fair solutions. Although public choice theory explains why it seldom happens, politicians do occasionally take ownership of an initiative. Anyone trying to take ownership of a water conflict, though, faces extraordinary barriers. There are no individual heroes in this story, just as there are no real individual villains. Instead, the story of the Klamath conflict is one of individuals caught in a maze of multiple government agencies with conflicting mandates. The basin's fragmented legal regimes ensure that there is no simple way through the maze because no one has jurisdiction over the complete range of problems.

The incentives are stacked against anyone—government agency, individual irrigator, local elected official, tribe, or environmental group—taking ownership of this conflict. The Bureau of Reclamation is the most powerful player in the basin's water management, but for it taking ownership would mean alienating its core constituency, the irrigators. One does not have to subscribe to any fancy academic theory of rational actors to realize that administrative agencies are not suicidal.

The closest precedent does not look as promising as it once did. During the 1990s, Betsy Reike, then assistant secretary for water and science in the Department of the Interior, decided to broker a solution to the problems of the Bay-Delta in northern California. She was able to forge a public-private cooperative process known as CalFed that seemed to make strides toward a solution. Any solution that depends on political leadership can falter with a change in administrations, though, and CalFed did. It was unable to secure long-term funding; and once the Clinton administration was out of office, the federal government failed to meet its early financial commitments. In addition, CalFed failed to produce the win-win solution that the proponents of consensus processes tend to promise. Its constituencies fragmented as the ecosystem failed to recover and water users failed to see substantial increases in the security of their supplies. Within a few years, the process and the institutions created to govern it fell apart. California is gamely trying to continue parts of it without federal help, but prospects are dim.

Meanwhile, the Bay-Delta ecosystem has suffered an unforeseen collapse that has a Klamath-style crisis looming. The delta smelt, a tiny minnow listed under both the state and federal endangered species acts, has declined drastically. Early in 2007, a state court judge ruled that the state could not continue to run the massive pumps that export water from the delta to the croplands of the San Joaquin Valley and the cities of Southern California without a permit from the state Department of Fish and Game. An appeal by the state has stayed that order, but federal court trouble looms as well. A federal district court ruled that the BiOp for the federal Central Valley Project, which is closely intertied with California's State Water Project, is invalid but so far has refused to enjoin pumping while a new BiOp is prepared. Pumping was briefly halted voluntarily in May 2007 to limit its impacts on the delta smelt, but it was ramped up again later as demand increased and the fish were thought to have moved away from the immediate vicinity of the pumps. In sum, as of mid-2007, the once much-vaunted Bay-Delta process is where no one wanted it to be, in the courts, and Governor Schwarzenegger and the legislature have begun a debate about water policy that revives decades of conflict about how to deal with the geographic disconnect between the state's water resources and its population and farms.

In the Klamath Basin, the Bureau of Reclamation and the Department of the Interior have taken ownership of only one side of the problem: protecting irrigation deliveries. They have pushed that goal rather than trying to solve the problem of a deteriorating ecosystem by eliminating underlying causes. Taking ownership requires commitment to finding a sustainable path, not just preservation of the status quo. Outside of the Department of the Interior, no other government agency or private party in the Klamath Basin has the political will, power, or vision to take ownership of the problem as a whole.

Never Enough Science

The problems of using science to solve disputes such as the Klamath water conflict are discussed in detail in chapter 6. We add here only that the search for scientific perfection in ecosystem management is fundamentally misguided. As sensible ecologists have frequently warned, ecology and the related biological sciences will never reach the precision of physics and mathematics. The science of the natural world will never be a matter of formulaic prediction or perfect understanding. The search for impossibly perfect science-based decisions deflects attention from the more important issue of legitimacy. One of the strengths of law is that it has never demanded perfection or even truth in the absolute sense, being satisfied with the more attainable goal of legitimacy. Although reasonably accurate data, transparency, and reasoned conclusions are necessary components of legitimacy, absolute certainty or precision is not.

All that can be asked of decision makers in the face of incomplete scientific information is that they make a good-faith effort to reach a justifiable decision in light of the available information. In the context of natural resource regulation, the key legitimacy question is not whether the variety of judgments that go into regulatory decisions are objectively correct or certain, but whether they are adequately serving legitimately chosen societal goals. To ensure that, the process of decision making must be appropriately controlled, with adequate support and effective oversight.

In some cases, oversight should involve independent scientific review.[16] "Peer review," as it is called in the scientific world, takes a variety of forms, from individual review of the claims made on the basis of a single set of data to in-depth multidisciplinary review of the questions asked, the data consulted, and the conclusions drawn, which is the approach usually taken by NRC committees. There are also fundamentally different models, such as special research and monitoring centers, supported by independent advisory groups, with mandates to synthesize and apply relevant information to the target management objective.[17]

We believe that peer review can be helpful but should not become a fetish. Outside review in any form introduces a style of discipline that can protect against tunnel vision or the unquestioning propagation of assumptions that may be wrong. Outside review can spur learning by inspiring new thinking, demanding accountability, and highlighting significant gaps in the existing database that could be filled. Resource-intensive reviews on the NRC model are most likely to be justified when the costs (economic and environmental) of error are high and there is substantial disagreement within the scientific community or a substantial risk that scientific consensus is being ignored in favor of unacknowledged political concerns.

The NRC review of the Klamath BiOps drew everyone's attention to the paucity of data to support any water management decisions. The committee's final report included a detailed set of recommendations for research and monitoring.[18] The report triggered a series of meetings focusing on the data and data gaps, and helped bring in funding, primarily through the bureau, to support additional studies. At a minimum, the report increased awareness of important unanswered questions and of the limits of science as a guide to management decisions.

Peer review has its limits, however, and carries its own risks. Outside reviews may by their very nature carry more credibility than they deserve. Outside reviewers may be expert in fields implicated by a regulatory decision, but they will frequently be relative newcomers to the details of the particular system. While they can provide a valuable perspective, they might easily miss or misunderstand important details. In the face of high uncertainty, when outside review is most likely to be sought, it provides another opinion but nothing more. There is no reason to automatically give a reviewer's opinion special weight, but it may be natural to do so. Like the authors of peer-reviewed journal articles, resource management agencies should have the opportunity to respond to external reviews. Reviews of regulatory decisions should move the conversation forward, not be expected to automatically supply the final word.

In addition, just as agency decisions can unconsciously or covertly reflect agency policy judgments, outside reviews can themselves reflect the hidden policy judgments of the reviewers. Reviews should be carefully performed and presented to minimize that risk. Review committees should not simply be invited to critique an agency decision. They should be asked instead to evaluate the degree of scientific support for a particular decision; identify gaps or weaknesses in the available data; highlight what interpretive judgments were made and how the agency dealt with uncertainty; quantify to the extent possible the likelihood of errors on either side; and consider what value additional data would carry for the regulatory decision. Explicitly charging the review committee with revealing policy judgments made in the course of the regulatory process should discourage the committee from (unconsciously) substituting its own policy views for those of the regulatory agency under the guise of scientific review. It could also help avoid mischaracterization and misunderstanding of the review.

In chapter 6, we highlighted the possibility that committee members' policy views may have unconsciously influenced the NRC committee's conclusions and the way those conclusions were presented. In our view, though, the most troubling aspect of the Klamath NRC review was the way the committee's interim report was portrayed as showing that the regulatory agencies had engaged in junk science. Had the committee been more conscious of distinctly separating its review of the scientific support for the regulatory decisions from review of the decision itself, its interim report might have been less vulnerable to such misuse.

Change from the Outside

In evaluating the effect of environmental law on the Klamath Basin, it is important not to fall into the trap of assuming that, but for the ESA, the status quo would continue indefinitely. Even if the ESA disappeared tomorrow, broader social and economic trends would continue to put pressure on Upper Basin farms, especially those on the most marginal land. With or without environmental law, agriculture is likely to have a smaller footprint in the Klamath Basin of the future.

The most immediate external threat is an impending increase in electricity rates, touched on in chapter 3. In 2006, both the California and Oregon Public Utility Commissions decided that the subsidized electric rates established in the 1917 contract between the predecessor of PacifiCorp and the Bureau of Reclamation should be revised because they are now inappropriately compelling power users outside the basin to subsidize basin farming.[19] Irrigators unsuccessfully asked FERC to include the 1917 rates, which amount to a subsidy of about $10 million per year, as a condition of relicensing for the Klamath Hydropower Project. Thus, after a transition period in each state, power rates for Upper Basin irrigators could increase by nearly an order of magnitude unless some other way to subsidize them is found.[20]

The impact of these new rates will depend on the ability of irrigators to conserve energy or water, and the profitability of the crops grown. The crunch will likely come on lower-quality, sprinkler-irrigated lands. Some farmers may convert to flood irrigation or install more energy-efficient pumps and irrigation technologies. Others may have to fallow their lands, perhaps selling or leasing their water rights for other uses. In the short term, some compromise or additional transition time is likely before the irrigators face truly market electricity rates. A larger lesson remains. Marginal agriculture in areas without large-scale processing facilities or exporting ability will inevitably shrink in the face of unstoppable global economic transitions.

The Vision Thing

In telling the tale of the Klamath conflicts, we have repeatedly said that the basin suffers from the lack of a viable vision for the landscape. Actually, the problem is not that there is no vision, it is that there are too many small visions and no big one. Everyone sees the world that would be ideal for him or her. The irrigators see a second century of business as usual on the Klamath Project. Downstream fishermen and tribes see a healthier river with fewer dams supporting stronger salmon runs. The Klamath tribes also see a landscape closer to the extensive wetlands complex their ancestors learned to inhabit, supporting not only suckers but a robust tribal culture and a modern economy. Just as no one has taken ownership of the whole suite of problems affecting the basin, no one has articulated a broader vision that takes account of each of these perspectives and provides a platform for trade-offs among them.

Any effort to "fix the Klamath" must start from some realistic alternative vision of the landscape that focuses on the whole, rather than on one or more component parts. There is no single "right" or "optimum" vision. The final political choice must, like the ecosystem itself, work and integrate with other systems at a variety of scales. It must recognize that the Klamath is both a unique and valuable natural system and a working landscape.[21]

The Forgotten Ecosystem

Perhaps the most striking aspect of the Klamath story is the almost complete absence of a focus on the ecosystem as a whole. In its final report, the NRC committee strongly emphasized the need for, and noted the utter lack of, a holistic perspective. That aspect of the NRC review, which we regard as the most important, was utterly missed by the media and the larger public discussion in the furor over the conclusions about lack of scientific support for the 2001 shutoff. NMFS tried to expand the regulatory focus in its 2002 BiOp, calling for coordinated ecosystem restoration projects and the initiation of a joint state-federal process to identify non-project water that might be used to maintain flows needed by the coho.[22] That effort is still limited, focusing only on the coho. Even so, its success lies entirely beyond the Bureau's control and, as a practical matter, almost entirely beyond NMFS's control.

The challenges of crafting and implementing the 2002 BiOp illustrate the difficulties of undertaking anything approaching true ecosystem management in the Klamath Basin. The construct of the ecosystem is science's most important contribution to environmental protection, but the teachings of ecology do not translate readily into effective laws and management institutions. Landowners and agencies are stuck trying to do ecosystem management with a set of laws and institutions too narrowly focused for that task. In part that is a matter of timing. Environmental law enjoyed a burst of creativity in the 1970s, before the notion of dynamic ecosystems was widely appreciated, and has fallen into legislative gridlock more recently. But it is also because ecosystem management requires a broad and flexible view that is at odds with existing institutions and with the stability that law itself is supposed to provide.

The result is that ecosystem management remains at best a messy process of "muddling through" involving the courts; small-scale democratic experiments; and a complex web of agencies, jurisdictions, laws, regulations, and incentives. Commentators on western resource management routinely bemoan the maze of overlapping, conflicting, and in many ways outdated laws and institutions. We can only echo dismay over the fossilized geological formation called natural resources law. Like imperial Chinese dynastic history, which told the story of each dynasty seriatim, layer after layer of law has been piled one on top of the last with no serious effort at integration or correction. The net result is a historical accident more than a coherent, planned whole. On the bottom layer are the nineteenth-century legal regimes designed to encourage and facilitate resource exploitation that Charles Wilkinson has dubbed the "Lords of Yesterday."[23] Despite decades of reform efforts and widespread recognition that the conditions that justified them are long past, the Lords of Yesterday endure. The most relevant for the Klamath Basin is the Reclamation Act of 1902.

The next layer includes the conservation efforts of the early twentieth century, including the creation of the national wildlife refuge system and the national forest system, designed to restrain and rationalize resource exploitation. Finally, there are the modern environmental laws, designed to address specific problems such as species conservation or water quality protection. It is not surprising that these various regimes are often themselves in tension. Since the 1980s, federal agencies have tried not only to reconcile the conflicts, but also to adapt the entire mass to an ecosystem management approach. There have been some successes where federal lands predominate and a local "new West" constituency supports the transition.[24] Otherwise, attempts at ecosystem management are swimming upstream against a strong current of vested rights and political resistance.

The Evolution of Nature Protection

In the United States, nature protection policy has evolved over time. It began in the late nineteenth and early twentieth centuries with the creation of large nature reserves walled off from exploitation, with humans allowed only to visit and appreciate. The effort to focus more holistically on ecosystems developed in two stages beginning in the 1960s. First, the environmentalist successors to the early-twentieth-century preservation movement took the idea of awe-inspiring natural areas and gave it a scientific twist by shifting the focus from scenery to the functioning ecosystem.[25] Following Aldo Leopold, some posited rights for those natural systems, but that project made little headway in law.[26] Instead, lawyers and legislators took a rationalist approach, tackling the persistent marginalization of environmental concerns with laws like the National Environmental Policy Act (NEPA), which required recognition and consideration of the impacts of human actions on the natural world.

While it at least brought environmental effects into the decision-making process, the courts construed NEPA not to impose any substantive limits on environmental degradation.[27] Science, combined with a measure of self-conscious advocacy, again stepped in. In the 1980s, ecologists invented a term and a concept, *biodiversity*, to marshal public support for a broader form of conservation, highlighting the importance of the full range of species and natural processes. Biodiversity conservation attempts to provide an organizing concept for a variety of uncoordinated resource management objectives,[28] as well as a theory that can compete with economics, which has long emphasized the obvious costs of nature protection and its uncertain material benefits.[29] A biodiversity approach to conservation requires that ecosystems be viewed as integrated functioning units rather than collections of discrete species. Beyond that, it provides maddeningly little specific guidance.

Environmentalism, and especially the idea of biodiversity conservation, eventually changed economic thinking. It sensitized economists to the idea that resources can be valuable even if they are not traded in any market. [30]

Ecosystems provide "services" with measurable monetary value—for example, in the way wetlands filter pollution and retain waters that otherwise would flood human settlements. That recognition led to a movement to create markets that would accurately reflect at least some of these previously overlooked values, encouraging their protection.[31] Ecosystem service provision is different from the broader effort to sustain healthy, functioning ecosystems. The ecosystem services recognized by economists are limited to those functions that provide concrete, measurable benefits to human welfare.[32] An ecosystem service approach seeks to protect and perhaps even increase the output of high-value goods and services from ecosystems but is content to ignore their other functions.[33] In practice, though, the line between ecosystem function and service is hazy.

The New Western Commodities

Conceptually, one way to improve the Klamath ecosystem for the benefit of farmers, as well as the ecosystem and those who rely on it, is to create a market for ecosystem services. Ecosystem services represent the "new West" version of a resource economy. An ecosystem service economy seeks to capitalize on the natural resources that make an area unique, rather than removing them or modifying them out of existence. The idea is hardheaded and pragmatic in a way that earlier environmentalist calls to see and consider the heritage and opportunity values of natural systems were not. The motivation for the ecosystem services approach is to attach "real" hard economic value to natural resources in place by valuing what they do for us humans so that they can put cash in the pockets of the people who would otherwise feel the need to exploit those resources.

As a basin in economic transition, the Klamath would seem to be a good test case to see how well the ecosystem services idea translates from theory to practice. Elsewhere, there are some emerging examples of private provision of ecosystem services for profit. The one that is most often trotted out is the decision of New York City to buy land and conservation easements in the watershed that provides its drinking water rather than build a costly filtration plant. Others are developing. The Nez Perce Tribe in Idaho, for example, may be able to sell carbon sequestration credits from its forestlands.[34] But constructing functional markets for ecosystem services is a challenge. In economic terms, ecosystems are usually public goods like roads, national defense, and consumer regulation, meaning that they cannot be provided to one person without providing them to others as well. Public goods are systematically underproduced by private markets; because a proportion of the beneficiaries will always free-ride, private producers can never capture all the benefits of public good provision.[35] The government, which can compel all the beneficiaries to contribute through the tax system, has traditionally been the preferred supplier of public goods.

The problems of moving to a private ecosystem service provision model in the Klamath are almost insurmountable at the present time.[36] There are no easy win-win market options in the Klamath. It is unfair to make private parties provide a service if the return is only hypothetical, no matter how valuable the service may be.[37] But it is nearly impossible to give Upper Basin farmers concrete market incentives to switch their crop mix from familiar commodities to ecosystem services.

Klamath water interests can be conceptually divided into upstream "tortfeasors" and downstream "victims."[38] The tortfeasors are the Klamath irrigators, who have long, albeit never consciously, shifted the external costs of irrigation downstream. The victims are downstream tribes and commercial and recreational salmon fishermen, who have suffered lowered flows and impaired salmon runs. Upstream, the Klamath tribes and the wildlife refuges also fall into the victim category. The geographic and social isolation of the two groups, combined with the reasonable belief of each side that it holds the stronger entitlement, encourages litigation rather than the voluntary negotiation of a market solution. In the ideal world of economics, the initial assignment of property rights does not matter. The famous Coase theorem posits that, absent transaction costs, the parties will bargain to an efficient allocation of resources regardless of who has the property right.[39] The Klamath experience shows why the Coase theorem rarely applies to real natural resource conflicts. The ecosystem impacts of human actions are typically acceptable or even undetectable at low levels. As a result, expectations develop on both sides that cannot be fulfilled as pressures on the resource increase. Entitlement holders who have historically been allowed to exercise their entitlements without concern for the ecosystem resist any suggestion that they are obligated to provide ecosystem services without compensation. By the same token, though, beneficiaries accustomed to getting ecosystem services without charge resist the idea that they should suddenly purchase those services. The more entrenched the initial entitlement, psychologically or legally, the greater the resistance to negotiations. That leaves forced reallocation or "bribes" as the other available options.[40]

Forced reallocation only stiffens resistance, and bribing, although it is widely endorsed in the ecosystem services literature, raises a moral hazard problem. We briefly discussed moral hazard in chapter 7 in connection with natural disaster policy. In the ecosystem services context, it refers to the discomfort that accompanies a decision to reward people for having engaged in behaviors now deemed socially undesirable. As a leading student of ecosystem service provision has asked, "Are we not essentially paying off the bad actors and thereby encouraging undesirable behavior?"[41] While we recognize this concern, we believe that carefully structured bribes may be both necessary and fair.

Public providers of ecosystem services are in a different legal position than private ones, but the outcome is often the same. Public ownership often carries with it the discretion to dedicate land or water to ecosystem service provision but seldom the duty to do so. Because there are inevitably costs to ecosystem service provision and the benefits typically accrue to political outsiders, governments are often just as reluctant as private parties to provide ecosystem services. They may also face practical constraints. In the Klamath Basin, federal water rights holders could potentially be the major ecosystem service providers. However, as discussed in chapter 6, both the Upper Basin's wildlife refuges and the Klamath Tribe can claim federal reserved water rights that can be dedicated to service provision, but their potential to provide consistent long-term ecosystem services is limited.

From Federal to Local Control

As we have explained, we are pessimistic about the prospects that litigation alone will catalyze lasting transition in the Klamath Basin. In some situations an ecosystem services approach may provide the needed additional leverage, but not in the context of water conflicts like this one, where significant aspects of the environmental improvements sought cannot be translated into economic benefits and both sides believe (with some justification) that they hold the stronger entitlement. Although we are hardly sanguine about its prospects in the Klamath Basin, we believe bioregionalism holds more promise.

There is a long history of intense local opposition to the federal government's management of its western "colonies." High proportions of federal land in the western states give the federal government power different in kind and degree from its power in the East. In many respects, federal land law allows generous private access to public lands for commodity production, but it also selectively restricts and blocks access. Worse from the prospect of the "old West," that law can be changed in distant Washington, at the urging of easterners and environmentalists who do not bear the costs of change.

Deep resentment of federal interference with western autonomy (to give it a sympathetic spin) or with the culture of grabbing (from a less sympathetic perspective) has been part of the western landscape since the frontier era. It ebbs and flows on the political scene. The most recent flare-up began in the 1980s with the "Sagebrush Rebellion" and continued in the 1990s under the rubric of the "county supremacy movement." The demand that the federal government cede large hunks of public lands to the states has once again died down, but federal power has quietly eroded as congressional and executive support for the traditional missions of federal land management agencies has declined and no strong alternative missions have emerged. The Bureau of Reclamation has done a bit better on the national political scene than the Forest Service and the Bureau of Land Management because in places like the Klamath Basin it continues to support, rather than disrupt, local economies. But the Bureau's grand "civilizing" mission is dead. It is now a local service provider rather than the regional leader it once was.

As resource disputes have intensified in the power vacuum of a shrinking federal government, "native" westerners, from ranchers to environmentalists, have searched for alternative landscape visions. The notion that the majority of westerners, whatever their political leanings, are deeply attached to the region's unique and magnificent landscapes gave rise to the idea of place-based solutions. The idea has several variants, but at its core is the progressive conservation era heresy that westerners should be trusted to manage their landscape heritage.[42] Advocates of place-based solutions are essentially trying to adapt the ideas of the patron saint of rational western settlement, John Wesley Powell, to a modern, urban West integrated into the global economy.

Powell, the first person to navigate the Colorado River through the Grand Canyon,[43] is best known for his unsuccessful efforts to design a rational western land and water policy around the fundamental fact of aridity,[44] or more accurately of highly variable precipitation. As Powell's first biographer, Wallace Stegner, put it,

> Almost alone among his contemporaries, he looked at the Arid Region and saw neither desert nor garden. What he saw was a single compelling unity that the region possessed: except in local islanded areas its rainfall was less than twenty inches a year, and twenty inches he took, with slight modifications for the particularly concentrated rainfall in the Dakotas, to be the minimum to support agriculture without irrigation.[45]

Powell's famous *Report on the Lands of the Arid Region* concluded that only a small percentage of the West was irrigable, and thus that settlement should be limited, concentrated, and organized by cooperative irrigation districts. He pressed that claim at the Second Irrigation Congress in 1893, to the disgust and boos of the faithful. In the end, the federal government and the West rejected this early version of locally driven placed-based governance, in part because it was at the time "unpatriotic in a Westerner to admit that his country was dry."[46] Nonetheless, the legacy of Powell's proposals lie at the core of modern environmental thinking and the rhetoric of resource limits.[47]

Daniel Kemmis, a leading proponent of place-based governance, envisions the urban West's cities, supported by institutions such as watershed trusts, leading the governance of the western landscape. Place-based institutions, many of which already exist in some form, would emerge. Federal power would be partially devolved to those entities in return for "a guarantee that the land would be managed for ecosystem viability and sustainability, perhaps [even] promising that each succeeding generation would inherit healthier ecosystems than the generation before."[48] A number of stakeholder stewardship initiatives have been launched. Some, notably the Quincy (California) Library Group, have managed to convince Congress to authorize or mandate variations on traditional management practices.[49] Even there, implementation has been slow, satisfying no one. Successful examples of collaborative governance are still few on the public lands, and the list of successful aquatic ecosystem collaboration efforts is even shorter. The Klamath serves as a strong cautionary tale to this latest chapter in western romanticism.[50]

Bioregionalism and Place-Based Experimentation

As environmental historians have documented, human beings have long preferred modifying nature to adapting settlement and resource-use patterns to nature's realities. In places like the Klamath Basin, the costs of that fundamental choice to fight rather than adapt are becoming apparent. Bioregionalism is one possible response. In brief, bioregionalism begins by defining the appropriate geographic scale of management for natural systems such as river basins. Next, the stresses to the system are identified and ways to relieve those stresses detailed. The final, and most difficult, step is to devise institutions capable of implementing needed management steps at the appropriate scale.

Bioregionalism is, unfortunately, a term with many meanings. To some, it is an up-to-date version of traditional autarkical utopian arguments for returning to and living off the land.[51] As a leading proponent of this view has put it, people should become "dwellers in the land."[52] To others, bioregionalism is a management theory that actually tries to revive large-scale degraded ecosystems by putting the horse before the cart.

The Klamath is a promising place to try to implement the idea of bioregionalism. Because we are keenly aware of Wallace Stegner's conclusion that so much damage has been done to the West "that neither nostalgia nor boosterism can any longer make the case for it as a geography of hope,"[53] we favor the second, less utopian, version of bioregionalism. We are also aware, as William Rodgers has suggested, that the idea of combining a working ecosystem with an ecosystem that works may be a fatal delusion,[54] but we see no alternative to the attempt. Our version of bioregionalism strives for realism. It is conscious of the national and global connections that influence local landscapes, and it resists calling for impractical conversion of the region's residents to "deep ecology." The focus is on ecosystem health rather than local self-sufficiency and an ethic of restrained consumption. It is enough if a significant number of resource users are convinced (through either carrots or sticks) to act in ways that move the system toward revival.

The Murray-Darling Basin

The best example of bioregionalism at work can be found in the Murray-Darling Basin in Australia. The Murray-Darling is a version of the Klamath, and many other stressed western basins, writ large with the added complication of a significant rural-urban conflict. Australia is the driest continent, and its severe cycles of wet and drought years are expected to be made worse by global warming. The Murray-Darling is the commonwealth's largest river system and supplies much of the country's agriculture. Agricultural water diversions, which already place considerable stress on the system, are increasing. The environmental problems connected to agricultural withdrawals include downstream salinity at the river's mouth, where the city of Adelaide takes its water, wetlands loss, increased algal blooms, and reduced breeding and survival opportunities for native fish and waterbirds.

A federal-state commission was charged in 1992 with improving the river's health. It eventually established a series of artificial base flows after a long consultation process using three flow scenarios based on a variety of environmental and human factors including river health. The base flows recognized that the river's hydrograph has been substantially altered by dams and diversions. The commission asked two crucial questions in a far more direct way than they have been raised in the Klamath Basin: To what extent did withdrawals need to be reduced, and how could the needed reductions be fairly distributed among water users throughout the basin? In 1996, the commission announced a withdrawal cap, which became the "cornerstone of a number of policies designed to manage water resources for scarcity: water trading, environmental flows and the security of property rights."[55] The cap imposes yearly diversion limits on the four states and the Australian Capital Territory, which share the basin. Responsibility for achieving the cap rests with the states, which are much stronger under Australia's federal structure than are the U.S. states.

Achieving the cap will require many innovative management strategies, such as conjunctive use of ground and surface water, reservoir reoperation, abandonment of the "use it or lose it" tradition in the administration of water licenses, and implementation of an accounting system to balance water use over a period of time. Initially, several sub-basins in New South Wales exceeded the cap, but by 2002 a water audit showed all but one in compliance. The ultimate test of the cap will be whether it leads to reductions in claimed entitlements. The initiative is still a work in progress with uneven and incremental advancement, but the important point is that the commonwealth has consistently used a vision of a healthier river basin, initially expressed in base flows, to drive a complex restoration process. That process appears to be on track, even in the face of extreme stresses such as the 2006–7 drought.

A Short Checklist for Effective Bioregionalism

We reiterate that many in the West have lost faith in the ability of Congress and the federal resource management agencies to respond to the need for greater ecosystem conservation, and that others have always resisted federal control. From both sides, there are now constituencies for place-based solutions, hopeful that local stakeholders can agree on new, environmentally sustainable regimes. We join this group with some trepidation. We know that the earliest experiment with place-based governance of the federal lands, the Taylor Grazing Act, led to badly degraded grazing lands on which no effort was made to sustain aspects of the ecosystem without clear economic value. Mindful of that example, the strength of the status quo, and the power of human beings to engage in self-delusion, we suggest that experiments in bioregionalism must be carefully hedged. In the following paragraphs, we suggest five essential elements for such experiments.

A Federal Charter and Oversight

The first issue is whether these experiments must operate within the context of existing federal mandates or should be allowed to displace those mandates. Strong arguments for each position exist, but we argue that any solution must be consistent with existing federal laws unless Congress grants an exemption in the form of a monitored experiment. We recognize that the law may seem to present obstacles to implementation of a bioregional vision. The Clinton administration's discovery of a surprising degree of administrative flexibility in the ESA,[56] though, convinces us that it is often possible to adapt existing statutes to encourage responsible innovation. The few firm mandates that exist are often instrumental in supplying the political backbone needed to counter the status quo.[57] They should not be lightly supplanted.

One promising model comes from the Valles Caldera National Preserve and Trust in north-central New Mexico.[58] In 2000, the United States acquired 89,000 acres of a Spanish land grant, the Baca Ranch, which is surrounded by the Santa Fe National Forest and Bandelier National Monument. To manage this spectacular volcanic area, Congress created the Valles Caldera National Reserve with a unique governance structure. The reserve is managed by a trust with the mandate to preserve its scenic, cultural, watershed, and fish and wildlife resources while permitting the multiple use and sustained yield of renewable resources, primarily grazing and timber production. The nine-person board of trustees includes the superintendents of the national forest and national monument, along with seven other members with specific expertise. The trust is subject to all the laws that apply to the Forest Service, including NEPA.

Some Attention to Property Rights

The Klamath experience suggests that any process solution that is indifferent to the initial assignment and reassignment of property rights is likely to fail. The less tolerance existing entitlement holders have for increased risk, the more likely that litigation and political resistance will block innovation. The broader lesson of the focus on property rights is that any solution must candidly admit that some property rights will be reassigned. The issue of reassignment can be separated from the issue of who will pay for the reassignment.

Change in the Klamath, we hope, will come through a mix of regulation, market transactions, and private and government subsidies. Compensation for those newly required to provide ecosystem services is often the most controversial aspect of environmental law transitions. On the plus side, it is often faster and cheaper to pay than to bludgeon rights holders into submission through the legal system.[59] It may also be the fair thing to do. Property rights protect against sudden changes in policy regardless of the merits of the new policy.[60] Clearly established rights must be respected in order to protect against the ability of the majority to impose the costs of conservation on an unlucky few. The major argument against compensation is that it seems to reward past bad behavior and resistance to necessary change.[61]

As we have explained in some detail, in the Klamath and other contested water basins, the assignment of property rights is ambiguous and the identification of "antisocial" behavior hotly contested. That blunts the force of the moral arguments both for and against compensation. In general, people should be entitled to make decisions on the basis of their reasonable understanding of the legal rules in effect at the time. But that intuition must be tempered by an accompanying understanding that the world and social goals change. Property rights should not be so strong that they prevent change. The goal should be to strike a workable balance between impulsiveness, or changing the governing rules too much and too often, and inertia, or excessive resistance to change.[62] Inertia has been the operative rule, but it would be a mistake to swing too far the other direction. Change imposes real psychological as well as economic costs. Compensation should not be the only response to a crisis, but properly calibrated and appropriately tied to changes in the legal rules, it can ease the transition to a new regime that favors ecosystem revival.

Money Well Spent

The existence of firmly entrenched rights, and the political resistance that accompanies them, pushes the political branches toward solutions that carry a high risk of "suboptimization" if not outright failure. The most immediate problems are identified and patched over, often at considerable expense and with insufficient attention to long-term solutions. We have spent countless hours in meetings and conferences about ecosystem revival hearing the simple message "It's the money, stupid!" Of course it is. It took a huge investment of private and federal capital to create irrigation economies, and it will take even greater amounts—thanks to inflation—to undo even part of the damage from this social experiment. The real issue, though, is how well money is spent. The public coffers should not be opened until after specific goals and benchmarks for ecosystem improvement are adopted and there is a concrete plan for meeting those goals and evaluating progress. This is a deceptively simple suggestion, one that runs against the grain of the American system of small fixes without systematic monitoring and adaptation.

The water bank established by the Bureau of Reclamation in the wake of the 2001 crisis is an example of the usual approach. As we explained in the previous chapter, lack of monitoring makes it impossible to determine whether the considerable expense of the bank has bought the intended environmental improvement. An even more telling story of misspent money comes from a private water trust. In 2002, the Bureau of Reclamation paid a generous contributor to Senator Gordon Smith's campaign over six times the regional market value of water not to irrigate his hobby ranch. The rancher set up a nonprofit trust with a few of his neighbors and was able to sell water twice, once for not irrigating and again for the water that the pastures did not soak up![63] It is not clear if the government, or more accurately the downstream fish, actually got any increased flow from the deal. The Valles Caldera experiment holds similar risks. A recent review reported that although the trust has issued the required general framework plan, it has developed neither a process for making the inevitable trade-offs between use and preservation nor measurable restoration targets.[64]

Science-Driven Adaptive Management

Science must continue to inform water management decisions in the Klamath Basin, but it will never deliver the firm answers that all parties would like. It cannot identify a precise, perfect balance between agricultural withdrawals and basin-wide environmental protection and improvement. But we also reject the view that direct democracy in the form of citizen participation can dispense with science.[65] To close the gap between the supply of and demand for information, the currently preferred analytical tool is adaptive management, which is part theology and part science. As an early proponent observed, with perspicacity, "Adaptive management is not really much more than common sense. But common sense is not always in common use."[66]

Adaptive management was developed in the late 1970s as a response to the prevailing static model of environmental assessment. It is derived from established methods of decision analysis.[67] The basic argument was that "a fixed review of an independently designed policy" was inconsistent with the experience of resource managers worldwide that initial judgments were often later proved incorrect, and with what has come to be called nonequilibrium ecology, which points out that nature itself is not static.[68]

Adaptive management remained primarily an academic construct until the late 1980s and early 1990s, when the ESA emerged as a major barrier to a wide variety of private and public activities. The hope was that adaptive management would permit decision makers to avoid the paralysis that scientific uncertainty can create by opening a path for incremental action with the promise of progressively reducing the initial scientific uncertainty. The technique was embraced by agencies eager to approve activities that posed some risk to listed species. Adaptive management provided a "science-based" justification for allowing such activities in the face of high uncertainty, backstopped with an empty promise that corrective measures could be taken later if need be. In contrast, "true" adaptive management is a rigorous, continuous process of acquiring and evaluating scientific information.[69] Adaptive management was strongly recommended for the Klamath by the National Research Council's final 2004 report.[70]

We agree that adaptive management is necessary, but we are under no illusion that it is easy. Because it requires that management decisions be regarded as tentative and subject to change, adaptive management is inconsistent with the fundamental urge for stability that underlies property law. It cannot succeed without a long-term commitment of funding for monitoring; a scientific program with credibility in the eyes of all stakeholders, preferably backed by periodic independent review; and a common vision of the goals of management.

Structured Democracy

In chapter 7, we sketched the emerging theory of modular regulation, which tries to marry faith in scientific expertise with more democratic, or at least more responsive, decision-making processes. The Klamath offers a lesson in the pitfalls of "recreational" modularity. As early as 1995, former senator Mark Hatfield persuaded Congress to create and fund an Upper Klamath Basin Working Group to focus on ecosystem restoration, water quality enhancement, economic stability, and "drought proofing" the basin.[71] In more than a decade, despite substantial funding and high awareness of the need for change, neither that group nor elected officials in the basin or outside interests have been able to launch a useful process involving all the relevant stakeholders.

In the end, old-fashioned closed-door negotiation in which parties can cut deals without revealing fully who blinked first may offer the best hope for moving the sustainability project forward. In the spring of 2007, there was a great deal of optimism that settlement negotiations associated with the FERC hydropower relicensing mentioned in chapter 7 would help move the basin along the path to sustainability. Settlement negotiations offer an opportunity to take a broad look at the basin, to get commitment to steps that cannot be mandated by regulatory fiat, and to make trade-offs between environmental and economic goals short of consigning the listed species to jeopardy. In order to have those extra-regulatory effects, however, the negotiations must command a consensus that is difficult to maintain. By summer, some of the optimism had faded as PacifiCorp backed off some early public statements suggesting it was open to dam removal, and the coalition of environmental interests frayed. As this book goes to press, the outcome of the settlement negotiations is not yet known.

The Klamath experience teaches that the search for more flexible ways to address resource conflicts is most likely to succeed if the major parties are not deeply invested in the status quo. Entrenched entitlement holders may join such a process but have little incentive to change the status quo. Talk is not exactly cheap, especially when lawyers and experts must be hired, but the process can become an end in and of itself to the detriment of the ecosystem. In California, millions of dollars have been spent on the Bay-Delta process seeking to balance water demands with ecosystem protection. Major agricultural users were willing to talk but did not give up water rights. The ecosystem, as we previously mentioned, has continued to worsen, to the point that in late May 2007 state and federal officials temporarily shut down the pumps that send water from northern California to thirsty Los Angeles and the San Joaquin Valley. In short, there is a risk that these processes will suffer a variant of the economist's "second best" problem:[72] The new solution may be worse than what would result from the application of conventional regulation.

Nonetheless, the Klamath does suggest some guidelines for the practice of structured democracy, novel processes designed to achieve otherwise elusive substantive outcomes. First, there must always be a default decider. In the case of the Klamath, the Departments of the Interior and Commerce would continue to apply the ESA if no agreed-upon, basin-specific alternative emerged. Any departure from "normal" enforcement of the relevant statutes must produce a net environmental improvement. Second, there must be a deadline for producing an initial vision statement and a strategy for achieving it. This does not mean that the respective constituencies ultimately must accept that product, but it does mean that, by contrast with the Bay-Delta experiment, the process must put forward a vision for addressing the long-term needs of the irrigation community, the ecosystem, and the tribes.[73] At a minimum, such a plan must include performance targets and a monitoring process. Third, the participants must commit to meaningful participation, which means that existing water rights holders must be prepared at least to consider in good faith the possibility of substitutes for their entitlements. This does not mean that they must self-destruct. Rather, it means that they must be prepared to consider alternatives such as temporary fallowing; permanent, fully compensated land retirement; job retraining; and new operating plans for the Klamath Project, presented with transparent descriptions of risk distribution.

Cautious, but not Blind, Optimism

It would be tempting to end the Klamath story with the tag line from the old Looney Tunes cartoons, "That's All Folks," or just to trail off as the TV drama *The Sopranos* did. In one sense, we have no other choice, as events continue to unfold and the underlying problem of too little water to meet all competing demands remains unsolved. Still, we think it is possible to draw some lessons from this dramatic ESA-driven crisis about the practice of ecosystem management in an inhabited landscape.

As we have acknowledged throughout this volume, most of those lessons are negative. Even negative lessons are important, however, as the West struggles to strike a new balance between human use and ecosystem conservation. After all, much of history, especially environmental history, is a chronicle of mistakes made, harm done, and opportunities missed, producing learning in fits and starts.

Maintaining healthy aquatic ecosystems in working landscapes is a hard job. Glossing over the difficulties does not make it easier. It must begin with the articulation of a new vision for the landscape, one that neither enshrines forever our historical lack of concern for the environment nor reads people out of the picture. Both the vision and the strategies for achieving it must be science based but recognize the limits of science and the need for forthright value judgments. Finally, and most dauntingly, it will require the development of institutions and laws capable of taking a broader view of the landscape and empowered to make necessary trade-offs. The current overlay of environmental protection laws on the earlier resource exploitation regimes does not offer effective ways to find middle ground between the two extremes. It is probably too much to ask that Congress fund a new commission, modeled on the Public Land Law Review and National Water Commissions of a generation ago as a prelude to broadscale reform, although we would prefer that course. As a second-best solution, Congress can, as it has started to do in places like Valles Caldera and the Everglades, create place-specific governance regimes or support broad-based local initiatives for such regimes. Such experiments potentially offer the hope of combining a broad vision with correspondingly broad authority and clear lines of responsibility, although those lines must be carefully drawn so that they do not become an excuse to further insulate the status quo from change.

In sum, our examination of the Klamath conflict leaves us hopeful that ways can be found to move forward but mindful of the barriers to creating a sustainable landscape. Crisis may be necessary to motivate change, but it is not sufficient. Change will not come without a new vision, which the environmental laws that triggered the crisis do not provide.

Articulating a new vision will be a challenge, because it will require trust and compromise. All participants must be ready to surrender some of the security of the macho legal regimes on which they have relied. All must move beyond seeing science as a weapon with which to bludgeon one another, to seeing science as a shared tool for understanding trade-offs. Scientific work in the basin should be a collective effort, overseen and directed collaboratively, rather than a form of cage fighting, pitting one set of scientists or one collection of data against another. Finally, all participants must be willing to engage in political discourse and give-and-take, without crossing the line into "dirty" politics by taking advantage of their own special access to decision makers to make end runs around other participants. We hope this difficult process will begin in earnest soon, in the Klamath Basin and beyond, because we know that in the West the next drought is never far off.

Afterword

We noted in chapter 8 that the story of water conflict in the Klamath basin is an ongoing one. Events since this book went to press have confirmed that observation, while continuing to demonstrate the difficulty of ultimately resolving this sort of environmental conflict. Time has not stood still, but neither have the problems been magically resolved.

The most important, and exciting, news comes out of the hydropower negotiations we alluded to at several points. Negotiations over renewal of PacifiCorp's FERC license for the Klamath dams have produced a draft agreement calling for removal of four of those dams (Copco I, Copco II, JC Boyle, and Iron Gate).[1] The newspaper in Eureka immediately declared the Klamath water war over,[2] but that assessment comes too soon. Wars can end while the underlying causes of conflict remain to fester and trigger new conflicts in the future.

There are many positive features of the complex proposed settlement, which runs more than 250 pages. In addition to the grand compromises among the major interests, there are provisions for adaptive management and long-term monitoring. However, as skeptical lawyers and students of natural resource conflicts, we must reserve judgment for now. A series of important caveats remain. PacifiCorp is conspicuously not a party to the agreement, and has maintained publicly that it will not agree to removal unless it and its customers are made whole; the agreement will not become fully effective until its terms are incorporated into federal and state legislation; it envisions a win-win solution where fish can be restored to the upper and lower basins without taking water from irrigators; and it calls for almost $1 billion in funding over the next ten years, with no indication where that money will come from. In other words, strong political leadership is still needed to move the agreement forward, and it could fall apart if the win-win solution it envisions turns out not to be feasible.

Still, even if it does not go into effect precisely as currently set out, the draft agreement marks a milestone. It shows that the fishing communities, farming communities, tribes, and government agencies can reach broad consensus and make modest but important adjustments in the risks of future shortages, at least when none of them is directly confronting the costs. And it takes a broad view of the basin's water challenges, calling for restoration of anadromous fish to the Upper Klamath Basin, suggesting resolutions for several contentious water rights issues in the Oregon adjudication, providing for more secure water allocation to the National Wildlife Refuges, setting targets for nonproject irrigation water use in the upper basin and establishing a framework for looking into retirement of nonproject irrigated lands, and calling for advance planning on how to survive future droughts. If funding can be obtained and PacifiCorp gets on board, the agreement holds great promise for moving the basin forward.

Two other developments deserve mention, one within the Klamath Basin, the other without. Within the basin, understanding of the information needs for evaluating the effects of Klamath Project operations on anadromous fish in the Klamath River has been advanced by a new NRC report.[3] Issued late in 2007, this latest report examined the models used to estimate preproject baseline flows and predict the flows needed by the listed coho. It found that the Bureau of Reclamation's model for estimating baseline flows provided "some basis for understanding unimpaired flows" but lacked the detail needed to support management decisions and did not follow best modeling practices. The committee felt that the instream flow models used to evaluate Klamath project impacts on salmon were more scientifically credible, but still lacked needed resolution and detail. The report should improve the scientific dialogue in the basin by providing an outside perspective on the type of information needed to support credible management decisions.Outside the Klamath Basin, the next big water conflict has heated up to at least a fierce simmer, and is just on the edge of boiling over. Running through our analysis of the Klamath conflict is a brief comparison with the longer running Sacramento–San Joaquin Bay Delta process. If the Klamath is a Verdi tragedy, the Bay Delta is a Wagnerian one. The two watersheds are in fact connected; water from the Trinity River, a major tributary of the lower Klamath River, has been diverted into the Sacramento. However, the principal reason for comparison is that the Bay Delta process has been hailed as the model for the revival of stressed watersheds under the gun of the ESA. As we reported in the book, the listed species that triggered the crisis, the Bay Smelt, has continued to decline as the process was unable to reach a consensus on the necessary remedy-reduced diversions from the Delta. The Bay Delta merits a separate book, if not a multivolume history. We only report that in December, 2007, a federal district judge in California, who had earlier agreed with the Natural Resources Defense Council that the federal and state agencies had failed to protect the smelt, issued an order that requires the agencies reduce their diversions when necessary to protect the fish. On Christmas Day, 2007, one of the triggers popped and diversions to the Central Valley and southern California were halved for ten days.[4] Whether diversions can continue at or close to present levels hinges on California's increasingly uncertain winter rainfall. If the Klamath water knot has been tough to untangle, the Bay-Delta will be even tougher. Perhaps, though, the Klamath experience can point the way toward the good-faith compromises necessary to promote more sustainable watersheds, large and small. Stay tuned.

Notes

Chapter 1

1. Between October 2000 and August 2001, the basin received less than 7 inches of rain, just over half its normal rainfall—6.93 compared to 13.05 inches. Michael Milstein, "Clearing Up Water Issues in the Klamath Basin," *Portland Oregonian*, August 29, 2001.

2. A detailed description and history of the Klamath Project can be found on the Bureau of Reclamation Web site, at http://www.usbr.gov/dataweb/html/klamath.html.

3. For a history of the legal events that led to the 2001 crisis, see Reed D. Benson, "Giving Suckers (and Salmon) an Even Break: Klamath Basin Water and the Endangered Species Act," *Tulane Environmental Law Journal* 15 (2002): 197.

4. The Klamath Project has some 233,625 acres of irrigable land, but only about 210,000 of those acres were in production in 2000.

5. Jeff Head, "I Was an Eyewitness to the Stand at Klamath Falls," July 16, 2001, http://www.freerepublic.com/forum/a3b5497383a6f.htm.

6. Patrick May, "Oregon Families Wage Water War," *San Jose Mercury News*, August 22, 2001, A1.

7. "Federal Officials Leave A Canal Headgates," *Klamath Falls Herald and News*, September 26, 2001. The Bureau of Reclamation subsequently spent $750,000 to guard the headgates; in late December 2001 the bureau installed a $90,000 fence, camera, and motion detector. Associated Press, "Tight Security Goes Up around Irrigation System," *St. Louis Post-Dispatch*, January 3, 2002, A6.

8. Michael Milstein, "Raising Crops Instead of a Fuss," *Portland Oregonian*, September 9, 2001, A19.

9. The Upper Klamath Basin is a marginal agricultural area and does not contain the large corporate farms found in the Great Plains, California, and the Midwest. In 1997, the average net return per farm was $36,094, or about $34 per acre. One-third of the farms

had a net average loss of $19,139. These figures are taken from Ernie Niemi, Anne Fifield, and Ed Whitelaw, *Coping with Competition for Water* (Eugene, OR: ECONorthwest, November 2001), 12.

10. William Snape III, Michael Senatore, and John M. Carter II, "Sabotaging the Endangered Species Act: How the Bush Administration Uses the Judicial System to Undermine Wildlife Protections," report of Defenders of Wildlife, Washington, DC, Fall 2003, 23.

11. Peter Skene Ogden led the first trapper party into the area between 1826 and 1827. See Jeff LaLande, *First over the Siskiyous: Peter Skene Ogden's 1826–1827 Journey through the Oregon-California Borderlands* (Portland: Oregon Historical Society Press, 1987).

12. Ed Austin and Tom Dill, *The Southern Pacific in Oregon* (Edmonds, WA: Pacific Fast Mail, 1987).

13. U.S. Department of the Interior, *Water 2025: Preventing Crises and Conflict in the West* (Washington, DC: Author, May 5, 2003).

14. Rachel Carson, *Silent Spring* (Boston: Houghton Mifflin, 1962), 49.

15. Oregon Progress Board, *State of the Environment Report 2000* (Salem: Author, 2000), 178, http://egov.oregon.gov/DAS/OPB/soer2000index.shtml.

16. George Woodward and Jeff Romm, "A Policy Assessment of the 2001 Klamath Reclamation Project Water Allocation Decisions," in *Water Allocation in the Klamath Reclamation Project, 2001: An Assessment of Natural Resource, Economic, Social, and Institutional Issues with a Focus on the Upper Klamath Basin,* a report by Oregon State University and the University of California (Oregon State University Extension Service, Special Report 1037, reprinted May 2003), http://extension.oregonstate.edu/catalog/html/sr/sr1037/report.pdf.

17. Tupper Ansel Blake, Madeleine Graham Blake, and William Kittredge, *Balancing Water: Restoring the Klamath Basin* (Berkeley: University of California Press, 2000), 135.

18. See *Kandra v. United States*, 145 F. Supp. 2d 1192, 1197 (D. Or. 2001).

19. Oregon Department of Water Resources, *Resolving the Klamath: Special Supplement–Klamath Basin General Stream Adjudication 1999* (Salem: Author), 6.

20. *Klamath Irrigation District v. United States*, 75 Fed. Cl. 677, 688 (Ct. Cl. 2007).

21. *Clean Water Act*, U.S.C. 33 § 1362(14).

22. National Research Council, *A New Era for Irrigation* (Washington, DC: National Academy Press, 1996), 17.

23. Rebecca Clarren, "No Refuge in the Klamath Basin," *High Country News*, August 13, 2001.

24. See Robert H. Nelson, *Economics as Religion: From Samuelson to Chicago and Beyond* (University Park: Pennsylvania State University Press, 2001), 168–69.

25. National Research Council, *A New Era for Irrigation* (Washington, DC: National Academy Press, 1996), 28.

26. "The Basin and the Bay," *Washington Post*, July 28, 2004, A18.

27. The prevalence of vague legislative language acknowledging the state interest in water allocation has led to a widespread belief that federal law generally defers to state water allocation decisions. That purported deference is, as a matter of law, mythical. See David H. Getches, "The Metamorphosis of Western Water Policy: Have Federal Laws and

Local Decisions Eclipsed the States' Role?" *Stanford Environmental Law Journal* 20 (2001): 3, 6; Reed D. Benson, "Deflating the Deference Myth: National Interests versus State Authority under Federal Laws Affecting Water Use," *Utah Law Review* (2006): 241. Nonetheless, it carries undeniable political power.

28. ESA-driven litigation over groundwater pumping in the Edwards Aquifer in Texas, for example, eventually persuaded the state to abandon its historic rule of capture and regulate groundwater withdrawals for the first time, at least in this one area. See Todd H. Votteler, "Raiders of the Lost Aquifer? or The Beginning of the End to Fifty Years of Conflict over the Texas Edwards Aquifer," *Tulane Environmental Law Journal* 15 (2002): 257; Todd H. Votteler, "The Little Fish That Roared: The Endangered Species Act, State Groundwater Law, and Private Property Rights Collide over the Texas Edwards Aquifer," *Environmental Law* 28 (1998): 845.

29. Former secretary of the interior Stewart Udall describes Victor Yannacone, the first lawyer to try and stop the use of DDT, as follows: "Yannacone was a brilliant tactician, but from the beginning he had no illusions that litigation would produce resounding legal victories. His maverick motto was 'Sue the Bastards,' and he envisioned his lawsuits as show trials to dramatize environmental truths that would ultimately compel members of the legislative and executive branches of government to act. He was willing to lose court decisions if his cause prevailed in the court of public opinion." Stewart L. Udall, *The Quiet Crisis and the Next Generation* (Layton, UT: Gibbs-Smith, 1988), 224.

30. James E. Krier and Edmund Ursin, *Pollution & Policy: A Case Essay on California and Federal Experience with Motor Vehicle Air Pollution, 1940–1975* (Berkeley: University of California Press, 1977), 263–67.

31. The decision is *West Virginia Division of the Izaak Walton League of America, Inc. v. Butz*, 522 F.2d 945 (4th Cir. 1975). For a discussion of the connection between that decision and enactment of NFMA, see Charles F. Wilkinson, "The National Forest Management Act: The Twenty Years Behind, the Twenty Years Ahead," *University of Colorado Law Review* 68 (1997): 659; Oliver A. Houck, "The Water, the Trees and the Land: Three Nearly Forgotten Cases That Changed the American Landscape," *Tulane Law Review* 70 (1995): 2279.

32. Warren I. Choen, *America in the Age of Soviet Power*, vol. 4, *The Cambridge History of American Foreign Relations* (Cambridge: Cambridge University Press, 1993), 88.

33. In *Massachusetts v. EPA*, 415 F.3d 50 (D.C. Cir. 2005), for example, the court of appeals ruled that the Environmental Protection Agency is not obligated by the Clean Air Act to regulate emissions of carbon dioxide and other greenhouse gases from automobiles. That decision seems to fly in the face of the plain language of the act, which requires regulation of automobile emissions of pollutants that cause or contribute to "air pollution which may reasonably be anticipated to endanger public health or welfare" (42 U.S.C. § 7521(a)(1)). The Supreme Court reversed it in *Massachusetts v. EPA*, __ U.S. ___, 127 S. Ct. 1438 (2007).

34. *Bennett v. Spear*, 520 U.S. 154, 176 (1997).

35. Garrett Hardin, "Carrying Capacity As an Ethical Concept," *Soundings* 59 (1976): 120, http://www.garretthardinsociety.org/articles_pdf/cc_ethical_concept.pdf.

36. Count Carlo Sforza, *Italy and the Italians* (New York: E.P. Dutton, 1949), 86.

37. Ed Marston, "Reclaiming the Spirit of Reclamation," *Natural Resources Journal* 44 (2004): 681, 683.

Chapter 2

1. National Research Council, *Endangered and Threatened Fishes in the Klamath River Basin: Causes of Decline and Strategies for Recovery* (Washington, DC: National Academies Press, 2005), 46 (hereafter cited as NRC Final Report).

2. We first heard the basin described this way by UC Davis geology professor Jeff Mount.

3. David Rains Wallace, *The Klamath Knot* (San Francisco: Sierra Club Books, 1983), 23–24, 53.

4. Only 12 percent of the annual runoff in the watershed originates in the Upper Basin. Wallace, *Klamath Knot*, 52.

5. NRC Final Report, 41.

6. Marc Reisner, *Cadillac Desert: The American West and Its Disappearing Water* (New York: Viking, 1986), 277.

7. Samuel F. Dicken and Emily Dicken, *The Legacy of Ancient Lake Modoc: A Historical Geography of the Klamath Lakes Basin* (Eugene: University of Oregon Bookstore, 1985).

8. Kenneth Rykbost, "Water Resources," in *Water Allocation in the Klamath Reclamation Project, 2001* (Oregon State University Extension Service, Special Report 1037, reprinted May 2003), http://extension.oregonstate.edu/catalog/html/sr/sr1037/report.pdf.

9. Agriculture is the only important consumptive use of water in the basin, accounting for more than 95 percent of total consumptive use. See U.S. Department of the Interior, Bureau of Reclamation, *Final Biological Assessment: The Effects of Proposed Actions Related to Klamath Project Operation (April 1, 2002–March 31, 2012) on Federally-Listed Threatened and Endangered Species* (Washington, DC: Author, February 25, 2002), 25 (hereafter cited as *Final 2002 Biological Assessment*).

10. Harry L. Carlson et al., "Soil Resources in the Klamath Reclamation Project," in *Water Allocation in the Klamath Reclamation Project, 2001* (Oregon State University Extension Service, Special Report 1037, reprinted May 2003), http://extension.oregonstate.edu/catalog/html/sr/sr1037/report.pdf.

11. Mark Clark and Earl D. Miller, "Notes on Early Water Use in the Klamath Basin," in *A River Never the Same: A History of Water in the Klamath Basin* (Klamath Falls: Shaw Historical Library, Oregon Institute of Technology, 1999), 19.

12. U.S. Fish and Wildlife Service, *Klamath Basin National Wildlife Refuges, California / Oregon* (Washington, DC: Department of the Interior, 1999), 3.

13. Ibid., 4.

14. Ibid., 2.

15. Blake, Blake, and Kittredge, *Balancing Water*, 128.

16. Carlson et al., "Soil Resources."

17. Blake, Blake, and Kittredge, *Balancing Water*, 26.

18. Woodward and Romm, "A Policy Assessment."

19. NRC Final Report, 191.

20. U.S. Fish and Wildlife Service, "Determination of Endangered Status for the Shortnose Sucker and Lost River Sucker," *Federal Register* 53 (1998): 27130, 27131 (hereafter cited as Sucker Listing).

21. E. D. Cope, "On the Fishes of the Recent and Pliocene Lakes of the Western

Part of the Great Basin, and of the Idaho Pliocene Lake," *Proceedings of the Academy of Natural Sciences of Philadelphia*, 35 (1884): 134. Cited in U.S. Fish and Wildlife Service, Klamath Falls, "Formal Consultation on the Effects of the Long-Term Operation of the Klamath Project on the Lost River Sucker, Shortnose Sucker, Bald Eagle, and American Peregrine Falcon," July 22, 1992.

22. C. H. Gilbert, "The Fishes of the Klamath Basin," *Bulletin of the U.S. Fish Commission* 17 (1898): 1, http://www.krisweb.com/biblio/klamath_usfc_gilbert_1898.pdf.

23. Sucker Listing, 27131.

24. See Peter D. Nichols, Megan K. Murphy, and Douglas S. Kenney, *Water and Growth in Colorado: A Review of Legal and Policy Issues* (Boulder: Natural Resources Law Center, University of Colorado School of Law, 2001), 1–4.

25. See Denise Lach et al., "Effects of the 2001 Water Allocation Decisions on Project-Area Communities," in *Water Allocation in the Klamath Reclamation Project, 2001* (Oregon State University Extension Service, Special Report 1037, reprinted May 2003), http://extension.oregonstate.edu/catalog/html/sr/sr1037/report.pdf.

26. Bruce Weber and Bruce Sorte, "The Upper Klamath Basin Economy and the Role of Agriculture," in *Water Allocation in the Klamath Reclamation Project, 2001* (Oregon State University Extension Service, Special Report 1037, reprinted May 2003), http://extension.oregonstate.edu/catalog/html/sr/sr1037/report.pdf.

27. Weber and Sorte, "Upper Klamath Basin Economy," 7. The significance of the current agricultural base is discussed in the next section.

28. See Niemi, Fifield, and Whitelaw, *Coping with Competition*, 15.

29. Niemi, Fifield, and Whitelaw, *Coping with Competition*, 9. Of those irrigated farms, 1,400 are irrigated by the Klamath Project; irrigated acres represent only about a fourth of total farm acreage, but they are the most productive acres. Weber and Sorte, "Upper Klamath Basin Economy," 10, 12.

30. Weber and Sorte, "Upper Klamath Basin Economy," 16.

31. See A. Dan Tarlock, "Can Cowboys Become Indians? Protecting Western Communities as Endangered Cultural Remnants," *Arizona State Law Journal* 31 (1999): 539.

32. Mark Sagoff, *Price, Principle, and the Environment* (Cambridge: Cambridge University Press, 2004), 12.

33. The philosophical basis of individual versus group rights is explored in Vernon Van Dyke, "The Individual, the State, and Ethnic Communities in Political Theory," in *The Rights of Minority Cultures*, ed. Will Kymilca, 31 (Oxford, England: Oxford University Press).

34. Wallace, *Klamath Knot*, 13.

35. Frances Turner McBeth, *Lower Klamath Country* (Berkeley, CA: Anchor Press, 1950).

36. These numbers come from the U.S. Census Bureau's Web site, http://censtats.census.gov.

37. D. H. Wagner, "Klamath-Siskiyou Region, California and Oregon, U.S.A.," in *Centres of Plant Diversity*, vol. 3, *The Americas*, ed. S. D. Davis, V. H. Heywood, O. Herrera-MacBryde, J. Villa-Lobos, and A. C. Hamilton, 74–76 (Oxford, England: Information Press, 1977).

38. Wallace, *Klamath Knot*, 6.

39. As Wallace puts it, "Miners ransacked the Klamaths as violently as they did the

Mother Lode in the Sierra. . . . Many river beds are now undulating heaps of cobbles left by big companies that washed away entire bluffs with giant hoses and extracted millions of dollars worth of gold." *Klamath Knot*, 28.

40. The Klamath Basin was "the third most important salmon producing river system in the nation, producing an estimated 660,000 to 1,100,000 adult fish annually." Water Management and Endangered Species Issues in the Klamath Basin: Oversight Field Hearing Before the Committee on Resources, U.S. House of Representatives, One Hundred Seventh Congress, First Session, June 16, 2001, in Klamath Falls, Oregon, Statement of William F. "Zeke" Grader Jr. on Behalf of the Pacific Coast Federation of Fishermen's Associations, http://frwebgate.access.gpo.gov/cgi-bin/getdoc.cgi?dbname=107_house_hearings&docid=f:73135.pdf.

41. Blake, Blake, and Kittredge, *Balancing Water*, 35.

42. NRC Final Report, 250–52.

43. Peter B. Moyle, *Inland Fishes of California* (Berkeley: University of California Press, rev. exp. ed., 2002), 245–47.

44. NRC Final Report, 254–55.

45. Ibid., 256.

46. Ibid.

47. Moyle, *Inland Fishes*, 250.

48. National Research Council, *Scientific Evaluation of Biological Opinions on Endangered and Threatened Fishes in the Klamath River Basin* (Washington, DC: National Academy Press), 17.

49. Larry R. Brown, Peter B. Moyle, and Ronald M. Yoshiyama, "Historical Decline and Current Status of Coho Salmon in California," *North American Journal of Fisheries Management* 14 (1994): 237, 241–43.

50. Moyle, *Inland Fishes*, 252.

51. NRC Final Report, 263–64.

52. Ibid., 268; John O. Snyder, "Salmon of the Klamath River, California," *Fish Bulletin* no. 34 (Division of Fish and Game of California, 1931), http://www.krisweb.com/biblio/klamath_cdfg_snyder_1931.pdf.

53. NRC Final Report, 264.

54. Ibid., 265.

55. Department of Commerce, National Oceanic and Atmospheric Administration, "Proposed Endangered Status for Two Chinook Salmon ESUs and Proposed Threatened Status for Five Chinook Salmon ESUs; Proposed Redefinition, Threatened Status, and Revision of Critical Habitat for One Chinook Salmon ESU; Proposed Designation of Chinook Salmon Critical Habitat in California, Oregon, Washington, Idaho," *Federal Register* 63 (1998): 11482, 11487–88.

56. Carlos M. Gutierrez, "Declaration Concerning the Klamath River Fall Chinook Salmon Fishery," August 10, 2006, http://www.commerce.gov/opa/press/Secretary_Gutierrez/2006_Releases/August/Klamath.pdf.

57. NRC Final Report, 270–71.

58. Peggy J. Busby, Thomas C. Wainwright, and Robin S. Waples, "Status Review for Klamath Mountains Province Steelhead," NOAA Technical Memorandum NMFS-NWFSC-19 (December 1994), http://www.nwfsc.noaa.gov/publications/techmemos/tm19/tm19.html.

59. Moyle, *Inland Fishes*, 110.

60. Wallace, *Klamath Knot*, 55.

61. Moyle, *Inland Fishes*, 111.

62. U.S. Department of Commerce, National Oceanic and Atmospheric Administration, "Threatened Status for Southern Distinct Population Segment of North American Green Sturgeon," *Federal Register* 71 (2006): 17757.

63. Wallace, *Klamath Knot*, 57.

64. David A. Close, Martin S. Fitzpatrick, and Hiram W. Li, "The Ecological and Cultural Importance of a Species at Risk of Extinction, Pacific Lamprey," *Fisheries* 27 (2002): 19.

65. Moyle, *Inland Fishes*, 97.

66. McBeth, *Lower Klamath Country*, 48–50.

67. Ibid., 51.

68. See http://swr.nmfs.noaa.gov/fmd/bill/land_06.htm.

69. Glen Spain, "Public Property Rights Must Prevail," *Environmental Forum* (March/April 2002): 50.

70. Pacific Fishery Management Council, *Review of 2004 Ocean Salmon Fisheries* (Portland, OR: Author, 2005), 117.

71. California Board of Equalization, "California Timber Harvest Statistics," http://www.boe.ca.gov/proptaxes/pdf/harvyr2.pdf.

72. See U.S. Department of Commerce, National Oceanic and Atmospheric Administration, "Natural Resource Damage Assessments under the Oil Pollution Act of 1990," *Federal Register* 58 (1993): 4610 (including as Appendix I the Report of the NOAA Panel on Contingent Valuation).

73. Aaron J. Douglas and Andrew Sleeper, "Estimating Recreational Trip Related Benefits for the Klamath River Basin with TCM and Contingent Use Data," http://www.krisweb.com/biblio/klamath_usgs_douglasetal_xxxx_economics.pdf.

74. National Park Service, Public Use Statistics Office, *Statistical Abstract*, 2006 (Denver: Author, undated), 13, http://www2.nature.nps.gov/stats/abst2006.pdf.

75. One of many examples is the salmon and tuna boat captain out of Port Angeles, Washington, who explained to a researcher, "You've heard of the expression . . . 'being called to the sea'? That's exactly what I had. . . . When I get away from the water, anyplace, I feel like I'm landlocked. I've gotta be near the water." Charlene J. Allison, "Women Fishermen in the Pacific Northwest," in *To Work and to Weep: Women in Fishing Economies*, ed. Jane Nadel-Klein and Dona Lee Davis, 230, 234 (St. John's, Newfoundland, Canada: Institute of Social and Economic Research, 1988).

76. Indeed, people may be, or may have been in the past, drawn to fishing by the perception that it is largely unregulated, a haven for the paradigmatic western values of independence and self-reliance. Benjamin G. Blount, "Perceptions of Legitimacy in Conflict between Commercial Fishermen and Regulatory Agencies," in *Values at Sea: Ethics for the Marine Environment*, ed. Dorinda G. Dallmeyer, 127, 129 (Athens: University of Georgia Press, 2003).

77. Jack Sutton, *The Mythical State of Jefferson: A Pictorial History of Early Northern California and Southern Oregon* (Medford, OR: Josephine County Historical Society, 1965), 58.

78. Sutton, *The Mythical State*, 1–3.

Chapter 3

1. *Coffin v. Left Hand Ditch Co.*, 6 Colo. 443 (1882).

2. The Mormon settlement of the intermountain west was a carefully planned, collective process. Irrigation was a central part because of the aridity of the region and the relative scarcity of arable land. Leonard J. Arrington and Davis Britton, *The Mormon Experience: A History of the Latter-Day Saints* (New York: Knopf, 1979), 109–26.

3. *Lux v. Haggin*, 69 Cal. 255 (Cal. 1886); *Hough v. Porter*, 51 Or. 318 (Or. 1909).

4. Oregon Revised Statutes § 539.010.

5. *Hough v. Porter*.

6. *California Oregon Power Co. v. Beaver Portland Cement Co.*, 295 U.S. 142 (1935).

7. Between 1996 and 1998, author Tarlock was the principal report writer for the Western Water Policy Review Advisory Commission. He urged the states to reconsider the whole idea of deference in light of the rise of environmental programs such as the Clean Water Act and the Endangered Species Act, which do not defer to state water law. A modified version of his initial language survives in Western Water Policy Review Advisory Commission, *Water in the West: The Challenge for the Next Century* (Denver, CO: Author, 1998), 3-38–3-39.

8. Robert Dunbar, *Forging New Rights in Western Waters* (Lincoln: University of Nebraska Press, 1983).

9. James R. Kluger, *Turning On Water with a Shovel—The Career of Elwood Mead* (Albuquerque: University of New Mexico Press, 1992).

10. Elwood Mead, "Recollections of Irrigation Legislation in Wyoming," in *Selected Writings of Elwood Mead on Water Administration in Wyoming and the West* (Cheyenne: Wyoming State Engineer's Office and Wyoming Water Association, 2000), http://seo.state.wy.us/PDF/FinalMeadBooklet.pdf.

11. Kluger, *Turning On Water*, 3–26. Mead was given the opportunity to develop irrigation colonies in Australia and California. He had some initial success in both places, but the California settlements did not take. Ibid., 14–73. He had more success in Australia due to the strong support of the state of Victoria. John Rutherford, "The Interplay of American and Australian Ideas for Development of Water Projects in Northern Victoria," *Annals of the Association of American Geographers* 54 (1964): 88.

12. Kluger, *Turning On Water*, 33.

13. Wells A. Hutchins, *Water Rights Laws in the Nineteen Western States*, vol. 2 (Washington, DC: Department of Agriculture, Economic Research Service, Natural Resource Economics Division, 1974), 2–14.

14. Oregon Revised Statutes §§ 539.230 to 539.240.

15. Reed Marbut, "Legal Aspects of Upper Klamath Basin Adjudication" in *Water Allocation in the Klamath Reclamation Project, 2001*, 75, 77 (Oregon State University Extension Service, Special Report 1037, reprinted May 2003), http://extension.oregonstate.edu/catalog/html/sr/sr1037/report.pdf.

16. Klamath River Basin Compact, Article III.

17. Klamath River Basin Compact, Article III(B)(3).

18. John E. Thorson, Ramsey Laursoo Kropf, Dar Crammond, and Andrea Gerlack, "Dividing Western Waters: A Century of Adjudicating Rivers and Streams," *University of Denver Water Law Review* 8 (2005): 355, 413–14.

19. American Bar Association, *Environment, Energy, and Resources Law: The Year in Review 2000* (Chicago: Author, 2001), 154.

20. Marbut, "Legal Aspects," 87.

21. *United States v. State of Oregon Water Resources Department*, 44 F.3d 758 (9th Cir. 1994).

22. Quoted in Debra L. Donahue, *The Western Range Revisited: Removing Livestock from Public Lands to Conserve Biodiversity* (Norman: University of Oklahoma Press, 1999), 24.

23. The ideological, political, and economic forces that came together to overcome opposition to a federal reclamation program are traced in Donald J. Pisani, *Water and American Government: The Reclamation Bureau, National Water Policy, and the West, 1902–1935* (Berkeley: University of California Press, 2002), 1–29.

24. Pisani, *Water and American Government*, 279.

25. See Kevin Starr, *Material Dreams: Southern California through the 1920s* (New York: Oxford University Press, 1990).

26. Pisani, *Water and American Government*, 2.

27. Frederick Merk, *History of the Westward Movement* (New York: Knopf, 1978), 508.

28. 28 Stat. 372, 43 U.S.C. §§ 641 et seq.

29. President's Water Resources Policy Commission, *Water Resources Law* (Washington, DC: U.S. Government Printing Office, 1950), 181.

30. Pisani, *Water and American Government*, 51.

31. Frederick H. Newell, *Irrigation in the United States* (New York: T.Y. Crowell, 1902), 406.

32. 43 U.S.C. § 372-600e.

33. Blake, Blake, and Kittredge, *Balancing Water*, 51.

34. NRC Final Report, 53.

35. Paul W. Gates, *History of Public Land Law Development* (Washington, DC: U.S. Government Printing Office,1968), 321.

36. Clark and Miller, "Notes on Early Water Use," 27.

37. Ibid.

38. See Act of February 9, 1905, 33 Stat. 714 (1903–1905).

39. Donald J. Pisani, *To Reclaim a Divided West: Water, Law, and Public Policy, 1848–1902* (Albuquerque: University of New Mexico Press, 1992), 30.

40. Marbut, "Legal Aspects." However, one company, the Van Brimmer Ditch Company, remained independent and secured a contractual right to have its pre-project vested water right served by the project. Clark and Miller, "Notes on Early Water Use," 33.

41. Clark and Miller, "Notes on Early Water Use," 38–39.

42. *Kansas v. Colorado*, 206 U.S. 46 (1907).

43. Eric A. Stone, "Construction of the Klamath Project," in *A River Never the Same: A History of Water in the Klamath Basin* (Klamath Falls: Shaw Historical Library, Oregon Institute of Technology, 1999), 43, 46.

44. Because these lakes were navigable under federal law, title to their beds had passed to the states upon admission to the Union under the "equal footing" doctrine.

45. Woodward and Romm, "A Policy Assessment."

46. Joseph L. Sax, "Federal Reclamation Law," in *Waters and Water Rights: A*

Treatise on the Law of Waters and Allied Problems: Eastern, Western, and Federal (Indianapolis, IN: A. Smith, 1967), 121.

47. See generally Thomas Capek, *The Cechs (Bohemians) in America* (New York: AMS Press, 1969).

48. Dorothy Swaine Thomas and Richard S. Nishimoto, *Spoilage: Japanese-American Evacuation and Resettlement During World War II* (Berkeley: University of California Press, 1946).

49. *Final 2002 Biological Assessment*, 26.

50. William K. Jaeger, "Water Allocation Alternatives for the Upper Klamath Basin," in Water Allocation in the Klamath Reclamation Project, 2001 (Oregon State University Extension Service, Special Report 1037, reprinted May 2003), http://extension.oregonstate.edu/catalog/html/sr/sr1037/report.pdf.

51. Niemi, Fifield, and Whitelaw, *Coping with Competition*, 10.

52. Ibid., 11. The Western Water Policy Review Advisory Commission estimated in 1998 that across the West about 54 percent of water withdrawn for irrigation was consumed by crops. *Water in the West*, 2-24.

53. Keith O. Fuglie, "International Potato Marketing: North American Perspective," paper presented at the Symposium on Potato Storage, Processing and Marketing, Global Conference on the Potato, New Delhi, India, December 9, 1999.

54. In fact, those facilities had departed before 2001, and many farmers had not planted potatoes in 2000.

55. U.S. Department of the Interior, Fish and Wildlife Service, "Integrated Pest Management Plan for the Lower Klamath and Tule Lake NWRs" (draft, 1997), http://library.fws.gov/Pubs1/IPM/intropest.html.

56. Pisani, *Water and American Government*, 59.

57. Weber and Sorte, "Upper Klamath Basin Economy," 221 .

58. Glen Martin, "The California Water Wars: Water Flowing to Farms, not Fish," *San Francisco Chronicle*, October 23, 2005, A15.

59. Weber and Sorte, "Upper Klamath Basin Economy," 221.

60. Martin, "California Water Wars," A15.

61. Renee Sharp and Simona Carini, *Double Dippers: How Big Ag Taps Into Taxpayers' Pockets—Twice* (Washington, DC: Environmental Working Group, 2005).

62. U.S. Fish and Wildlife Service, "Biological/Conference Opinion Regarding the Effects of Operation of the U.S. Bureau of Reclamation's Proposed 10-Year Operation Plan for the Klamath Project and Its Effect on the Endangered Lost River Sucker (*Delistes luxatus*), Endangered Shortnose Sucker (*Chamistes brevirostris*), Threatened Bald Eagle (*Haliaeetus leucocephalus*) and Proposed Critical Habitat for the Lost River and Shortnose Suckers" (Klamath Falls, OR, 2002), 21 (hereafter cited as 2002 Sucker BiOp). See http://www.usbr.gov/mp/mp150/envdocs/kbao/Final_2002_KPOP_BO.pdf.

63. See *Kandra v. United States*, 145 F. Supp. 2d 1192.

64. *Final 2002 Biological Assessment*, 22.

65. Ibid., 24.

66. U.S. Department of the Interior, Bureau of Reclamation, Klamath Project Historic Operation (November 2000), 17, 23. See http://www.usbr.gov/mp/kbao/docs/Historic%20Operation.pdf.

67. *Final 2002 Biological Assessment* (p. 28) recommended a screen, and in 2003

the bureau completed a screen, which diverts fish into a pumping system and deposits them on the west shore of Upper Klamath Lake.

68. U.S. Department of the Interior, Bureau of Reclamation, Klamath Project Historic Operation (November 2000), 24.

69. PacifiCorp's Klamath River hydroelectric operations are currently undergoing FERC relicensing. The implications of that process are further discussed in chapter 7.

70. See *Final 2002 Biological Assessment*, 34.

71. Kenneth A. Rykbost and Rodney Todd, "An Overview of the Klamath Reclamation Project and Related Upper Klamath Basin Hydrology," in *Water Allocation in the Klamath Reclamation Project, 2001*, 45, 62 (Oregon State University Extension Service, Special Report 1037, reprinted May 2003), http://extension.oregonstate.edu/catalog/html/sr/sr1037/report.pdf.

72. Oregon Revised Statutes § 757.227. This law does not name the Klamath Basin as its target, but it applies only to rate increases imposed on those customers who had enjoyed stable rates since before 1960.

73. Public Utility Commission of Oregon, In the Matter of Pacific Power & Light (dba PacifiCorp), Request for a General Rate Increase in the Company's Oregon Annual Revenues (Klamath River Basin Irrigator Rates), Order No. 06-172, April 12, 2006.

74. Federal Energy Regulatory Commission, Order Denying Petition for Declaratory Order and Issuing Notice of Proposed Readjustment of Annual Charges for the Use of a Government Dam, Project Nos. 2082-039 and 2082-040, 114 FERC ¶ 61,051 (January 20, 2006); Order Denying Rehearing, Project No. 2082-041 (April 20, 2006).

75. Richard N. L. Andrews, *Managing the Environment, Managing Ourselves: A History of American Environmental Policy* (New Haven, CT: Yale University Press, 1999), 202.

76. See generally Jack A. Stanford et al., "A General Protocol for Restoration of Regulated Rivers," *Regulated Rivers—Research & Management* 12 (1996): 391.

77. See generally Chris Bromley, "A Political and Legal Analysis of the Rise and Fall of Western Dams and Reclamation Projects," *University of Denver Water Law Review* 5 (2001): 204; Christine A. Klein, "On Dams and Democracy," *Oregon Law Review* 78 (1999): 641.

78. See National Research Council, *The Missouri River Ecosystem: Exploring the Prospects for Recovery* (Washington, DC: National Academy Press, 2002), 58–62, for a description of the ecosystem benefits provided by the flood pulses on the Missouri prior to the construction of six main-stem dams from the 1940s through the 1960s.

79. Walter E. Hecox and E. Patrick Holmes III, eds., *The 2004 Colorado College State of the Rockies Report Card* (Colorado Springs: Colorado College Rockies Project, 2004), 13, http://www.coloradocollege.edu/stateoftherockies/04Reportcard/2004ReportCard.pdf.

80. Transcription of Klamath Project Tour hosted by Bureau of Reclamation for Humboldt State University, September 11, 2003, http://www.klamathbasincrisis.org/tours/humboldtprojtour/toc.htm.

Chapter 4

1. Dale D. Goble and Eric T. Freyfogle, *Wildlife Law: Cases and Materials* (New York: Foundation Press, 2002), 832.

2. 44 Stat. 187 (1900).

3. Charles Wilkinson, *American Indians, Time, and the Law* (New Haven, CT: Yale University Press, 1987). The Rehnquist Supreme Court was much more hostile to Indian tribal rights than previous supreme courts because of its hostility to preferential treatment for racial minorities and its veneration of states' autonomy. David H. Getches, "Beyond Indian Law: The Rehnquist Court's Pursuit of States' Rights, Color-Blind Justice and Mainstream Values," *Minnesota Law Review* 86 (2001): 267.

4. *Worchester v. Georgia*, 31 U.S. 515, 555 (1832).

5. That attitude persisted despite the fact that the Klamaths sometimes traded food for Modoc slaves. Philip L. Fradkin, *The Seven States of California: A Human and Natural History* (New York: H. Holt, 1995), 124.

6. See Francis Paul Prucha, *The Great Father: The United States Government and the American Indians* (Lincoln: University of Nebraska Press, 1984), 536–38.

7. See Brian W. Dippie, *The Vanishing American: White Attitudes and U.S. Indian Policy* (Middletown, CT: Wesleyan University Press, 1982).

8. Clarence Hill, "The History of Early Irrigation in the Klamath Basin," in Clifford Miller, *History of the Pacific Northwest* (1958), 3. Cited in Clark and Miller, "Notes on Early Water Use," 4. See also Mark Clark and Earl D. Miller, "Notes on Early Water Use in the Klamath Basin," *Journal of the Shaw Historical Library* 13 (1999): 19.

9. See Arthur Quinn, *Hell with the Fire Out: A History of the Modoc War* (Boston: Faber & Faber, 1988).

10. Quinn, *Hell with the Fire Out*, is the most complete history of the war.

11. Prucha, *Great Father*, 1015–66.

12. D. W. Meinig, *The Shaping of America: A Geographical Perspective on 500 Years of History*, vol. 3, *Transcontinental America, 1850–1915* (New Haven: Yale University Press, 1998), 172.

13. 24 Stat. 388 (1887).

14. Dippie, *Vanishing American*.

15. Charles Wilkinson, *Blood Struggle: The Rise of Modern Nations* (New York: Norton, 2005), 77–78.

16. Klamath Tribes, "Termination of the Tribes," http://www.klamathtribes.org/TerminationStatement.html.

17. Wilkinson, *Blood Struggle*, 79. See Patrick Haynal, "Termination and Tribal Survival: The Klamath Tribes of Oregon," *Oregon History Quarterly* 101 (2000): 217.

18. Act of August 13, 1954, as amended, 68 Stat. 718, 25 U.S.C. §§ 564–564x.

19. Emphasis supplied.

20. Wilkinson, *Blood Struggle*, 83.

21. Prucha, *Great Father*, 1054–56.

22. 25 U.S.C. § 564w-1.

23. Klamath Indian Tribe Restoration Act, 25 U.S.C. § 566.

24. Michael Milstein, "U.S. Will Negotiate with Tribe," *Portland Oregonian*, March 20, 2002, A1.

25. Arthur F. McEvoy, *The Fisherman's Problem: Ecology and Law in the California Fisheries, 1850–1980* (New York: Cambridge University Press, 1986), 25.

26. McEvoy, *Fisherman's Problem*, 42, 51–61.

27. The story is told by Mr. Justice Harry Blackmun in *Mattz v. Arnett*, 412 U.S. 481 (1973).

28. The history of the Lower Basin tribes is concisely related in two judicial opinions: *Mattz v. Arnett*, 412 U.S. 481, and *Karuk Tribe of California v. Ammon*, 209 F.3d 1366 (Fed. Cir. 2000).

29. Act of March 8, 1853, 10 Stat. 238 (1851–1855).

30. *Karuk Tribe of California v. Ammon*, 209 F.3d 1366, 1371–72.

31. *United States v. Forty-Eight Pounds of Rising Star Tea*, 35 Fed. 403 (N.D. Cal. 1888), aff'd 38 Fed. 400 (C.C. N.D. Cal. 1889).

32. *Mattz v. Arnett*, 412 U.S. 481, 493–94.

33. Act of June 17, 1892, 27 Stat. 52 (1891–1893).

34. Hoopa-Yurok Settlement Act, Public Law 100-580, 102 Stat. 2924 (1988).

35. 25 U.S.C. § 1300i-5.

36. *Karuk Tribe of California v. Ammon*, 209 F.3d 1366.

37. 21 U.S. 543 (1823).

38. *Tee-Hit-Ton Indians v. United States*, 348 U.S. 272 (1955).

39. *Hoopa Valley Tribe v. Special Trustee, Interior Board of Indian Appeals*, Docket No. IBIA 07-90-A (April 20, 2007).

40. See John M. Glionna, "Rural Tribe Gives New Meaning to 'Wireless,'" *Portland Oregonian*, August 12, 2001, A25. Cited in Robert J. Miller, "Economic Development in Indian Country: Will Capitalism or Socialism Succeed?" *Oregon Law Review* 80 (2001): 757, 759n3.

41. This idea is clearly articulated in Australia's recent aboriginal rights jurisprudence. *Mabo v. Queensland* (1992) 175 *Commonwealth Law Reports* 1.

42. *Winters v. United States*, 207 U.S. 564 (1908).

43. See Norris Hundley, "The Winters Decision and Indian Water Rights: A Mystery Reexamined," *Western History Quarterly* 13 (1982): 17; and John Shurts, *Indian Reserved Water Rights: The Winters Doctrine and Its Social and Legal Context* (Norman: University of Oklahoma Press, 2000).

44. In *A Final Promise: The Campaign to Assimilate the Indians 1888–1920* (Lincoln: University of Nebraska Press, 1984), 171, Frederick E. Hoxie argues that the decision is contrary to the fundamental assumption of Social Darwinistic assimilation: Indians who could not prosper under white rules deserved to have their resources shifted to the superior whites.

45. *In re the General Adjudication of All Rights to Use Water in The Gila River System and Source*, 201 Ariz. 307, 35 P.3d 68 (Ariz. 2001).

46. *United States v. Adair*, 723 F.2d 1394 (9th Cir. 1983).

47. *Adair*, 723 F.2d 1394.

48. 25 U.S.C. § 564m.

49. The rights of non-Indian allottees had been previously recognized in *Colville Confederated Tribes v. Walton*, 647 F.2d 42 (9th Cir. 1981).

50. Reed D. Benson, "Maintaining the Status Quo: Permitting Established Water Uses in the Pacific Northwest, Despite the Rules of Prior Appropriation," *Environmental Law* 28 (1998): 881, 891–93.

51. *United States v. Adair*, 187 F. Supp. 2d 1273, 1276 (D. Or. 2002). This decision was subsequently vacated by the Ninth Circuit, which ruled that the district court should have waited for a definitive ruling in the Oregon adjudication. While it is not currently binding law, the district court's decision signals the likely outcome of a challenge should the Oregon adjudication adopt the standard proposed.

52. 43 U.S.C. §666(a). For a history of the amendment, see John E. Thorson et al., "Dividing Western Waters: A Century of Adjudicating Rivers and Streams, Part II," *University of Denver Water Law Review* 9 (2006): 303, 452–59.

53. *United States v. District Court for Eagle County*, 401 U.S. 529 (1971).

54. *Colorado River Water Conservation Dist. v. United States*, 424 U.S. 800 (1976). *Arizona v. San Carlos Apache Tribe*, 463 U.S. 545 (1981), extended *Colorado River*'s dubious holding to states that had disclaimed all rights to Indian lands. See also *United States v. Oregon*, 44 F.3d 758 (9th Cir. 1994).

55. Michael C. Blumm, David H. Becker, and Joshua D. Smith, "The Mirage of Indian Reserved Water Rights and Western Streamflow Restoration in the McCarran Amendment Era: A Promise Unfulfilled," *Environmental Law* 36 (2006): 1157, 1161.

56. Indian tribes around the explosively growing Phoenix metropolitan area have benefited from Indian water rights settlements that give them the authority to transfer water to non-Indian urban use. See John Thorson, Sarah Britton, and Bonnie Colby, eds., *Tribal Water Rights: Essays in Contemporary Law, Policy and Economics* (Tucson: University of Arizona Press, 2006).

57. *Parravano v. Babbitt*, 70 F.3d 539, 543 (9th Cir. 1995).

58. *Parravano* 70 F.3d 539.

59. Kari Marie Norgaard, "The Effects of Altered Diet on the Health of the Karuk People: A Preliminary Report," report prepared for the Karuk Tribe of California, Department of Natural Resources Water Quality Program, August 2004, http://www.klamathwaterquality.com/Norgaard_%20Health%20Effects%20of%20Altered%20Diet.pdf.

60. Eric Posner, "Agencies Should Ignore Distant-Future Generations," *University of Chicago Law Review* 74 (2006): 139, 143.

61. "Fishing Rights of the Yurok and Hoopa Valley Tribes," Department of the Interior, Solicitor's Memorandum M-36979, October 4, 1993, 29.

62. Order, *Pacific Coast Federation of Fishermen's Associations v. U.S. Bureau of Reclamation*, Civ. No. C 02-02006 SBA, March 8, 2005, http://www.klamathbasincrisis.org/pdf-files/pcffayurokOrder%20030905.pdf.

63. Act of March 10, 1934, ch. 55, § 2, 48 Stat. 401 (codified as amended at 16 U.S.C. § 661–667e).

64. Act of March 10, 1934, § 3(b).

65. Michael J. Bean and Melanie J. Rowland, *The Evolution of National Wildlife Law*, 3rd ed. (Westport, CT: Praeger, 1997), 405.

66. Act of Aug. 14, 1946, ch. 965, 60 Stat. 1080 (1946).

67. Public Law 85-624, 72 Stat. 563 (1958).

68. 16 U.S.C. § 661.

69. 16 U.S.C. § 662(b).

70. Public Law 89-304, 79 Stat. 1125 (1965).

71. 16 U.S.C. § 797(e).

72. *Udall v. Federal Power Commission*, 387 U.S. 428 (1967).

73. Michael C. Blumm, "Saving Idaho's Salmon: A History of Failure and a Dubious Future," *Idaho Law Review* 28 (1991–92): 667.

74. Joel C. Baiocchi, "Use It or Lose It: California Fish and Game Code Section 5937 and Instream Fishery Resources," *UC Davis Law Review* 14 (1980): 431, 433–34. Oddly, a 1915 amendment imposed the "good condition" requirement only on dams with fishways. In 1937, it was broadened to cover "any dam."

75. McEvoy, *Fisherman's Problem*, 176–77.

76. This discussion draws on "Iron Gate Dam, Its Effect on the Klamath River Fisheries," the transcript of a meeting of the Subcommittee on Fish and Game of the California Senate Fact Finding Committee on Natural Resources, August 31, 1961.

77. The law is presently codified at California Fish and Game Code § 11036.

78. Klamath River Basin Fisheries Task Force, *Long Range Plan for the Klamath River Basin Conservation Area Fishery Restoration Program*, January 1991, 2–77, http://www.krisweb.com/biblio/gen_usfws_kierassoc_1991_lrp.pdf.

79. "Iron Gate Dam, Its Effect on the Klamath River Fisheries," 75.

80. Testifying at a state legislative hearing, an FWS representative said, "You may infer from the fact that temperature is not mentioned in our reports that we have concluded that it was not of significance." "Iron Gate Dam, Its Effect on the Klamath River Fisheries," 77.

81. *Final 2002 Biological Assessment*.

82. See U.S. Fish and Wildlife Service, "Biological/Conference Opinion," 35.

83. NRC Final Report, 190–91.

84. Eric Jay Dolin, *The Smithsonian Book of National Wildlife Refuges* (Washington, DC: Smithsonian Institution Press, 2003), 65.

85. National Wildlife Refuge System Improvement Act of 1997, 16 U.S.C. § 668d. See Robert L. Fischman, "The National Wildlife Refuge System and the Hallmarks of Modern Organic Legislation," *Ecology Law Quarterly* 29 (2002): 457; and Robert L. Fischman, *The National Wildlife Refuges: Coordinating a Conservation System Through Law* (Washington, DC: Island Press, 2003).

86. Fischman, "The National Wildlife Refuge System," 498.

87. Blake, Blake, and Kittredge, *Balancing Water*, 77.

88. Tule Lake historically ranged from 55,000 to 110,000 acres, depending on the year, while Lower Klamath Lake ranged from 85,000 to 94,000 acres, much of it marsh rather than open water. Today, Tule Lake covers only about 10,000 to 13,000 acres, while Lower Klamath Lake covers a mere 4,700 acres. *Final 2002 Biological Assessment*, 22.

89. This bleak appraisal was made by William A. Finley, founder of the Portland chapter of the National Audubon Society, in the wake of a 1922 dust storm aggravated by the burning of peat in the refuge. The quote appears in Stephen Most, "Putting Nature to Work: Birds of a Feather," Oregon History Project, http://www.ohs.org/education/oregon history/narratives/subtopic.cfm?/subtopic_ID=282.

90. Robert M. Wilson, "Directing the Flow: Migratory Waterfowl, Scale, and Mobility in Western North America," *Environmental History* 7 (2002): 247.

91. 16 U.S.C. § 695n.

92. The Blumenauer-Thompson-Shays Amendment to the Interior Appropriations Bill in 2003 would have taken an important step toward balance in the Klamath Basin by phasing out those crops grown on the basin's NWRs that consume the most water; use the most pesticides; and provide little, if any, benefit to wildlife. The amendment, which was rejected by the House, would have required that new farming lease agreements on the Klamath Basin NWRs not allow growing of onions, potatoes, horseradish, or alfalfa.

93. Andrew Laughland and James Caudill, *Banking on Nature: The Economic Benefits to Local Communities of National Wildlife Refuge Visitation* (Washington, DC: U.S. Fish and Wildlife Service, 2003), 35.

94. 438 U.S. 690 (1978).

95. 16 U.S.C. § 473 et seq.

96. *In re Matter of the Amended Applications of the United States for Reserved Rights in the Platte River*, Case No. W-8439-76 (February 12, 1993). See Teresa A. Rice, "Colorado Water Court Denies Reserved Rights Claims for Channel Maintenance," *Rivers* 4 (1993): 146.

97. Lois G. Witte, "Still No Water for the Woods," *Stream Notes* (Stream Systems Technology Center; April 2002), http://www.stream.fs.fed.us/news/streamnt/pdf/SN_4_02.pdf.

98. Executive Order 4851, April 3, 1928.

99. 16 U.S.C. § 695k.

100. Memorandum from Walter Perry, assistant attorney general, Natural Resources Section, Oregon Department of Justice, to Richard Bailey, adjudicator, Oregon Water Resources Department, September 19, 1999.

101. A. Dan Tarlock, *Law of Water Rights and Resources* § 9.53 (New York: Clark Boardman, 1988 with annual updates).

102. Public Law 106-530, s 9(b)(2)(B), 114 Stat. 2527 (2000). See John D. Leshy, "Water Rights for New Federal Land Conservation Programs: A Turn-of-the-Century Evaluation," *University of Denver Water Law Review* 4 (2001): 271, 285–86.

Chapter 5

1. Although largely ignored by modern environmentalists, the roots of the need for a new human-nature balance can be traced to the New Deal's efforts to conserve the nation's soil resources and sustain local farming communities. See Sarah T. Phillips, *This Land, This Nation: Conservation, Rural America, and the New Deal* (New York: Cambridge University Press, 2006); Henry L. Henderson and David D. Woolner, *FDR and the Environment* (New York: Palgrave MacMillan, 2005).

2. 42 U.S.C. §§ 4321–4370f.

3. 33 U.S.C. § 1251(a).

4. National Forest Management Act, 16 U.S.C. §§ 1600–1614; Federal Land Management and Policy Act, 43 U.S.C. §§ 1701–1785.

5. *Tennessee Valley Authority v. Hill*, 437 U.S. 153 (1978). In *Pyramid Lake Paiute Tribe of Indians v. United States*, 898 F.2d 1410 (9th Cir. 1999), the court rejected the navy's argument that it need not comply with the ESA if its primary mission would be frustrated. The court indicated that federal agencies had some discretion to decide how to fulfill its species conservation duties but avoided a fuller exploration of the scope of discretion by holding that the navy's action would not jeopardize the species.

6. 16 U.S.C. § 1532(6).

7. 16 U.S.C. § 1532(20).

8. The precise words of the statute require that listing decisions be made "on the basis of the best scientific and commercial data available." Public Law 93-205, § 4, 87 Stat. 884 (1973). In 1973, it was understood that "commercial data" meant scientific data supplied by industry or trade groups. See *Bills to Prevent the Importation of Endangered Species of Fish or Wildlife into the United States: Hearings Before the Subcomm. on Fisheries and Wildlife Conservation of the House Comm. on Merchant Marine and Fisheries*, 91st

Cong., 107. Later, a congressional committee explained that "commercial data" refers to objectively verifiable data concerning the impact of commercial trade on the species. House Committee on Merchant Marine and Fisheries, 97th Cong., 2d Sess., 1982, H. Rep. No. 567, p. 20.

9. Public Law 97-304, § 2(a)(2), 96 Stat. 1411 (1982).

10. House Conference Report, 97th Cong., 2d Sess., 1982, No. 835, p. 19.

11. 16 U.S.C. § 1532(5)(A).

12. "Notice of Intent to Clarify the Role of Habitat in Endangered Species Conservation," *Federal Register* 64 (1999): 31871, 31872.

13. Critical habitat designation must be preceded by analysis of the economic impacts. The Clinton administration took the position that this economic analysis could be fairly perfunctory because most economic effects would follow from listing alone, regardless of whether critical habitat were designated, and therefore need not be considered. The Bush administration, however, has supported recent judicial decisions requiring broader economic analysis. See, for example, *New Mexico Cattle Growers Association v. U.S. Fish and Wildlife Service*, 248 F.3d 1277 (10th Cir. 2001).

14. As of July 2007, critical habitat had been formally designated for 489, or just over one-third, of the 1,314 listed U.S. species.

15. 16 U.S.C. § 1532(19); 50 C.F.R. § 17.3. The ESA expressly forbids the take only of endangered animals. 16 U.S.C. § 1538(a)(1)(C). Threatened animals are protected more flexibly; the law gives the services discretion to regulate take as necessary or advisable for the conservation of those species, up to the full level of protection provided for endangered species. 16 U.S.C. § 1533(d). For terrestrial and freshwater species, FWS typically relies on a general regulation applying the full force of section 9 to threatened species, rather than issuing specific take regulations tailored to each threatened species. See 50 C.F.R. § 70.31(a). NMFS, which has many fewer species to keep track of, has made more aggressive use of the flexibility allowed by the law. Plants, which the law has long regarded as the property of the owner of the land on which they grow, get much less protection. They cannot be removed from or destroyed on federal lands, or damaged on or removed from other lands in knowing violation of state law. 16 U.S.C. § 1538(a)(2). In general, landowners are free to destroy listed plants on their land.

16. 16 U.S.C. § 1539(a)(1)(B).

17. 16 U.S.C. § 1536(a)(2).

18. 467 U.S. 837 (1984).

19. 50 C.F.R. § 402.02.

20. "Destruction or adverse modification [of critical habitat] means a direct or indirect alteration that appreciably diminishes the value of critical habitat for both the survival and recovery of a listed species." 50 C.F.R. § 402.02.

21. *Gifford Pinchot Task Force v. U.S. Fish and Wildlife Service*, 378 F.3d 1059 (9th Cir. 2004); *Sierra Club v. U.S. Fish and Wildlife Service*, 245 F.3d 434 (5th Cir. 2001). For an excellent discussion of the meaning and significance of critical habitat under the ESA and its implementing regulations, see Jason Patlis, "Paying Tribute to Joseph Heller with the Endangered Species Act: When Critical Habitat Isn't," *Stanford Environmental Law Journal* 20 (2001): 133.

22. 16 U.S.C. § 1536(a)(2); 50 C.F.R. § 402.14(a).

23. 16 U.S.C. § 1536(b)(3)A); 50 C.F.R. § 402.14(g)(4).

24. 16 U.S.C. § 1536(b)(4); 50 C.F.R. § 402.14(h). The Fish and Wildlife Service must find that the proposed activity will minimize the impacts of a taking to the maximum extent possible. *Gerber v. Norton*, 294 F.3d 173 (D.C. Cir. 2002).

25. See 16 U.S.C. § 1536(o)2.

26. *Ramsey v. Kantor*, 96 F.3d 434 (9th Cir. 1996).

27. See 16 U.S.C. § 1536(b)(3)(A); 50 C.F.R. § 402.14(h)(3).

28. 50 C.F.R. § 402.02.

29. *Bennett v. Spear*, 520 U.S. 154 (1997).

30. U.S. Fish and Wildlife Service and National Marine Fisheries Service, *Endangered Species Consultation Handbook: Procedures for Conducting Section 7 Consultations and Conferences* (Washington, DC: U.S. Fish and Wildlife Service, 1998), 1–6.

31. See, for example, *Center for Marine Conservation v. Brown*, 917 F. Supp. 1128 (S.D. Tex. 1996); *American Rivers v. NMFS*, No. 96-384-MA (D. Or. 1997). For a general discussion of the extent of agency discretion in this context, see Daniel J. Rohlf, "Jeopardy Under the Endangered Species Act: Playing a Game Protected Species Can't Win," *Washburn Law Journal* 41 (2001): 114, 146–50.

32. 50 C.F.R. § 402.03.

33. 437 U.S. 153, 193–94 (1978) (holding that closing the gates on a federal dam that was nearly complete before enactment of the ESA was a federal action subject to section 7).

34. *Sierra Club v. Babbitt*, 65 F.3d 1502, 1512 (9th Cir. 1995).

35. *National Wildlife Federation v. National Marine Fisheries Service*, 481 F.3d 1224, 1233–35 (9th Cir. 2007).

36. 16 U.S.C. § 1536(a)(1).

37. "Interagency Cooperation–Endangered Species Act of 1973, as Amended; Final Rule," *Federal Register* 51 (1986): 19926, 19934.

38. See, for example, *Pyramid Lake Paiute Tribe v. U.S. Department of the Navy*, 898 F.2d 1410 (9th Cir. 1990); *Hawksbill Sea Turtle v. Federal Emergency Management Agency*, 11 F. Supp. 2d 529 (D. V.I. 1998).

39. See, for example, *Sierra Club v. Glickman*, 156 F.3d 606, 617 (5th Cir. 1998); *Defenders of Wildlife v. Babbitt*, 130 F. Supp. 2d 121 (D. D.C. 2001); *Florida Key Deer v. Stickney*, 864 F. Supp. 1222, 1238 (S.D. Fla. 1994).

40. *Carson-Truckee Water Conservancy Dist. v. Clark*, 741 F.2d 257 (9th Cir. 1984).

41. 33 U.S.C. § 1251(g).

42. *Missouri v. Holland*, 252 U.S. 416, 434 (1920).

43. 756 F.2d 508 (10th Cir. 1986).

44. *Riverside Irrigation District v. Andrews*, 756 F.2d 513 (10th Cir. 1986).

45. Ibid.

46. 16 U.S.C. § 1531(c)(2).

47. See A. Dan Tarlock, "The Endangered Species Act and Western Water Rights," *Land and Water Law Review* 20 (1985): 1, 19.

48. *United States v. Glenn-Colusa Irrigation Dist.*, 788 F. Supp. 1126, 1134 (E.D. Cal. 1992).

49. See Martha C. Knack and Orner C. Stewart, *As Long As the River Shall Run: An Ethnohistory of Pyramid Lake Indian Reservation* (Berkeley: University of California Press, 1984).

50. See William D. Rowley, *Reclaiming the West: The Career of Francis G. Newlands* (Bloomington: Indiana University Press, 1996), for a history of the founding of the district by the leading sponsor of the Reclamation Act of 1902. California Resources Agency, Department of Water Resources, *Truckee River Atlas* (Sacramento: Author, 1991), is a valuable source of the geography, hydrology, and history of the river and its use.

51. The tribe subsequently sought to reopen the 1944 Orr Ditch Decree on the grounds that the federal government was too worried about protecting irrigation to adequately represent the tribe's interests, but the Supreme Court refused to reopen because water rights had vested in the project beneficiaries. *Nevada v. United States*, 463 U.S. 110 (1983).

52. The Department of the Interior had begun to develop more efficient operating criteria in 1966. In 1973, a federal district court held that the department had a trust duty to implement those criteria. *Pyramid Lake Paiute Tribe of Indians v. Morton*, 354 F. Supp. 252 (D. D.C. 1973). This duty was reaffirmed by the Ninth Circuit in *Pyramid Lake Paiute Tribe of Indians v. Hodel*, 878 F.2d 1215 (9th Cir. 1989).

53. TCID's efficiency increased from about 40 percent in 1964, when the Department of the Interior began investigating Newlands's operations, to 68.4 percent in 1992. Annual diversions fell over that time period from 370,000 to 320,000 acre-feet. Jeremy Pratt, *Truckee-Carson River Basin Study: Final Report* (Springfield, VA: Western Water Policy Review Advisory Commission, 1997), 91.

54. *Carson-Truckee Water Conservancy Dist.*, 741 F.2d 257, 259.

55. Ibid., 262.

56. Ibid., 262 n5.

57. *Platte River Whooping Crane Critical Habitat Maintenance Trust v. Federal Energy Regulatory Commission*, 962 F.2d 27 (D.C. Cir. 1992).

58. 50 F.3d 677 (9th Cir. 1995).

59. 204 F.3d 1206 (9th Cir. 1999).

60. *Klamath Water Users Protective Association*, 204 F.3d 1213 (9th Cir. 1999).

61. Memorandum from regional solicitor, Pacific Southwest Region, to regional director, Bureau of Reclamation, Mid-Pacific Region, "Certain Legal Rights and Obligations Related to the U.S. Bureau of Reclamation, Klamath Project for Use in Preparation of the Klamath Project Operations Plan (KPOP)" July 25, 1995, p. 7. Emphasis supplied.

62. See *Klamath Water Users Protective Association*, 204 F.3d 1213.

63. Holly Doremus, "Water, Population Growth, and Endangered Species in the West," *Colorado Law Review* 72 (2001): 361, 399–400; Joan E. Drake, "Contractual Discretion and the Endangered Species Act: Can the Bureau of Reclamation Reallocate Federal Project Water for Endangered Species in the Middle Rio Grande?" *Natural Resources Journal* 41 (2001): 487.

64. 127 S. Ct. 2518 (2007).

65. It does not seem likely to prevail in many other situations, either. So long as Reclamation maintains some control over the extent and allocation of water deliveries, operation of water projects will continue to be a federal action for section 7 purposes.

66. 50 F.3d 677 (9th Cir. 1995).

67. Memorandum from regional solicitors to regional directors, "Oregon Assistant Attorney General's March 18, 1996, Letter Regarding Klamath Basin Water Rights Adjudication and Management of the Klamath Project," January 9, 1997, 9n10.

68. *United States v. Winstar Corp.*, 518 U.S. 839, 896 (1996); see also *Winstar Corp.* 898 (stating that "governmental action will not be held against the Government for purposes of the impossibility defense so long as the action's impact upon public contracts is . . . merely incidental to the accomplishment of a broader government objective").

69. 49 Fed. Cl. 313 (2001).

70. 458 U.S. 419, 435 (1982).

71. Ibid., 436. Emphasis in original.

72. *Penn Central Transportation Company v. City of New York*, 438 U.S. 104 (1978).

73. *Klamath Irrigation District v. United States*, 67 Fed. Cl. 504 (Ct. Cl. 2005).

74. Ibid., 538.

75. Presentation of Greg Jaeger, Marzulla and Marzulla, at the Natural Resources Law Center 25th Anniversary Conference and Natural Resources Law Teachers 14th Biennial Institute, University of Colorado School of Law, June 7, 2007.

76. Sucker Listing, 27130.

77. Ibid., 27132.

78. Ibid., 27131.

79. "Proposal to Determine Endangered Status for the Shortnose Sucker and the Lost River Sucker," *Federal Register* 52 (1987): 32145, 32148.

80. Sucker Listing, 27133.

81. Sucker Listing, 27132.

82. U.S. Department of the Interior, Fish and Wildlife Service, Region One, "Recovery Plan: Lost River Sucker, *Deltistes luxatus*, and Shortnose Sucker, *Chasmistes brevirostrus*," April 1993, http://ecos.fws.gov/docs/recovery_plans/1993/930317.pdf.

83. "Threatened Status for Southern Oregon/Northern California Coast Evolutionarily Significant Unit of Coho Salmon," *Federal Register* 62 (1997): 24588, 24589.

84. "Policy on Applying the Definition of Species Under the Endangered Species Act to Pacific Salmon," *Federal Register* 56 (1991): 58612.

85. "Proposed Threatened Status for Three Contiguous ESUs of Coho Salmon Ranging from Oregon Through Central California," *Federal Register* 60 (1995): 38011, 38016.

86. "Designated Critical Habitat: Central California Coast and Southern Oregon/Northern California Coasts Coho Salmon," *Federal Register* 64 (1999): 24049.

87. Ibid., 24059.

88. 515 U.S. 687 (1995).

89. See NRC Final Report, 325–29. Although the NRC committee noted that there are circumstances in which regulatory authorities have used the threat of section 9 enforcement against dispersed actions, few such examples involved are water diversion or pollution.

90. As Jim Rasband explains, "Federal agencies have not been eager to seek civil penalties or even to impose injunctive relief" under the ESA on individual water users. James R. Rasband, "Priority, Probability, and Proximate Cause: Lessons from Tort Law about Imposing ESA Responsibility for Wildlife Harm on Water Users and Other Joint Habitat Modifiers," *Environmental Law* 33 (2003): 595, 638.

91. *Klamath Water Users Protective Association*, 204 F.3d 1206, 1231.

92. U.S. Department of the Interior, Bureau of Reclamation, "Klamath Project Historic Operation" (November 2000), 36.

93. *Bennett v. Spear*, 520 U.S. 154 (1997).
94. *Bennett v. Spear*, 5 F. Supp. 2d 882, 885–86 (D. Or. 1998).
95. 2002 Sucker BiOp.
96. Benson, "Giving Suckers an Even Break," 197, 218.
97. *Klamath Water Users Protective Association*, 204 F.3d 1206.
98. 138 F. Supp. 2d 1228 (2001).
99. *Kandra*, 145 F. Supp. 2d 1192, 1210–11.
100. Benson, "Giving Suckers an Even Break," 232.

Chapter 6

1. Kyna Powers et al., *Klamath River Basin Issues and Activities: An Overview* (Washington, DC: Congressional Research Service, 2005), 33.

2. John Passmore, *The Perfectibility of Man* (New York: Charles Scribner's Sons, 1970), 320. See also Dick Taverne, *The March of Unreason: Science, Democracy, and the New Fundamentalism* (New York: Oxford University Press, 2005).

3. See A. Dan Tarlock, "Is There a There There in Environmental Law?" *Journal of Land Use and Environmental Law* 19 (2004): 213. For a detailed discussion of the difficulties environmental problems create for the traditional model of law, see Richard J. Lazarus, *The Making of Environmental Law* (Chicago: University of Chicago Press, 2004), 1–42.

4. More than three-quarters of American adults sampled in a 2006 Harris Poll indicated that they generally trust scientists. Scientists were the third–most trusted group in the poll, just behind doctors and teachers and well ahead of presidents and members of Congress. Harris Interactive, Harris Poll no. 61, August 8, 2006.

5. Luntz Research Companies, "Straight Talk: The Environment: A Cleaner, Safer, Healthier America," http://www.luntzspeak.com/graphics/LuntzResearch.Memo.pdf.

6. Cary Coglianese and Gary E. Marchant, "Shifting Sands: The Limits of Science in Setting Risk Standards," *University of Pennsylvania Law Review* 152 (2004): 1255, 1260–61; Wendy E. Wagner, "Science in the Regulatory Process: The 'Bad Science' Fiction: Reclaiming the Debate over the Role of Science in Public Health and Environmental Regulation," *Law and Contemporary Problems* 66 (2003): 63, 66.

7. Horst W. Rittel and Melvin M. Webber, "Dilemmas in a General Theory of Planning," *Policy Sciences* 4 (1973): 155, 160–67.

8. See, for example, Russell B. Korobkin and Thomas S. Ulen, "Law and Behavioral Science: Removing the Rationality Assumption from Law and Economics," *California Law Review* 88 (2000): 1051, 1093; Jeffrey J. Rachlinski, "The Psychology of Global Climate Change," *University of Illinois Law Review* 2000: 299, 304–6.

9. See Dan M. Kahan and Donald Braman, "Cultural Cognition and Public Policy," *Yale Law and Policy Review* 24 (2006): 149, 165.

10. See Daniel Sarewitz, "How Science Makes Environmental Controversies Worse," *Environmental Science and Policy* 7 (2004): 385.

11. For a general explanation of these contrasting approaches to the role of science in regulation, see J. B. Ruhl, "The Battle over Endangered Species Act Methodology,"

Environmental Law 34 (2004): 555; Holly Doremus, "Science Plays Defense: Natural Resource Management in the Bush Administration," *Ecology Law Quarterly* 32 (2005): 249.

12. See, for example, 16 U.S.C. § 1533(b)(1)(A) (listing decisions must be made "solely on the basis of the best scientific and commercial data"); 16 U.S.C. § 1533(b)(5)(C) (when they propose to list a species or designate critical habitat, wildlife agencies must give notice of their proposals to appropriate scientific organizations); 16 U.S.C. § 1536(a)(2) (requiring that all federal agencies use the best scientific data available in determining whether their proposed actions would jeopardize the continued existence of a listed species).

13. Department of the Interior, Fish and Wildlife Service, and Department of Commerce, National Oceanic and Atmospheric Administration, "Notice of Interagency Cooperative Policy on Information Standards under the Endangered Species Act," *Federal Register* 59 (1994): 34271.

14. Klamath Falls Fish and Wildlife Office, "Biological/Conference Opinion Regarding the Effects of Operation of the Bureau of Reclamation's Klamath Project on the Endangered Lost River Sucker (*Deltistes Luxatus*), Endangered Shortnose Sucker (*Chasmistes Brevirostris*), Threatened Bald Eagle (*Haliaeetus Leucocephalus*), and Proposed Critical Habitat for the Lost River/Shortnose Suckers," sec. 3, part 2, April 2001, 124.

15. Ibid., 144–45.

16. National Marine Fisheries Service, Southwest Region, "Biological Opinion: Ongoing Klamath Project Operations," April 6, 2001, 25.

17. Ibid., 26.

18. See Eric Bailey, "Outside Group to Review Status of Three Fish Species," *Los Angeles Times*, October 3, 2001, B7 (quoting Glen Spain of the Pacific Coast Federation of Fishermen's Associations).

19. *Kandra*, 145 F. Supp. 2d 1192, 1199.

20. The authors have both served on multiple NRC committees, and Professor Tarlock has been a member of the council's Water, Science, and Technology Board.

21. National Research Council, *The Missouri River Ecosystem: Exploring the Prospects for Recovery* (Washington, DC: National Academy Press, 2002).

22. Michael S. Cooperman and Douglas F. Markle, "The Endangered Species Act and the National Research Council's Interim Judgment in Klamath Basin," *Fisheries* 28 (2003): 10, 11.

23. National Research Council, *Scientific Evaluation of Biological Opinions on Endangered and Threatened Fishes in the Klamath River Basin* (Washington, DC: National Academy Press, 2002), 26.

24. Ibid., 3.

25. NRC Final Report, 10.

26. *Final 2002 Biological Assessment*, 55.

27. Ibid., 56.

28. Ibid., 72.

29. Thomas B. Hardy and R. Craig Addley, "Evaluation of Interim Instream Flow Needs in the Klamath River, Phase II Final Report," November 21, 2001, 244.

30. Hardy and Addley, "Evaluation," 80.

31. U.S. Department of the Interior, Fish and Wildlife Service, "Final Biological Opinion for the Bureau of Reclamation's Proposed Operation of the Klamath Project for the Period April 1 through May 31, 2002," March 28, 2002, 2.

32. *Final 2002 Biological Assessment*, 79.

33. "Given the conclusions expressed by the NRC, NMFS currently has no basis for contradicting your determination. . . . Letter from James H. Lecky, assistant regional administrator, Protected Resources Division, National Marine Fisheries Service, to David Sabo, area manager, U.S. Bureau of Reclamation, March 28, 2002.

34. 2002 Sucker BiOp.

35. Douglas F. Markle et al., "Review of Biological Opinion and Conference Report for the Continued Operation of the Bureau of Reclamation's Klamath Project as it Effects [sic] Endangered Lost River Sucker (*Delistes luxatus*), Endangered Shortnose Sucker (*Chasmistes brevirostris*), Threatened Bald Eagle (*Haliaeetus leucocephalus*) and Proposed Critical Habitat for the Suckers (dated April 5, 2001)," (Corvallis: Oregon State University, Department of Fisheries and Wildlife, July 5, 2001).

36. "University of California Peer Review of: Biological/Conference Opinion Regarding the Effects of Operation of the Bureau of Reclamation's Klamath Project on the Endangered Lost River Sucker (*Deltistes laxatus*) Endangered Shortnose Sucker (*Chasmistes breirostris*) Threatened Bald Eagle (*Haliaeetus leucocephalus*) and Proposed Critical Habitat for the Lost River/Shortnose Suckers" (Berkeley: University of California, 2001).

37. 2002 Sucker BiOp, 118.

38. PacifiCorp, which generates power from two hydroelectric diversions on the Link River, opposes fish screens because the cost might make power generation uneconomical. Michael Milstein, "PacifiCorp Opposes Call for Intake Screens," *Portland Oregonian*, March 22, 2002.

39. National Marine Fisheries Service, "Biological Opinion: Klamath Project Operations," May 31, 2002, 34–37 (hereafter cited as 2002 Coho BiOp).

40. Ibid., 38.

41. Ibid., 39–40.

42. Ibid., 6.

43. Ibid., 7.

44. Ibid., 49.

45. Michael S. Kelly, "Narrative Statement of Michael S. Kelly, Fishery Biologist, National Marine Fisheries Service," http://www.peer.org/docs/noaa/kelly_narrative.pdf.

46. 2002 Coho BiOp, 55.

47. Memorandum from Kirk Rodgers, regional director, U.S. Bureau of Reclamation, to Rodney R. McInnis, acting regional administrator, National Marine Fisheries Service, "Decision Regarding the Proposed Action Addressed in the National Marine Fisheries Service's May 31, 2002 Biological Opinion on the Proposed Operation of the Klamath Project," June 3, 2002; memorandum from Kirk Rodgers, regional director, U.S. Bureau of Reclamation, to Steve Thompson, manager, U.S. Fish and Wildlife Service, "Decision Regarding the Proposed Action Addressed in the U.S. Fish & Wildlife Service's May 31, 2002 Biological Opinion on the Proposed Operation of the Klamath Project," June 3, 2002.

48. Robert F. Service, "'Combat Biology' on the Klamath," *Science* 300 (2003): 36, 37.

49. Ibid., 36 (quoting FWS fisheries biologist Ron Larson).

50. Ibid.

51. Cooperman and Markle, "Endangered Species Act," 14.

52. Jacob Kann and Larry K. Dunsmoor, "Comments on: Scientific Evaluation of Biological Opinions on Endangered and Threatened Fishes in the Klamath River Basin; Interim Report from the Committee on Endangered and Threatened Fishes in the Klamath River Basin, February 6, 2002," February 12, 2002.

53. William M. Lewis Jr., "Klamath Basin Fishes: Argument Is No Substitute for Evidence," *Fisheries* 28, no. 3 (2003): 20, 24–25.

54. Ibid., 21.

55. Ibid., 25.

56. Independent Multidisciplinary Science Team, "IMST Review of the USFWS and NMFS 2001 Biological Opinions on Management of the Klamath Reclamation Project and Related Reports," Technical Report 2003-1 (Salem: Oregon Watershed Enhancement Board, April 16, 2003), 2.

57. Ibid.

58. Ibid.

59. Quoted in Sharon Levy, "Turbulence in the Klamath River Basin," *BioScience* 53 (2003): 315, 320.

60. Thomas O. McGarity, "Substantive and Procedural Discretion in Administrative Resolution of Science Policy Questions: Regulating Carcinogens in EPA and OSHA," *Georgetown Law Journal* 67 (1979): 729, 748.

61. NRC Final Report, 239.

62. Ibid., 225.

63. Ibid.

64. Ibid., 323–39.

65. Ibid., 327–29.

66. Department of Commerce, National Oceanic and Atmospheric Administration, "Policy on Applying the Definition of Species Under the Endangered Species Act to Pacific Salmon," *Federal Register*, 56 (1991): 58612.

67. Department of Commerce, National Oceanic and Atmospheric Administration, "Proposed Threatened Status for Three Contiguous ESUs of Coho Salmon Ranging from Oregon Through Central California," *Federal Register* 60 (1995): 38011, 38016.

68. Ibid., 38013–14.

69. 16 U.S.C. § 1532 (6).

70. 16 U.S.C. § 1532 (20).

71. Department of Commerce, National Oceanic and Atmospheric Administration, "Threatened Status for Southern Oregon/Northern California Coast Evolutionarily Significant Unit (ESU) of Coho Salmon," *Federal Register* 62 (1997): 24588, 24591.

72. Department of the Interior, FWS, "Determination of Endangered Status for the Shortnose Sucker and Lost River Sucker," *Federal Register* 53 (1988): 27130, 27131.

73. This is the operative language of ESA § 7(a)(2), 16 U.S.C. § 1536(a)(2).

74. 50 C.F.R. § 402.02.

75. NRC Final Report, 314.

76. Lewis, "Klamath Basin Fishes," 21.

77. Any number of studies have concluded that the wildlife agencies do not list species whose conservation obviously conflicts with economic activities unless and until forced to do so by litigation. See, for example, Amy Whritenour Ando, "Waiting to Be Protected Under the Endangered Species Act: The Political Economy of Regulatory Delay,"

Journal of Law and Economics 42 (1999): 29; Andrew Metrick and Martin L. Weitzman, "Patterns of Behavior in Endangered Species Preservation," *Land Economics* 72 (1996): 1; David S. Wilcove, Margaret McMillan, and Keith C. Winston, "What Exactly Is an Endangered Species? An Analysis of the U.S. Endangered Species List, 1985–1991," *Conservation Biology* 7 (1993): 87; Steven L. Yaffee, *Prohibitive Policy: Implementing the Federal Endangered Species Act* (Cambridge, MA: MIT Press, 1982); U.S. General Accounting Office, *Endangered Species: A Controversial Issue Needing Resolution* (Washington, DC: General Accounting Office, 1979). Fewer studies have looked at section 7 jeopardy determinations, but it is clear that jeopardy determinations are rare and typically accompanied by extraordinary attempts to find alternatives that minimize regulatory intrusion. See Oliver A. Houck, "The Endangered Species Act and Its Implementation by the U.S. Departments of Interior and Commerce," *University of Colorado Law Review* 64 (1993): 277, 354.

78. NRC Final Report, 237.

79. *Bennett*, 5 F. Supp. 2d 882, 885–86.

80. *Kandra*, 145 F. Supp. 2d 1192.

81. Complaint for Declaratory and Injunctive Relief, Pacific Coast Federation of Fisherman's Associations, Civ. No. C02-2006 SBA.

82. See Deborah Schoch, "Klamath Farmers Applaud Ruling," *Los Angeles Times*, May 4, 2002.

83. *Pacific Coast Federation of Fisherman's Associations v. U.S. Bureau of Reclamation*, 138 F. Supp. 2d 1228 (N.D. Cal. 2001).

84. See Order, *Pacific Coast Federation of Fisherman's Associations v. U.S. Bureau of Reclamation*, No. C02-2006 SBA (N.D. Cal. 2006).

85. *Pacific Coast Federation of Fishermen's Associations v. U.S. Bureau of Reclamation*, 426 F.3d 1082 (9th Cir. 2005).

86. Order Granting Motion for Injunctive Relief Following Remand, *Pacific Coast Federation of Fishermen's Associations v. U.S. Bureau of Reclamation*, Civ. No. C02-2006 SBA (N.D. Cal., March 27, 2006), slip op. at 7. The government did not appeal that ruling. Klamath Project irrigators, who had intervened in support of the government, did, but the Ninth Circuit rejected their appeal. *Pacific Coast Federation of Fishermen's Associations v. U.S. Bureau of Reclamation*, No. 06-16296 (9th Cir., March 26, 2007) (not published).

87. Eric Bailey, "Eagles Back at Winter Home," *Los Angeles Times*, January 15, 2002, B6.

88. Klamath Basin Federal Working Group, Press Release, "Secretaries Norton and Veneman, Senator Smith Open 'A' Canal Headgates, Provide Water to Irrigators" (March 29, 2002).

89. Deborah Schoch, "A Race to Save Baby Salmon in Klamath," *Los Angeles Times*, May 2, 2002.

90. U.S. Department of the Interior, Bureau of Reclamation, Mid-Pacific Regional Office, News Release, "Reclamation Changes Water Year Type for Klamath Basin," July 10, 2002.

91. John Driscoll, "Reclamation Cuts Water as Klamath Salmon Start to Run," *Eureka Times-Standard*, August 3, 2002. Acceding to the reduced flows, NMFS's regional administrator for protected species observed, "If the water's not there, it's not there." Ibid.

92. According to FWS, "The most accurate estimate of the total number of observable fish that died . . . is 34,056." U.S. Fish and Wildlife Service, *Klamath River Fish Die-off, September 2002: Report on Estimate of Mortality*, Report No. AFWO-01-03 (Arcata, CA: U.S. Fish and Wildlife Service, 2003), ii. The California Department of Fish and Game subsequently estimated that twice that number or even more may have been killed. California Department of Fish and Game, Northern California–North Coast Region, *September 2002 Klamath River Fish-Kill: Final Analysis of Contributing Factors and Impacts*, July 2004 (hereafter cited as Final Fish-Kill Report). The vast majority of the casualties, more than 95 percent, were nonlisted chinook, representing (according to FWS's conservative estimate) nearly 20 percent of the chinook run. The dead included at least three hundred endangered coho. U.S. Fish and Wildlife Service, *Klamath River Fish Die-off*, ii.

93. Final Fish-Kill Report, 122.

94. Michael Milstein, "U.S. Official Pledges Study of Fish Die-Off," *Portland Oregonian*, October 3, 2002, D1.

95. Michael Milstein and Jim Barnett, "Salmon Die-Off Becomes Harsh Reality," *Portland Oregonian*, September 29, 2002, A1.

96. Glen Martin, "New Clash on Salmon Die-Off," *San Francisco Chronicle*, October 3, 2002, A3; Timothy Egan, "As Thousands of Salmon Die, Fight for River Erupts Again," *New York Times*, September 28, 2002, A1.

97. The die-off had already slowed by the time the pulse reached the lower river. The California Department of Fish and Game expressed concern that the pulse might even make matters worse by coaxing fish upstream, where they would be stranded in small pools when the pulse ended. See Eric Bailey, "U.S. Denies Blame for Die-Off of Salmon," *Los Angeles Times*, October 3, 2002, B1.

98. California Department of Fish and Game, Northern California–North Coast Region, "September 2002 Klamath River Fish Kill: Preliminary Analysis of Contributing Factors," January 2003, 52.

99. Final Fish-Kill Report, 158.

100. U.S. Fish and Wildlife Service, *Klamath River Fish Die-Off*, 40–42.

101. David Whitney, "Salmon Harvest Will Be Slashed," *Sacramento Bee*, May 31, 2005, A1.

102. Pacific Fishery Management Council and National Marine Fisheries Service, "Final Environmental Assessment for Pacific Coast Salmon Plan Amendment 15: An Initiative to Provide *De Minimis* Ocean Fishing Opportunity for Klamath River Fall Chinook," March 2007, 2.

103. Steve Chawkins, "Fishery 'Failure' Declaration Triggers Aid," *Los Angeles Times*, August 11, 2006, A3.

104. Pacific Fishery Management Council and National Marine Fisheries Service, "Final Environmental Assessment," 2.

105. David Whitney, "No U.S. Aid for Fishermen," *Sacramento Bee*, December 12, 2006.

106. Magnuson-Stevens Fishery Conservation Management and Reauthorization Act, Public Law 109-479, § 113(b), 16 U.S.C. § 460ss note.

107. NMFS, "Magnuson-Stevens Reauthorization Act Klamath River Coho Salmon Recovery Plan," July 10, 2007, http://swr.nmfs.noaa.gov/salmon/MSRA_Recovery Plan_Final.pdf.

108. Ibid., 5.

109. Ibid., 39.

110. Penn Herb Co., Ltd., "Project Category: Green Foods," http://www.pennherb.com/pennherb/info/Green%2520Foods.html.

Chapter 7

1. James M. Buchanan, "What is Public Choice Theory?" *Imprimis* 32 (2003): 3.

2. William Buzbee, "Recognizing the Regulatory Commons: A Theory of Regulatory Gaps," *Iowa Law Review* 89 (2003): 1.

3. Wilderness Society, "Economic Profile of Klamath County, Oregon" (2000), cited in Pacific Coast Federation of Fishermen's Associations, "Myths and Facts About the Klamath Water Issues" (March 30, 2002), http://www.pcffa.org/kl-myths.htm. Farm proprietor income in the Upper Basin represents only 0.5 percent of total personal income for the region. Bruce Weber and Bruce Sorte, "The Upper Klamath Basin Economy and the Role of Agriculture," in *Water Allocation in the Klamath Reclamation Project, 2001* (Oregon State University Extension Service, Special Report 1037, reprinted May 2003), pp. 213, 223, http://extension.oregonstate.edu/catalog/html/sr/sr1037/report.pdf.

4. William K. Jaeger, "What Actually Happened in 2001? Comparison of Estimated Impacts and Reported Outcomes of the Irrigation Curtailment in the Upper Klamath Basin," in *Water Allocation in the Klamath Reclamation Project, 2001*, 265, 269 (Oregon State University Extension Service, Special Report 1037, reprinted May 2003), http://extension.oregonstate.edu/catalog/html/sr/sr1037/report.pdf.

5. Kyna Powers et al., *Klamath River Basin Issues and Activities: An Overview*, report for Congress (Washington, DC: Congressional Research Service, 2005), 10–11.

6. Ibid., 270.

7. Ibid., 272.

8. Charles E. Merriam, *Political Power: Its Composition and Incidence* (New York: McGraw-Hill, 1934), remains a readable classic.

9. Harold D. Lasswell, *Politics: Who Gets What, When, Where* (New York: McGraw-Hill, 1936), 3.

10. Helen Ingram, *Water Politics: Continuity and Change* (Albuquerque: University of New Mexico Press, 1990).

11. As it turned out, Smith's popularity did not depend on his ability to deliver a knockout blow for the Klamath Basin; he was easily reelected. Tom Hamburger, "Oregon Water Saga Illuminates Rove's Methods with Agencies," *Wall Street Journal*, July 30, 2003.

12. Former representative Pombo was hired by the Department of the Interior as a special consultant. In March of 2007, Salon.com obtained a copy of a 117-page draft of new ESA regulations, which bore a strong resemblance to various bills introduced by Pombo. Rebecca Clarren, "Inside the Secretive Plan to Gut the Endangered Species Act," http://www.salon.com/news/feature/2007/03/27/endangered_species/index.html.

13. The Klamath Basin became the first place to experience the shutoff of a federal irrigation project, in large part because its upside-down topography provided no site for a deep Upper Basin reservoir.

14. Rutherford H. Platt, *Disasters and Democracy: The Politics of Extreme Natural Events* (Washington, DC: Island Press, 1999), 247.

15. John Barry, *Rising Tide: The Great Mississippi Flood of 1927 and How It Changed America* (New York: Simon and Schuster, 1997).

16. See Donald Worster, *The Dust Bowl: The Southern Plains in the 1930s* (New York: Oxford University Press, 1979), and R. Douglas Hurt, *The Dust Bowl: An Agricultural and Social History* (Chicago: Nelson-Hall, 1981).

17. Cooke was a protégé of the father of the modern Forest Service, Gifford Pinchot. After creating a program of low electricity rates and rural electrification in Pennsylvania, Cooke was recruited by then-governor Roosevelt for the New York Power Authority. After Roosevelt's election to the presidency, Cooke became the head of the Rural Electrification Administration.

18. Morris Cooke et al., *Report of the Great Plains Drought Area Committee* (Washington, DC: Great Plains Drought Area Committee, 1936), 3.

19. Ibid.

20. Ibid., 14.

21. Disaster Relief Act of 1969, Public Law 91-79, 53 Stat. 125 (1969), codified at 42 U.S.C. §§ 1855aaa–1855nnn.

22. Theodore Steinberg, *Acts of God: An Unnatural History of Natural Disaster in America* (New York: Oxford University Press, 2000), xix–xx.

23. Drought Policy Review Task Force, *National Drought Policy, Final Report* (Canberra: Australian Government Publishing Service, 1990).

24. Interim National Drought Council, "Catalog of Federal Drought Assistance Programs" (June 2001).

25. *Supplemental Appropriations Act of 2001*, Public Law 107-20 § 2014, 115 Stat 155 (2001). The act was not limited to the Klamath Basin; it provided a total of $65.5 million, mainly for watershed and flood prevention programs in several states. Ralph A. Chite, *Emergency Funding for Agriculture: A Brief History of Supplemental Appropriations FY1999–FY2006* (Washington, DC: Congressional Research Service, updated April 3, 2006).

26. James McCarty, *Crisis Profiteering: Inequities and Excesses of the Klamath Project Bailout* (Etna, CA: Klamath Forest Alliance, Nov. 2001), p. 9, http://www.klamathbasin.info/CrisisProfiteering.pdf.

27. Carolyn Dimitri, Anne Effland, and Neilson Conklin, *The 20th Century Transformation of U.S. Agriculture and Farm Policy* (Washington, DC: U.S. Department of Agriculture, Economic Research Service, 2005).

28. Chad A. Hart, "Risk Management Instruments for Water Reallocations" (Ames: Iowa State University, Center for Agricultural and Rural Development, February 2005), 5, http://www.card.iastate.edu.

29. Glenn D. Schaible, ed., *Agricultural Risks in a Water-Short World: Producer Adaptation and Policy Directions: A Workshop Summary for an Economic Research Service / Farm Foundation Workshop May 24–25, 2004* (Washington, DC: U.S. Department of Agriculture, Economic Research Service, 2004).

30. Natural Resources Conservation Service, *Conservation in the Klamath Basin: Partnership Accomplishments* (Washington, DC: Author, December 2003).

31. Natural Resources Conservation Service, *Agricultural Conservation Programs: A Scorecard*, 11 (Washington, DC: Author, 2006).

32. Tom Hamburger, "Water Saga Illuminates Rove's Methods," *Wall Street Journal*, July 30, 2003, A4.

33. "Klamath by Karl?" *Sacramento Bee*, August 9, 2003.

34. Jo Becker and Barton Gellman, "Leaving No Tracks," *Washington Post*, June 27, 2007, A1.

35. Irving Brant, *Adventures in Conservation with Franklin D. Roosevelt* (Flagstaff, AZ: Northland, 1988), 85–89.

36. During roughly the same period in which it reviewed the Klamath Basin BiOps, the NRC had been involved in reviews of a number of other controversial decisions at the intersection of science and conservation, including operation of federal water projects on the Missouri, Columbia, Colorado, and Platte rivers, a more general look at the Corps of Engineers water project policy, and an ongoing examination of the use of science in the Everglades restoration program.

37. Becker and Gellman, "Leaving No Tracks," A1.

38. *McNamara v. Rittman*, 107 Ohio State 3d 243, 838 N.E.2d 640, 644 (2005).

39. Joseph L. Sax, "We Don't Do Groundwater: A Morsel of California Legal History," *Denver Water Law Review* 6 (2003): 269, 270.

40. Government Accountability Office, *Klamath River Basin: Reclamation Met Its Water Bank Obligations, But Information Provided to Water Bank Stakeholders Could Be Improved* (Washington, DC: Author, 2005), 28–29.

41. This famous remark was quoted by the late Chief Justice William Rehnquist in a speech delivered at the Faculty of Law at the University of Guanajuato, Mexico in September 2001; see http://www.supremecourtus.gov/publicinfo/speeches/speeches.html.

42. 5 U.S. 137 (1803).

43. Merrick B. Garland, "Deregulation and Judicial Review," *Harvard Law Review* 98 (1985): 505, 532; Richard J. Pierce Jr., *Administrative Law Treatise*, 4th ed. (New York: Aspen Law and Business, 2002), section 11.4.

44. See, for example, Robert Dahl, *Who Governs? Democracy and Power in an American City* (New Haven, CT: Yale University Press, 1961).

45. These theories are associated with the political scientists V. O. Keys, David Truman, and Robert Dahl. For a trenchant criticism of them, see Gus diZerega, *Persuasion, Power and Polity* (Cresskill, NJ: Hampton Press, 2000).

46. Mark Seidenfeld, "A Civic Republican Justification for the Bureaucratic State," *Harvard Law Review* 105 (1992): 1511, 1566.

47. Seidenfeld, "Civic Republican Justification," 1566.

48. Doremus, "Science Plays Defense," 249, 268–69.

49. Reed Benson, "So Much Conflict, Yet So Much in Common: Considering the Similarities Between Western Water Law and the Endangered Species Act," *Natural Resources Journal* 44 (2004): 29, 51.

50. California Fish and Game Code, §§ 2800–2835.

51. Elizabeth Ann Rieke, "The Bay-Delta Accord: A Stride Toward Sustainability," *University of Colorado Law Review* 67 (1996): 341.

52. Todd H. Votteler, "Raiders of the Lost Aquifer? Or The Beginning of the End of the Fifty Years of Conflict Over the Texas Edwards Aquifer," *Tulane Environmental Law Journal* 15 (2002): 257, 276–78.

53. For insider accounts of these efforts to protect the ESA, see Joseph L. Sax, "Environmental Law at the Turn of the Century: A Reportorial Fragment of Contemporary

History," *California Law Review* 88 (2000): 2375; John D. Leshy, "The Babbitt Legacy at the Department of the Interior: A Preliminary View," *Environmental Law* 31 (2001): 199; Bruce Babbitt, *Cities in the Wilderness: A New Vision of Land Use in America* (Washington, DC: Island Press, 2005).

54. *Pacific Coast Federation of Fishermen's Associations v. Bureau of Reclamation*, No. Civ.C02-2006 SBA (N.D. Cal. Mar. 27, 2006), injunction upheld, 226 Fed.Appx. 715, (9th Cir. 2007). In 2005, the Ninth Circuit Court of Appeals held that the bureau's release plan (or nonplan) was arbitrary. *Pacific Coast Federation of Fishermen's Association v. U.S. Bureau of Reclamation*, 426 F.3d 1082 (9th Cir. 2005). The Bureau practically guaranteed the result by adopting in 2002 a biological opinion that phased in downstream protection over ten years and delayed the provision of the full amount of water necessary to protect the coho until year nine. The court easily found that the BiOp failed to analyze adequately the impact of the delay on the coho in years one through eight. The years of litigation that led to this decision are set out in Mary Christina Wood, "Restoring the Abundant Trust: Tribal Litigation in Pacific Northwest Salmon Recovery," *Environmental Law Reporter* 36 (2006): 10163.

55. Jody Freeman and Daniel A. Farber, "Modular Environmental Regulation," *Duke Law Journal* 54 (2005): 795, 876. See also Daniel A. Farber, *Eco-Pragmatism: Making Sensible Environmental Decisions in an Uncertain World* (Chicago: University of Chicago Press, 1999).

56. Donald Hornstein, "Complexity Theory, Adaptation and Administrative Law," *Duke Law Journal* 54 (2006): 913, 949–60, applies the insights of complexity and game theory to modular regulation, which is an example of governance as a complex adaptive system. The center of game theory, the famous prisoner's dilemma, combined with the tragedy of the commons, postulates that the rewards to any one stakeholder from cheating instead of cooperating are high. Thus, despite its shortcomings, government regulation may be preferable, especially because any process that promises the relaxation of regulatory mandates is an invitation for the most powerful stakeholder to capture the process. As Hornstein (p. 959) concludes, "It should come as little surprise that the empirical evidence on regulatory experiments that emphasize leniency is mixed at best."

57. Deborah L. Donahue, *The Western Range Revisited: Removing Livestock from Public Lands to Conserve Native Biodiversity* (Norman: University of Oklahoma Press, 1999).

58. Carol Hardy Vincent, *Grazing Fees: An Overview and Current Issues*, report to Congress RS21232 (Washington, DC: Congressional Research Service, May 10, 2006), 2.

59. *Public Lands Council v. Babbitt*, 167 F.3d 1287 (10th Cir. 1999).

60. April Reese, "The Big Buyout," *High Country News*, April 4, 2005.

61. Memorandum to the secretary of the interior from the solicitor of the interior, "Authority for the Bureau of Land Management to Consider Requests for Retiring Grazing Permits and Leases for Public Lands," October 4, 2002, http://www.rangebiome.org/genesis/myersmemo.html.

62. The opinion stands the idea of multiple use on its head, equates federal grazing lands with national parks, and ignores the public land reforms of the past forty years. The Secretary of the Interior has the express authority under the 1976 Federal Land Planning and Management Act (43 U.S.C. § 1903(b)) to determine that a federal land-use plan should be amended to eliminate grazing.

63. David G. Alderson, "Buyouts and Conservation Permits: A Market Approach to Address the Federal Public Land Grazing Problem," *New York University Environmental Law Journal* 12 (2005): 903, 928–29.

64. The U.S. Department of Agriculture classifies farm land on a five-point scale from I (the best lands) to V (the worst). There are no Class I lands in the Klamath Basin.

65. W. K. Jaeger, "The Value of Irrigation Water Varies Enormously Across the Upper Klamath Basin, Water Allocation in the Klamath Project," EM8843-E, Brief no. 1, January 2004, Oregon State University, Corvallis, http://arec.oregonstate.edu/jaeger/personal/EM8843-E.pdf.

66. Government Accountability Office, *Klamath River Basin*.

67. Charles Howe and Christopher Goemans, *Water Transfers and Their Impacts: Lessons from the Three Colorado Water Markets* (July 2003), 12. We are also indebted to Professor Howe for sharing with us his insights on the impacts of water transfers on the Arkansas and Platte basins.

68. Elizabeth and Mark Morris, *Moon Handbooks: Oregon*, 6th ed. (Emeryville, CA: Avalon Travel Publishing, 2004).

69. Government Accountability Office, *Klamath River Basin*, 25–28.

70. 16 U.S.C. § 811.

71. *Udall v. Federal Power Commission*, 387 U.S. 428, 440 (1967).

72. See *Confederated Tribes and Bands of Yakima Indian Nation v. FERC*, 746 F.2d 466 (9th Cir. 1984).

73. Electric Consumers Protection Act of 1986, 16 U.S.C. § 797(e).

74. 16 U.S.C. § 803(j).

75. 16 U.S.C. § 803(a)(2)(B).

76. Edwards Manufacturing Co. and City of Augusta, Me., Order Denying New License and Requiring Dam Removal, 81 F.E.R.C. P 61,255 (1997). The licensee withdrew its appeal after the state of Maine brokered a settlement among all dam owners and resource agencies on the Lower Kennebec to address the problems of anadromous fish migration.

77. As of the middle of 2005, FERC made a collaborative process the default procedure. Federal Energy Regulatory Commission, *Handbook for Hydroelectric Project Licensing and 5 MW Exemptions from Licensing* (Washington, DC: Author, 2004), 3–1.

78. "Final Klamath Hydroelectric Project, FERC no. 2082, Collaborative Process Protocol" (September 10, 2002), http://www.pacificorp.com/File/File17752.pdf.

79. See U.S. Department of the Interior and National Marine Fisheries Service, "Modified Prescriptions for Fishways and Alternatives Analysis Pursuant to Section 18 and Section 33 of the Federal Power Act for the Klamath Hydroelectric Project (FERC Project No. 2082)," January 26, 2007.

80. 16 U.S.C. § 823d(b). For an analysis of the Energy Policy Act's potential impact on the Iron Gate relicensing, see Adell Louise Amos, "Hydropower Reform and the Impact of the Energy Policy Act of 2005 in the Klamath Basin: Renewed Optimism or Same Old Song," *Journal of Environmental Law and Litigation* 22 (2007): 1.

81. 16 U.S.C. § 811.

82. Decision, In the Matter of Klamath Hydroelectric Project (License Applicant Pacific Corp), Docket Number 2006 NMFS 2006-0001, FERC Project No. 2082 (September 27, 2006).

83. Federal Energy Regulatory Commission, "Draft Environmental Impact Statement for Relicensing of the Klamath Hydroelectric Project No. 2082-027," issued September 25, 2006 (DEIS), xxix, xxxii, 2-2, http://www.ferc.gov/industries/hydropower/enviro/eis/2006/09-25-06.asp.

84. Eric Bailey, "Fields of Conflict in the Klamath," *Los Angeles Times*, May 7, 2007.

Chapter 8

1. Charles L. Mee Jr., *Meeting at Potsdam* (New York: M. Evans & Co., 1975), xiii.

2. The clearest explanation of the need for citizen suit provisions is found in Joseph L. Sax, *Defending the Environment: A Strategy for Citizen Action* (New York: Knopf, 1971), still a classic work.

3. Steven Yaffee has written an excellent analysis of the spotted owl crisis. Yaffee, *The Wisdom of the Spotted Owl: Policy Lessons for a New Century* (Washington DC: Island Press, 1994).

4. *Energy and Water Development Appropriations Act*, Public Law 108-137, 117 Stat. 1827 (2004).

5. Compare Joseph L. Sax and Robert B. Keiter, "Glacier National Park and Its Neighbors: A Study of Federal Interagency Relations," *Ecology Law Quarterly* 14 (1987): 207; with Joseph L. Sax and Robert B. Keiter, "The Realities of Regional Resource Management: Glacier National Park and Its Neighbors Revisited," *Ecology Law Quarterly* 33 (2006): 233.

6. Because there are few unmodified river systems to preserve, the modern focus is on returning highly modified systems to a more natural state. The popular term for this is *restoration*, but we prefer the term *revival* because it recognizes the value of improvements that fall short of a return to predisturbance conditions. See A. Dan Tarlock, "Slouching Toward Eden: The Eco-Pragmatic Challenges of Ecosystem Revival," *Minnesota Law Review* 87 (2003): 1173.

7. William B. Lord, "Conflict in Water Resources Planning," *Water Resources Bulletin* 15 (1979): 1226.

8. Matthew McKinney and William Harmon, *The Western Confluence: A Guide to Governing Natural Resources* (Washington, DC: Island Press, 2004), 18–21.

9. Helen Ingram and Ann Schneider, "Science, Democracy, and Water Policy," *Water Resources Update* 133 (1999): 21.

10. We borrow this wonderful phrase from John M. Volkman, "Rethinking Development and the Western Environment," in *Beyond the Mythic West*, ed. Stuart L. Udall, Patricia Nelson Limerick, and Charles F. Wilkinson, 105 (Salt Lake City, UT: Peregrine Smith Books, 1990). The distinction between working to serve human needs and working in an ecological sense is the organizing principle in the report *Water in the West: The Challenge for the Next Century* (Denver, CO: Western Water Policy Advisory Review Commission, 1998), 2-5–2-24.

11. Jones and Stokes, "Situation Assessment Memorandum for the Upper Klamath Basin Working Group Restoration Process" (October 2001), http://www.ecr.gov/pdf/KlamathAssessmentRpt.pdf.

12. Michael Milstein, "Farmers Fault Water Users Group," *Portland Oregonian*, June 22, 2002, D4.

13. Ryan Harper, "Group of Project Landowners Raises Issue with Water User Association," *Herald & News* (Klamath Falls), June 21, 2002.

14. The history of water conflict in the Truckee-Carson Basin is described in National Research Council, *Water Transfers in the West: Equity, Efficiency and the Environment* (Washington, DC: National Academy Press 1992), and Jeremy Pratt, *Truckee-Carson River Basin Study* (Denver, CO: Western Water Policy Review Advisory Commission, 1997).

15. *Fallon Paiute Shoshone Indian Tribes Water Rights Settlement Act*, Public Law 101-618, 104 Stat. 3289 (1990). See E. Leif Reid, "Ripples from the Truckee: The Case for Congressional Apportionment of Disputed Interstate Water Rights," *Stanford Environmental Law Journal* 14 (1995): 145.

16. J. B. Ruhl, "Prescribing the Right Dose of Peer Review for the Endangered Species Act," *Nebraska Law Review* 83 (2004): 398; J. B. Ruhl and James Salzman, "In Defense of Regulatory Peer Review," *Washington University Law Review* 84 (2006): 1.

17. Such a center was created to coordinate research on the environmental impacts of the operation of Glen Canyon Dam on the Colorado River ecosystem in the Grand Canyon. National Research Council, *Downstream: Adaptive Management of Glen Canyon Dam and the Colorado River Ecosystem* (Washington, DC: National Academy Press, 1999).

18. NRC Final Report, 345–350.

19. Proposed Decision, California PUC Docket No. 105-11-022, November 13, 2006, and Oregon Public Utility Commission Docket No. UE-170, Order No. 06-172, April 12, 2006.

20. W. K. Jaeger, "Energy Pricing and Irrigated Agriculture in the Upper Klamath Basin," Water Allocation in the Klamath Reclamation Project Brief no. 3, EM 8846-E, July 2004, Oregon State University, Corvallis, http://arec.oregonstate.edu/jaeger/personal/EM8846-E.pdf.

21. For a cogent argument that in the end environmental policy must be based on informed choices arrived at by processes that include those who must live in the landscape, see Sagoff, *Price, Principle*, chapter 9.

22. *Final 2002 Biological Assessment*, 107.

23. Charles F. Wilkinson, *Fire on the Plateau: Conflict and Endurance in the American Southwest* (Washington, DC: Island Press, 1999), 17. See also Wilkinson's pathbreaking *Crossing the Next Meridian: Land, Water, and the Future of the West* (Washington, DC: Island Press, 1992).

24. Sax and Keiter, "Realities of Regional Resource Management."

25. National park historians agree that the national park system was created to preserve geologic wonders, not large ecosystems, although later additions had more rational ecological boundaries. See Richard West Sellars, *Preserving Nature in the National Parks: A History* (New Haven, CT: Yale University Press, 1997).

26. Aldo Leopold, *A Sand County Almanac and Sketches Here and There* (New York: Oxford University Press, 1949).

27. *Strycker's Bay Neighborhood Council v. Karlen*, 444 U.S. 223 (1980).

28. See David Takacs, *The Idea of Biodiversity: Philosophies of Paradise* (Baltimore: Johns Hopkins University Press, 1996), for an informative history of the construction of the

term. A recent United Nations report links biodiversity conservation and ecosystem services. Millennium Ecosystem Assessment, *Living Beyond Our Means: Natural Assets and Human Well-Being* (March 2005), 12, http://www.millenniumassessment.org/documents/document.429.aspx.pdf.

29. Millennium Ecosystem Assessment, *Living Beyond Our Means.*

30. John Krutilla pioneered this idea in "Conservation Reconsidered," *American Economics Review* 57 (1967): 787.

31. See Gretchen C. Daily and Katherine Ellison, *The New Economy of Nature: The Quest to Make Conservation Profitable* (Washington, DC: Island Press, 2002), and James Salzman and J. B. Ruhl, "Currencies and the Commodification of Environmental Law," *Stanford Law Review* 53 (2002): 607.

32. The Millennium Ecosystem Assessment, for example, posits four categories of services: (1) the provision of food and water, (2) the regulation or prevention of adverse impacts such as disease, (3) support for other production activities, and (4) cultural services such as recreation. Millennium Ecosystem Assessment, *Living Beyond Our Means.*

33. Daily and Ellison, *New Economy of Nature*; Salzman and Ruhl, "Currencies and Commodification."

34. See Jim Robbins, "Sale of Carbon Credits Helping Land-Rich but Cash-Poor Tribes," *New York Times*, May 8, 2007, D3.

35. Mancur Olson, *The Logic of Collective Action* (Cambridge, MA: Harvard University Press, 1965).

36. Author Tarlock explores the prospects for an ecosystem service economy in the Klamath Basin in more detail in A. Dan Tarlock, "Ecosystem Services in the Klamath Basin: Battlefield Casualties or the Future?" *Journal of Land Use and Environmental Law* 22 (2007): 207.

37. Debates continue to swirl around how to measure nonuse values such as the existence value of the Arctic National Wildlife Refuge. Contingent valuation, asking people how much they would pay to preserve an environmental amenity, is the most commonly used method, but critics charge that it is inherently unreliable. Donald J. Boudreaux, Roger E. Meiners, and Todd J. Zywicki, "Talk Is Cheap: The Existence Value Fallacy," *Environmental Law* 29 (1999): 765.

38. We are not asserting that upstream irrigators are necessarily liable under common law tort doctrines. J. B. Ruhl, Steven E. Kraft, and Christopher L. Lant, *The Law and Policy of Ecosystem Services* (Washington, DC: Island Press, 2007), 267–71, are optimistic about the possibility of using the common law to penalize those who fail to maintain ecosystem services. On ecosystem scales, though, as the Lower Klamath fish kill described in chapter 6 illustrates, issues of causation will complicate any attempt to bring common law actions. As Judge Guido Calabresi pointed out in his classic book *The Costs of Accidents: A Legal and Economic Analysis* (New Haven, CT: Yale University Press, 1970), 239–43, the fault system makes liability decisions on an "all-or-nothing basis" and makes it difficult to allocate costs efficiently. If ecosystem service production must be enforced by the common law, ecosystems will surely be underproduced and overstressed.

39. Ronald Coase, "The Problem of Social Cost," *Journal of Law and Economics* 3 (1960): 1. Coase won the Nobel Prize in economics for this theorem.

40. We use the term *bribe* in the classic economic sense of a legal payment of money used to induce a person to change his or her behavior. We do not mean to imply that either the payment or its acceptance is immoral or illegal.

41. James Salzman, "A Field of Green? The Past and Future of Ecosystem Services," *Journal of Land Use and Environmental Law* 21 (2006): 133, 144.

42. Daniel Kemmis, *This Sovereign Land: A New Vision for Governing the West* (Washington, DC: Island Press, 2001), is the most thoughtful exposition of this thesis. See also J. Donald Hughes, *An Environmental History of the World: Humankind's Changing Role in the Community of Life* (New York: Routledge, 2001), 209–11, and Charles Sokol Bednar, *Transforming the Dream: Ecologism and the Shaping of an Alternative American Vision* (Albany: State University of New York Press, 2003).

43. The most gripping account of the journey remains Wallace Stegner, *Beyond the Hundredth Meridian: John Wesley Powell and the Second Opening of the West* (Boston: Houghton Mifflin, 1954).

44. John Wesley Powell, *Report on the Lands of the Arid Region of the United States*, ed. Wallace Stegner (Lincoln: University of Nebraska Press, 2004). Powell's latest biographer, the noted environmental historian Donald Worster, argues that Powell was impressed by the Mormon communitarian society that flourished in Utah in the 1870s. Donald Worster, *A River Running West: The Life of John Wesley Powell* (New York: Oxford University Press, 2001), 337–80.

45. Stegner, Beyond the Hundredth Meridian, 223–24.

46. Ibid., 321.

47. Hughes, *Environmental History of the World*, 209–11; Bednar, *Transforming the Dream*. This thinking can be traced in New Mexico water publications. See, e.g., Consuelo Bokum, Vickie Gabin, and Paige Morgan, *Living Within Our Means: A Water Management Policy for New Mexico in the 21st Century* (Santa Fe: New Mexico Environmental Law Center, 1992); Designwrights Collaborative, *People and Water in New Mexico* (Santa Fe, NM: Author, 1984).

48. Kemmis, *This Sovereign Land*, 191.

49. Sagoff, *Price, Principle*, 214–20.

50. In fairness to the advocates of place-based governance, it has yet to be tried in the form they envision, which would require larger-scale experiments with strong local and state government support.

51. Kirkpatrick Sale, *Dwellers in the Land: The Bioregional Vision* (San Francisco: Sierra Club Books, 1985).

52. Ibid., 41.

53. Wallace Stegner, *The American West as Living Space* (Ann Arbor: University of Michigan Press, 1987), 60.

54. William H. Rodgers Jr., "The Myth of the Win-Win: Misdiagnosis in the Business of Reassembling Nature," *Arizona Law Review* 42 (2000): 297.

55. Murray-Darling Basin Commission, *Annual Report, 1998–1999*, (Canberra, Australia: Author, 1999), 24.

56. J. B. Ruhl, "Who Needs Congress? An Agenda for Administrative Reform of the Endangered Species Act," *New York University Environmental Law Journal* 6 (1998): 367.

57. See Holly Doremus, "Adaptive Management, the Endangered Species Act, and the Institutional Challenges of 'New Age' Environmental Protection," *Washburn Law Journal* 41 (2001): 50.

58. The trust was created by the Valles Caldera Preservation Act, Public Law 106-248, 114 Stat 598 (2000).

59. Christopher S. Elmendorf, "Ideas, Incentives, Gifts, and Governance: Toward a

Conservation Stewardship of Private Land, in Cultural and Historical Perspective," *Illinois Law Review* (2003): 423.

60. See, for example, Jesse J. Richardson, "Downzoning, Fairness and Farmland Protection," *Journal of Land Use and Environmental Law* 19 (2003): 59. For a reply, see Mark W. Cordes, "Fairness and Farmland Preservation: A Response to Professor Richardson," *Journal of Land Use and Environmental Law* 20 (2005): 372.

61. See Joseph L. Sax, "Property Rights and the Economy of Nature: Understanding *Lucas v. South Carolina Coastal Council*," *Stanford Law Review* 45 (1993): 1433.

62. See Holly Doremus, "Takings and Transitions," *Journal of Land Use and Environmental Law* 17 (2003): 1, 14–21.

63. Michael Milstein, "Klamath Water Deal No Bargain for U.S.," *Portland Oregonian*, March 16, 2003, A1.

64. Government Accountability Office, *Valles Caldera: Trust Has Made Some Progress, but Needs to Do More to Meet Statutory Goals* (Washington, DC: Author, 2005), 22–23.

65. Sagoff, in *Price, Principle*, 229–31, argues that environmentalists must make a fundamental choice between science and democracy, but we find the choice to be a false one. As we explained in chapter 6, we believe that science must be combined with democracy (or, if you prefer, politics or value judgments) to make resource management decisions.

66. C. S. Holling, ed., *Adaptive Environmental Assessment and Management* (New York: Wiley, 1978), 136. See also Lance H. Gunderson and C. S. Holling, eds. *Panarchy: Understanding Transformations in Human and Natural Systems* (Washington, DC: Island Press, 2002); Carl Walters, *Adaptive Management of Renewable Resources* (New York: Macmillan, 1986).

67. Howard Raiffa, *Decision Analysis: Introductory Lectures on Choices Under Uncertainty* (Reading, MA: Addison-Wesley, 1968).

68. Holling, *Adaptive Environmental Assessment*, 1.

69. National Research Council, *Downstream: Adaptive Management of Glen Canyon Dam and the Colorado Ecosystem* (Washington, DC: National Academy Press, 1999), 52–54.

70. NRC Final Report, 332–35.

71. The group was formally authorized in the Oregon Resource Conservation Act of 1996, Public Law 104-208, 110 Stat. 3009 (2006).

72. "Second best" theory in economics posits that when all the conditions for an optimum or efficient solution are not met, attempts to solve a problem may result in a solution worse than the starting conditions. We use the term here as a metaphor for the risks that may be posed by new means of conflict resolution invented to fill the vacuum left by the collapse or calcification of regulatory regimes.

73. Lawrence Susskind and Jeffrey L. Cruikshank, *Breaking Robert's Rules: The New Way to Run Your Meeting, Build Consensus, and Get Results* (New York: Oxford University Press, 2006), 138. In the San Francisco Bay-Delta, that aspect of the process finally seems to be moving forward, catalyzed by an independent report that, for the first time, offered a series of alternative visions for the delta. Jay Lund et al., *Envisioning Futures for the Sacramento–San Joaquin Delta* (San Francisco: Public Policy Institute of California,

2007). A blue ribbon task force has now been empaneled to articulate a broadly acceptable vision.

Afterword

1. Proposed Klamath River Basin Restoration Agreement for the Sustainability of Public and Trust Resources and Affected Communities, January 15, 2008 (Draft 11).

2. Klamath Water War's Over (editorial), Eureka Times-Standard, Jan. 21, 2008. Other headlines were more measured, and even the Times-Standard editorial acknowledged that several additional steps would be needed before peace could truly be declared.

3. National Research Council, *Hydrology, Ecology and Fishes of the Klamath River Basin* (Prepublication Copy) (Washington, DC: National Academies Press, 2007), available at http://books.nap.edu/openbook.php?record_id=12072&page=R1

4. Matt Weiser, "Delta Exports Halved," *The Sacramento Bee*, Dec. 29, 2007.

Index

Island Press Board of Directors